To John
From Ella
Christmas 1979

PORTRAIT OF THE LOTHIANS

Portrait of
THE LOTHIANS

NIGEL TRANTER

Photographs by
Hamish Campbell

ROBERT HALE · LONDON

© Nigel Tranter, 1979

First published in Great Britain, 1979

ISBN 0-7091-7467-5

Robert Hale Limited
Clerkenwell House
Clerkenwell Green
London EC1

PRINTED IN GREAT BRITAIN
BY LOWE & BRYDONE LTD.,
THETFORD, NORFOLK

CONTENTS

ILLUSTRATIONS

between pages 32 and 33

Rich East Lothian farmlands
Preston
Gullane beach
North Berwick
Haddington
Tantallon Castle and the Bass Rock
Preston Mill, East Linton
Dunbar
Garleton
Athelstaneford
Gifford
Garvald
Sancta Maria Abbey, Nunraw

between pages 96 and 97

Lammermuir
Musselburgh
Pinkie House, Musselburgh
Dalkeith Palace
Newbattle Abbey
Roslin Chapel
Interior of Roslin Chapel
Hawthornden Castle
Penicuik
Borthwick
Rosebery
Stow-in-Wedale
Bavelaw Castle

All the photographs were taken by Hamish Campbell.

INTRODUCTION

THE LAND OF LOTHIAN

LOTHIAN is and always has been a name to ring in the ears, to challenge the imagination, an ancient name of colour and character and story which means so much more than a mere group of three Lowland Scottish counties, a tract of territory fifty miles long by fifteen miles wide on the south side of the Firth of Forth. For this is essentially a land on its own, distinct, peculiar, sandwiched between that other very individual and self-sufficient entity, the Borderland, and the rest of old Scotland beyond the Scottish Sea – as the Firth of Forth used to be named. It is so separate, in fact, that although now containing within it the capital of Scotland, it was the last area, apart from the Orcades, to be incorporated into the Kingdom of Scotland, this as late as 1018. Previously it had been the semi-independent northern portion of the Anglian Kingdom of Bernicia; and before that the homeland of the Southern Pictish nation which the Romans called the Votadini. So the distinction is of long standing.

It is not only historically and ethnically that Lothian is an entity of itself, but geographically also. For it is cut off from the rest of Scotland by salt water on the north and east, and wide ranges of hills to the south. Only to the west is there no major barrier, where it merges with modern Stirlingshire at the one-time province of Calatria; but this is at its narrowest point, and in the old days Calatria was a sort of no-man's-land anyway, on the southern edge of old Scotia or Alba. Moreover the Forth reached much further inland then than it does today, almost to Falkirk, and the marshes of the Carron estuary provided a sufficient barrier for anyone. This was where the Kingdom of the Scots stopped, for centuries.

The name Lothian is itself interesting, with an Arthurian note to it. Its origin is obscure. It does not appear to be either Brythonic nor typically Celtic, and it certainly is not Anglian.

9

The Romans do not seem to have given it a specific name, referring to it as the territory of the Votadini, a nation of the Southern Picts or Cruithne. The name Lothian always seems to have been a stumbling-block for scribes and chroniclers, especially in England, where it has been variously written as Looene, Loeneis, Leodwine, even Ybandonia and Loida. Perhaps the most absurd of all, as late as 1091, was when the English reporter dealing with a confrontation between Malcolm Canmore, King of Scots, and William Rufus, King of England, declared that it took place at Leeds – thus providing headaches for generations of bewildered historians. The Latin name was Laudonia, the Saxons called it Lothene and the Gaels of the North, Lethead. Be all that as it may, local tradition derives the name from Loth, King of the Southern Picts or Votadini, aforementioned, whose capital was on the summit – 32 acres of the abrupt hill of Dunpender, better known today as Traprain Law, which rises like a leviathan out of the vale of the East Lothian Tyne, a notable archaeological site of once-large population which shouts aloud for thorough excavation. It is known to have been occupied from the first millennium B.C. until at least the fifth century A.D., possibly considerably longer – so this, rather than Edinburgh with its renowned fortress of Dunedin, could be said to be the true Heart of Lothian. Indeed, in early times, East Lothian was the most important part of the whole. Whether in fact King Loth did provide the name, whether he even existed at all, is open to debate. He is claimed to be the pagan grandfather of the famous St Kentigern, or Mungo, the founder of Glasgow. Kentigern was born around A.D. 514; so it is just possible that his grandsire ruled Lothian from the top of Dunpender before the fort-city site was abandoned. At anyrate, for want of a better explanation of the name, let Loth stand.

The division of the territory into three unequally-sized sections was a comparatively late arrangement, and the terms East and West Lothian do not appear until fairly modern times – although oddly, Midlothian seems to have had an earlier genesis. Lothian appears to have remained a single entity until the division of the country into sheriffdoms or shires, for administration, legal and taxation purposes, presumably the whole being too much - and too rich - for any one officer to handle; although it is interesting to note that English King Edward, Hammer of the Scots, in his invasion of Scotland and consequent occupation, in 1292, decided that the countrzshould be put under three justiciars, one for Lothian, one for 'Scotland beyond the Scotswater' (that is all north of Forth and Clyde) and one for Galloway, by which he meant right up to Glasgow. Which gives some indication of the importance of Lothian in relation to the rest.

At first, the three divisions took their shire names from the most prominent towns therein - Haddingtonshire in the east, Linlithgowshire in the west and Edinburghshire or Midlothian in the centre. These styles survived into comparatively modern times.

I used the term rich, above. This is, of course, the key-note of the symphony. For in natural resources, as in much else, Lothian is the richest tract in Scotland; indeed, possibly the richest for its size in all the British Isles. Although perhaps one-third of the total area is hill or high moorland over 800 feet, the rest is astonishingly fertile. Indeed, in East Lothian especially, it used to be the wry boast that the farm-rentals were higher, per acre, than anywhere else in the United Kingdom, land so valuable that one can drive all day through a most lovely rural countryside and never see a cow or cattle-beast, the soil being so productive that it would be folly to use it as pasture. The cropping statistics and yields of barley, wheat and potatoes in especial, are all but fabulous. Small wonder that some of the world's most renowned agricultural improvers came from here. And beside the soil itself, what was under it, more particularly in Mid and West Lothian, has been treasure-trove also - whatever it has done to the landscape in places - great and rich seams of coal and oil shales.

Despite the blemishes, Lothian is rich in landscape - not in the dramatic scenery of the Highlands or the heart-breaking loveliness of the Hebrides or even the rugged beauties of the Borderland; but almost everywhere a warm and ample comeliness, an intensely characterful aspect of settled peace and ancient, heedful cherishing, a land lovingly tended, of wide prospects and great cloud-scapes, with the sea almost always evident on one side and the hills encircling on the other; and even in the level, fertile plain of it, the abrupt, towering volcanic outcrops such as Traprain Law and North Berwick Law, Edinburgh's Arthur's Seat and Castle Rock, West Lothian's Cairnpapple and Cockleroy, to give excitement and challenge to the scene. And, not to be forgotten, the ever-present back-cloth of the fair land of Fife soaring from its golden strands to the varied profile of its central lofty spine, across the Firth of Forth.

Lothian's own seaboard is no less attractive and varied, with great wildfowl-haunted bays, tidal estuaries, extensive sands, modest cliffs and offshore islands. There are at least seventy miles of this splendid coastline, with only a mile or two spoiled by such as Leith's docks and the Musselburgh-Cockenzie developments. Elsewhere it is all a priceless asset to Lothian, and a very present influence.

The hills towards which the entire territory lifts gently from the shore are as inescapable a factor and joy. There are many smaller groups and ridges and isolated heights; but basically three main ranges block off all to the south – the Lammer-muirs, the Moorfoots and the Pentlands. These three are of strangely differing character. The Lammermuirs cover the greatest area, something like 200 square miles – although square is the last adjective to employ about these long, rolling, rounded, sheep-strewn heights with their gentle, swelling, green contours and unbroken skylines, formed in seemingly endless parallel ranges. The Moorfoots, in the centre, extend to only half that area but are much more individual summits, jumbled, scattered, withdrawn, somehow making less impact than the other two – although containing the highest point, at 2,136 feet. And the Pentlands – which name is allegedly a corruption of the Pict-lands, like the far-away Pentland Firth which separates mainland Scotland from Orkney, the Pent-lands, R. L. Stevenson's 'hills of home', are the best-known and most characterful, steeper, more pronounced and rugged peaks forming a dramatic outline, some rising within a mile or so of Edinburgh's southern suburbs, a magnet and a dare to the city's young in heart of all ages. They are essentially a double range, some sixteen miles long by five in width, dotted with lochs converted into reservoirs, a changeless, smiling wilderness where the curlews wheeple, the larks shout and the grouse whirr off on down-bent wings – and all looking down on the fortunate capital of Scotland. Many areas of Britain lie between hills and sea. But few, surely, so comprehensively and kindly as Lothian.

Edinburgh, inevitably exercises a major influence, today, on all three Lothians, with a population of half-a-million against the 260,000 of the rest, and a sprawl of about nine miles in the centre of them. Yet it probably would be fair to say that the capital has not affected the Lothians, sucked their life's blood as it were, to anything like the same extent that London has done to a large part of the Home Counties, or even as Glasgow has done with contiguous parts of Lanarkshire and Renfrewshire. The pull is there, but possibly because Edinburgh itself is a somewhat reserved and restrained city, and because the Lothian character is strong and of age-old independence, the distinction remains pronounced. Even Musselburgh, the closest of all the Lothian towns to the city, only six miles from Edinburgh G.P.O., stoutly retains its individual identity and takes every opportunity to shout its slogan:

> Musselburgh was a burgh when Edinburgh was nane;
> Musselburgh will be a burgh when Edinburgh's gane!

Chanted with all the rhythm and fervour of any football-supporters' anthem, that couplet encapsulates in sixteen words the whole Lothian story.

I

EAST LOTHIAN – THE COASTAL FRINGE

FOR centuries the recognized boundary between Midlothian and East Lothian reached the coast just west of Prestonpans, at the shore of the Drummore estate. Within the last year or two, consequent upon the alleged reform of local government, our politicians have seen fit to change this, and a lot more, and have shifted the limits of the East Lothian region – no longer a county, such being outmoded from some reason – about two miles to the west, so as to include the ancient town of Musselburgh, for reasons said to be not unconnected with electoral votes, as most folk are convinced. Be that as it may, Musselburgh has always been a typical *Midlothian* burgh, indeed much the largest and most important of them; and for the purposes of this survey it is sensible, I think, to deal with it under that county/district – especially as, with the new dispensation so thoroughly unpopular on all hands, it seems not at all unlikely that it may not be long before Scotland decides to take its destiny into its own hands and reverts to something like the former situation.

So, for this volume at least, let East Lothian begin where it always did, just east of the Levenhall suburb of Musselburgh and about a mile west of Prestonpans, below the quite steep escarpment on top of which sits the handsome redstone Georgian mansion of Drummore, formerly the property of a family called Acheson, of whom more hereafter.

If Prestonpans is not the most typical or picturesque spot at which to commence a survey of East Lothian, it is at least a characterful and lively entity, as distinctive and controversial as was the famous battle fought here in 1745 when Prince Charles Edward sent the Hanoverian General Johnnie Cope scampering for the Border, to the enrichment of our heritage of story and song. The place, until recently its own burgh or municipality, stretches along the shoreline for well over a mile, really a

14

strung-together collection of villages and havens – Acheson's or Morison's Haven, the Pans or Salt Preston, Preston itself, Aldhamer and Cuthill, once described, with some truth as "a rueful feature of the landscape, zigzag at both ends and crooked in the middle". If there are towns and communities in the Lothians which might claim priority over this as beauty-spots, urban jewels and tourist-traps, it nevertheless has much to commend it, and few can have a more stirring history or be able to exhibit more authentic and remarkable vestiges of that notable past. Also it has a stout spirit, which all but scorns the rest of the county.

Prestonpans was the seat of industry for centuries – something few of its neighbours could claim, or might wish to. The land here and to the south, towards Tranent, belonged in the twelfth century to Holy Church, and was exploited for its coal by the monks of, first, Aldbotle or Eldbottle, near Dirleton, then Newbotle, or Newbattle Abbey, in the Esk valley – with some of the earliest coal-mines in the British Isles. But the Church was also interested in other means of gaining wealth, particularly the export of salted fish to France, the Low Countries and the Baltic. And here, at Aldhamer – which means the Old Settlement – they established a new settlement which they called Preston, the priests' town, for the manufacture of the necessary salt, made in great open-air heated pans for the evaporation of seawater. So Salt Preston, or the Pans developed. This salt trade burgeoned and continued for seven centuries, until in 1825, through the London government's repeal of the protective salt duties, it lost its trade to cheap foreign-mined salt. Salt Preston supplied the precious commodity to all Scotland and much of England and further afield, ten huge pans producing up to 900 bushels or 7000 dry gallons per week. A race of salt-wives used to carry the salt in creels on their backs, to Edinburgh for sale, like the fish-wives of nearby Fisherrow, tough and renowned characters. And that going outwith Scotland was exported from the harbour known as Acheson's Haven, after the family at nearby Drummore, who grew rich on the trade, after the Reformation, and in due course produced a Secretary of State for Scotland to Charles the First, who became a baronet, while his descendants 'warstled up the brae' to being, first, Viscounts Gosford and then Earls of

Gosford, in the peerage of Ireland – taking their title from their other old estate of Gosford to the east, rather than that of Drummore, for some reason. It is rather amusing that, when they began to get too big for their salty boots, Acheson's Haven was taken over and extended by a new entrepreneur, named John Morison, and the name changed to Morison's Haven. Salt paid well still and his son likewise rose in the world to become Sir Alexander and then a Lord of Session judge, under the title of Lord Prestongrange. All this land and industry had been bought from the representative of Holy Church, in the early stages of the Reformation – Mark Kerr, Abbot of Newbattle, who, like so many another, saw the Reformation coming and managed the transition from lord spiritual to lord secular with single-minded skill and much profit, *he* for his pains becoming Lord Newbattle and his son first Earl of Lothian. All largely from salt. *Gloria in sale!*

Other industries such as pottery, brick- and soap-making and brewing developed – not to mention the very individual trade of oyster-dredging, the Pan Door or Pandore beds becoming amongst the most famous in Scotland, the dredging-song thereof being renowned, a strange lilt of allegedly Scandinavian origin. Alas, like the oysters, nearly all this industry has passed away, even the local coal-pits being closed, so that the Pans folk now have to travel to work, some still to Midlothian mines, more commuting to Edinburgh. Sad that this is the price of centralizing progress. And that Prestonpans is unlikely again to become a nursery for future noble families. There is now a Museum of Mining on the site of the Prestongrange pit.

Actually the most prominent of all families here has been the Hamiltons of Preston, a branch of the illustrious Norman-Scots house of that name with its two dukedoms of Hamilton and of Abercorn. A cadet of the line married the Liddell heiress of Preston in the early sixteenth century, progenitor of a long and distinguished following, which also reached the baronetage. Preston Tower, their seat, in the centre of that part of the burgh, is unique in one respect and semi-unique in another. I know of only one other such tower, Niddrie Castle in West Lothian, where, when additional space was required, instead of building a wing or extension, the laird in the early seventeenth century merely built upwards, two storeys more on top of the already existing four and a garret-storey, producing one of the tallest fortalices in the land. The still more unusual development was the erection, within a stone's-throw, in the late sixteenth and early seventeenth centuries, of two more fortified houses, for sons of the then laird. So here, right in the midst of the community, are three very fine examples of the Scottish defensive mansion, cheek-by-jowl as it were. The likelihood of such a thing happening is by its very nature remote, since, for lairds of the defensive period of our turbulent past, the last thing they were apt to desire was to have another stronghold in their immediate vicinity. Presumably the Hamiltons trusted each other – and believed that their houses would never leave the family. Hamilton House, now National Trust property, and Northfield, privately-owned, are highly picturesque additions to our heritage of stone. Preston Tower itself, now a ruin but with some hopes of restoration, stands roofless within its fine walled-garden and orchard.

As it happens, almost within another stone's-throw is a further most handsome relic of the past which should be a magnet for visitors, the seventeenth century Mercat Cross of Preston, one of the finest in Scotland, indeed the only complete and unaltered example of its kind left. Its tall, unicorn-crowned shaft rises out of a splendid circular basement substructure, ornamented with pilasters and niches and containing a turnpike stair which rises to the parapet-surrounded platform from which official proclamations were made, a prize indeed.

If Prestonpans has retained these delightful windows into the past, amongst all its spread of council-housing and other innovations – including a highly modernistic Roman Catholic church – it is less to be congratulated on having failed to save Bankton House, just across the railway-line, occupied as a farmhouse until recent times, now a derelict ruin. This was the home of the famous Colonel James Gardiner, the only hero on the government side at the Battle of Prestonpans, who died gallantly trying to rally his fleeing dragoons, within half-a-mile of his own house. With its avenue of ancient trees, it could still be saved, to become a show-place – especially now that the great unsightly refuse-bing of the former coal-pit here has been laboriously cleared away and its sordid purlieus converted into a pleasant grass-park, for proposed recreational development, the Meadowmill Sports Complex. Surely late-seventeenth-century Bankton House, abutting, could be given some part to play in this project.

Altogether Prestonpans, instead of being a sort of decayed industrial problem-child of East Lothian, could, with a little imagination, turn itself into quite a mecca for tourists and visitors – for it has much more to show than I have touched on here, ancient and modern. With tourism an ever-growing industry and money-spinner, here is opportunity.

The next community, only a mile along the coast eastwards, now unfortunately dominated by the enormous Cockenzie coal-fired Power Station, is the small double-burgh of Cockenzie and Port Seton, so near to Prestonpans but quite different in character. Cockenzie, to the west, the older partner, is an ancient fishing-haven of redstone vernacular buildings clustering around the rambling old mansion and the quaint small harbour – this now enhanced by a quite well known boat-building yard. The main street is hardly beautiful but full of strong, functional character, preponderantly fishermen's houses with pantiled roofs. The through highway does not traverse this but passes to the south amongst the more modern parts. Port Seton, at the east end, is rather more outspread, and, as its name suggests, based upon a much larger and less tide-hampered harbour. This was constructed in 1880, partly at the expense of the then Earl of Wemyss, whose lands of Seton and Gosford are contiguous. It is still the base of a fleet of some fifteen or so fishing-vessels, mainly prawn-trawlers, whose constant comings and goings much add to the character of this seaboard – and towards which many Lothian folk's thoughts are apt to turn in wild weather.

Port Seton looks upon itself as more of a seaside resort than an industrial community, and manages to turn its back fairly effectively on the overpowering power-station to the west, preferring its fine outdoor swimming-pool and Pond Hall, its beach and even its Seton Sands chalet and caravan site half-a-mile to the east – not a beauty-spot either but having at least the patina of age, as these places go, it having been for many years a favourite holiday scene, especially of people from Glasgow and the west, with a great huddle of gaily-painted, semi-permanent buildings as well as the caravans.

If Port Seton has little of historical interest to show, it can at least boast of having Cope's Lane, where formerly stood the house in which the Hanoverian general spent the night before the battle in 1745, where he indeed left his military pay-chest – and in his headlong flight thereafter for the Border, had no time to recover it, so that the victorious Jacobites were able to collect a precious £2500 of much-needed cash to pay the Prince's troops.

Cockenzie folk may grumble about the vast bulk and soaring twin chimneys of the power-station which inevitably projects like a sore thumb on this level stretch of coastline. Nevertheless, as these very necessary places go, it is something of a model. And there were sound enough material reasons for siting it here – rock foundations on a mainly sandy shore, unlimited sea water for cooling – 30 million gallons an hour are used – supplies of coal nearby, and a main railway-line convenient. The site, too, was largely won from the sea, and by an ingenious system of lagoons, the fuel-ash is being used to reclaim more land, right to Musselburgh. Moreover, the un-sightly sea-probing bing of Prestonlinks colliery, to the west, was dug away to provide much of the site infilling, greatly improving the scene; and great quantities of the square concrete blocks, or so-called tank-traps, which had disfigured the East Lothian coast since the last war, were usefully got rid of here also. So the huge, 1200 megawatt monster, although so alien to the lovely coastline, still has much to be said for it. And the fine reclaimed sweep of grassland, now surrounding it is an asset, like the yacht marina included.

Actually this development might be said to be merely the postponement of a dream of two centuries earlier. In 1722 the first railway in the land was constructed here, with wooden rails and horse-drawn wagons, down from the Tranent coal-pits to Cockenzie harbour. Thereafter John Cadell bought Cockenzie House and estate. He was a major entrepreneur of his day. He foresaw a great industrial future for Cockenzie, in the iron-stone which crops up in various parts of Lothian – including the nearby Gullane Point – to smelt which demanded vast amounts of coal. However, the coal-owners, who had succeeded Holy Church at Tranent and Preston, were less on-the-ball than the late Abbot Mark Kerr, and refused to give Cadell his coal at the cut-price rates he required. So, although the family remained at Cockenzie House until recent times, Cadell removed his tremendous project thirty miles up-Forth to the mouth of the River Carron near Falkirk, where 'Abyssinian' Bruce of Kinnaird, needing money desperately for his explorations and discovery of the Nile, agreed to sell him unlimited coal from his lands there. And so the famous Carron Ironworks developed. It is interesting to speculate whether the renowned cannon at Waterloo might have been called something like 'Cockenny-ades' instead of carronades, and this part of East Lothian have had a very different aspect indeed, had the local coal-owners agreed to Cadell's price. Were the Cockenzie folk lucky or otherwise?

Inland a mile from Seton Sands is the highly interesting area of Seton itself, whence one of the most distinguished of Scots families take their name. There is now no township here, although once there was the important castleton of the Palace of Seton, now represented by a bulky Adam mansion in the castellated style; and also the fine fourteenth-century chapel thereof. The farms of Seton still remain, with their farm-touns of cottages; but the Setons themselves are gone, leaving only a trace or two of what was at the time the most magnificent seat in Scotland. The Lords Seton were notable supporters of the Stewarts, and sought to prop up Mary Queen of Scots when it would have been more profitable not to do so. Also they were staunch Roman Catholics, so they were doubly damned after the Reformation. The chiefly family is now represented by the Earls of Eglinton and Winton, in the west of Scotland, through the female line; but despite the vast lands they once held in East and West Lothian, they are landless here today. To Seton Palace came the hapless, beautiful Mary Stuart (she spelled her name that way because there was no 'w' in French), to take part in a lightsome archery contest only the week after the murder of her husband King Henry Darnley, at Kirk o' Field. And she had spent the night here after Rizzio's murder in her presence at Holyrood. Mary Seton, of course, was one of her Four Marys.

The chapel, wherein lie the effigies of Mary Seton's ancestors, stands close by. It was originally the parish church of Seton, but was raised to the status of a semi-monastic collegiate church in

1493, provided with "a provost, four prebendaries, a clerk and two singing boys". Unfortunately it suffered much at the hands of the invading English in 1544, and although being rebuilt, was never finished by the Reformation period. Its truncated spire looks rather odd, therefore; but internally it is very fine, with excellent stone tracery windows. It was restored last century by the same Earl of Wemyss who built Port Seton, and who lies buried here with his countess.

East of Seton lies the rapidly expanding community of Longniddry – it is scarcely to be called a village now, although it was only a year or two ago, so extensive are its environs becoming in the sphere of modern housing, mainly for commuting families from Edinburgh. After Prestonpans and Port Seton, industry ceases and immediately the countryside becomes rural, picturesque and fairly unspoiled; so that it is little wonder that this, only thirteen miles from the city, is a favourite area for so-called 'executive housing', especially as there is a good railway link. But spreading housing, however executive, can itself damage the scene; so it is to be hoped that this development does not go too far.

Longniddry has its roots in the past too. For here was the seat of a rival house to that of Seton, the Douglases; and they took the winning side in the Mary saga and the Reformation both. Indeed John Knox himself was tutor here to the young Douglases in 1643-7, and later preached in the church of which only a gable remains. This Douglas connection could be said to have survived, for the Earl of Wemyss is still proprietor here and his surname is Wemyss-Charteris-Douglas. The golf-course of the name, which lies between Longniddry and the shore, is quite renowned, and picturesque amongst its scattered Scots pines.

The three-mile stretch between Longniddry and Aberlady, with its attractive shoreline is taken up by the large estate of Gosford, the same that gives title to the Achesons over in Ireland, but now the home of the Earl and Countess of Wemyss, descended from the ancient Celtic Mormaors and Earls of Fife. It is a famous place, with a vast and splendid mansion but oddly, with little history. The resounding tale of the Wemyss family is not really centred on Gosford, which was only bought in unromantic fashion by the sixth earl in the eighteenth century, allegedly so that he was conveniently placed for playing golf. Certainly East Lothian abounds in golf-courses – a Prime Minister of Denmark on a visit to Scotland, was taken to North Berwick from Edinburgh for a respite, and is said to have told the Provost thereof that he noted that all the land totally unfit for golf-courses was given over to agriculture! With Longniddry course on one side and Kilspindie course on the other, both on Gosford land, there is certainly no lack of scope. The estate, once little more than sand, rabbit-warrens and marshland, has been effectively drained into a series of charming, tree-girt ponds, and richly planted parkland. Its miles-long high enclosing wall is well-known to all travellers on this North Berwick road for the extraordinary manner in which the prevailing winds off the Forth have moulded the tree-tops above the wall exactly as though they had been carefully clipped all the way.

Inland, but part of the property, are the contiguous farms of the Spittal and Redhouse, the latter with a lofty red-stone ruined fortalice overlooking the road. The name Redhouse does not refer to the colour of the stone however, for the place used to be called Reidspittal, that is the Hospital or Hospice of the Red or Trinitarian Friars. This was no doubt an offshoot of the monastery of that Order at Houston near East Linton. These spittals were, of course, not hospitals in the modern sense; more like hostelries, places of hospitality for strangers and travellers, maintained by the monks and providing a most valuable service to the country in days when no real inns existed. East Lothian, always a rich land, had many such.

Aberlady, happily, is still a village. Sandwiched pleasantly between the wooded estates of Gosford and Luffness, on the shores of the great tidal bay, it has also been protected by wise planning from any major present-day development, its modern housing tucked discreetly behind, its vernacular architecture and pantiled roofing much to the fore. It is an ancient place, once a burgh of barony and the port of Haddington, the county town five miles inland. Its most attractive parish church is at the west end; the site of a Carmelite nunnery, its fine walled pleasance or walled-garden, at the east; and the truncated but venerable stepped Mercat Cross in the middle – it no doubt having lost its cross-finial at the Reformation. The church is notable for its tall, square fifteenth-century tower crowned by a parapet and walk and with a vaulted stone basement, used as a vestry. In this is preserved the most ancient symbol of Aberlady's past, the shaft of an early Celtic cross with typical interlacing ornament. And at the gate is still the authentic 'louping-on stane', a flight of stone steps on the pavement to aid the less agile worshippers on to their horses after service and their wives to mount pillion behind them.

The community once was more extensive, ancient maps showing it to stretch along the shore westwards right to Kilspindie Point, where now is only grass flanking the private road to the golf-course. Here are the scanty remains of the Douglas fortalice of Kilspindie. The great bay, over 1000 acres of it drying out at low water, has always dominated the village, indeed was the reason for its existence. It forms the estuary of the West Peffer, the channel of which allowed fairly shallow-draft vessels to use this as a haven, although it is now largely silted up. The former custom-house is still at the Point. Always these tidal flats have been a noted haunt of wildfowl, vast numbers of wild geese in especial wintering here, so that from October to March their stirring gabble and honking is seldom stilled or the wavering ribbons of their V-shaped skeins absent from the East Lothian skies – save when forced down, and their trumpeting drowned out, by the thunder of the waves on the two-miles-long sand-bar at the mouth of the bay, a wild place in north-westerly gales. Today the area is renowned as a nature reserve, where visitors come from all over Europe.

Continued sand-blow from the bar has built up the great sand-hill formation which culminates in Gullane Hill – and the process still goes on, so that the bay is steadily filling itself up, of great interest to naturalists. Dutch visitors say that, in their country, long ago it would have been reclaimed as rich grain land. Once indeed it stretched far to the east, so that an English fleet in 1547 was able to sail far enough in to be bombarded by cannon from Luffness Castle, at the present head of the bay, where now trees grow.

Luffness is one of the most interesting places in Lothian. It once boasted a great twelfth-century Norman-style castle, one of the largest in the land, its moat and the outline of its extensive curtain-walls and angle-towers still evident, although it was deliberately 'spoiled' by the English after the disaster of Pinkie. The present late-sixteenth-century tower-house was thereafter built up on the two lower storeys of the keep, whose ten-foot-thick masonry had defied the demolishers. Originally erected by the well-known Scots-Norman family of de Lindsay, one of its early lairds, Sir David de Lindsay, Regent of Scotland for the young Alexander III, died on a crusade in 1268; and dying, promised a Scots monk dispossessed from the monastery on Mount Carmel by the Saracen that if he would carry his embalmed body back to Scotland, he would receive land at Luffness to establish a new Carmelite monastery. This was done and the Crusader's coffin and recumbent effigy still enhance the ruined chapel of the former monastery, near the castle. The up-and-coming Hepburn family got Luffness by marriage and in 1585 erected the present tall mansion. In 1713 the legal-luminary line of the Hopes gained the property, and are still there. East Lothian is a great place for fine estates and ancient families, who manage to retain them, despite modern pressures – largely undoubtedly because of the richness of the farmlands.

More golf-courses fill the space eastwards to the next village of Gullane, three of them – Luffness and Gullane Number One and Two – much of the land for which was once under Aberlady Bay's salt water, with the dramatic ruin of Saltcoats Castle almost two miles inland, but once, as the name implies another salt-making centre on the tide's edge. Gullane – pronounced Gillan, Gullan or Goolan, depending on where in it you live – is nevertheless no large centre of population, although now growing quickly, like Longniddry, thanks to the commuting fraternity. With its famous championship courses of Number One and Muirfield, it is a magnet for golfers; and its magnificent mile-long sandy beach, with its equally fine neighbour at Jovey's Neuk, provide some of Edinburgh's favourite recreation haunts. Gullane has a name for snobbery – that is, the Gillan end of it – established when only the most expensive Edinburgh folk could afford to live here; but that is dying out under present-day conditions.

It has a colourful history, too, like most other places in this vehement, ancient land. It was Church land again, until the

Reformation, and the ruin of St Andrew's Collegiate Church remains, less cherished than it ought to be – and no fewer than eight other religious establishments were administered from here. But in the early seventeenth century the parish church was transferred two miles eastwards to the next village, Dirleton – allegedly because James VI and I objected to Master McGill, the minister, smoking the noxious weed tobacco. Jamie did not like tobacco, admittedly, but I fear that he had more on his mind, down in London, to exercise himself with than the failings of Scots parish ministers; anyway, McGill remained in charge, but was forced to walk back and forth between his manse, which remained in Gullane, and his kirk – for which he put in a hurt demand to the Privy Council no less, for extra shoe-leather. No, the transference was really a much more murky business, an echo of the grim Gowrie Conspiracy of 1600 when King James engineered the murder of the Earl of Gowrie – to whom he owed £85,000 – and his brother Sandy Ruthven. The 'engineer' of it all was Sir Thomas Erskine, whose mother the Countess of Mar had fostered the young monarch. Erskine was rewarded by the gift of the forfeited Ruthven lands of Dirleton and Fentoun, became Viscount Fentoun, and desired the revenues of the rich parish of Gullane. Being able to blackmail the King, he was in a position to do more than merely shift parish ministers around. He continued to prosper, became Earl of Kellie, and his descendants still live at the other side of the Forth.

Gullane centres round its attractive Goose Green – where once was Master McGill's manse – and is, not unnaturally a place for hotels and holiday accommodation, although the largest hotel, the Marine, has been turned into a Fire Brigade school, and many of its largest houses sub-divided. Early documents show that the correct pronunciation, as so often is the case, rests with the humblest members of the population, Gulan or Goolan being correct.

Inland from Gullane the broad, splendid acres of the Vale of Peffer stretch, those of West and East Fenton, Fenton Barns and Fenton itself, or Kingston, amongst the richest. Fentoun Tower still stands proudly on high ground near the last, a fine fortalice, ruinous but which could yet be restored. Seawards the coastline changes character after Gullane, to rocks and skerries and little coves, but still some sands, very lovely, with no road within a mile or so.

Dirleton, or Dirlington as it used to be called, is deservedly recognized as one of the most picturesque villages in all Scotland, venue for artists, with its wide, tree-lined green and venerable castle – and the seventeenth-century church which replaced that of Gullane. Modern traffic was tending to spoil it all, but recently it has been relieved by a by-pass. There is no real main street here, no real street at all, for it is a small place, but full of character to draw the eye – and the gourmands, for it is nowadays enhanced by a renowed eating-house. The castle, on a mound in the centre, is an impressive pile of mellow stone, now in the care of the Department of the Environment, which well maintains it and its delightful garden, a place of peace so much at odds with its stormy past. Another Norman stronghold – our Celtic forebears did not go in for stone castles – it was built by the de Vaux family in the thirteenth century, later than and not quite so large as Luffness but retaining today many features which Luffness lost through the 'spoiling', including the massive drum-tower gatehouse and replaced drawbridge and the curious six-sided hall with domed ceiling. It was the last castle in Scotland's South to resist Edward, the Hammer of the Scots; and it stood out again against Cromwell 350 years later, until General Monk brought up his artillery to batter it into surrender, and hanged the captain. It was used, too, as a prison for a coven of witches, who were in due course 'worrit' or half-strangled and then burned at the stake on Dirleton Green – all in the cause of the better life. In 1355 Sir John Halyburton from the Borders married the de Vaux heiress; his grandson was Lord Treasurer of Scotland and the Regent Albany's son-in-law, yet he aided in the escape from the Regent of the young surviving son of Robert III, who became James I, organizing his transfer to the Bass Rock nearby – of which more later. Today the lands of the barony are incorporated in the Duke of Hamilton's estate of Archerfield, which stretches down to the very lovely coast, with its offshore islands of Eyebroughty and Fidra. Here, near the shore, was the site of the monastery of Eldbotle, the predecessor of Newbattle Abbey aforementioned. It grew here from a ferry maintained by the monks out to the island of

Fidra or Fetheray, on which was a Celtic cashel or monastery later Romanized by William the Lion in 1165 as the Priory of St Nicholas. For some reason it was a noted place for pilgrimage, and the Pilgrims' Road to it can still be traced in places. The St Nicholas monks soon found it more comfortable to have their own quarters on the mainland and only charge for ferrying the pilgrims, and out of this now commercial enterprise grew the great project which at Newbattle was to start the industrialization of much of Lothian. The ruins of the chapel now share the island with a lighthouse establishment.

A little way eastwards along the coast, and the fine Dirleton beach, is the hillock and woodland of Yellow Craig, in the vicinity of which is now one of the best caravan-parks in the land, landscaped and discreet – one of the few, surely, to have been graced by royalty. Yellow Craig itself, with its picnic facilities and nature-trail, it is not always realized, was the prototype for R. L. Stevenson's Spyglass Hill in *Treasure Island*. This coast was a favourite haunt of RLS, for he had relatives just at the other side of North Berwick. *Catriona* and *The Pavilion on the Links* also feature this Gullane-Dirleton area.

From Yellow Craig to North Berwick is just over two miles, all golden sands backed by dunes and another golf-course, seaward the skerry known as the Bubbly Buss and the larger islands of the Lamb and Craigleith. Beckoning ahead is the tall, green cone of Berwick Law, 613 feet high and crowned by a former Pictish fort and a whalebone arch. North Berwick is, to be sure, one of the most renowned and popular seaside resorts in Scotland, as well it might be, with so much to offer. Strangers often wonder about the name, assuming it to have some link with the other Berwick-on-Tweed, forty miles to the south. It has none. The name refers only to bere or barley having been grown at this *wic* or settlement.

The town clusters fairly tightly round its two bays, divided by the rocky headland, almost an island, on which is sited the small harbour, mecca of yachtsmen despite drying out at low water, and the popular outdoor swimming-pool – which could hardly be more attractively sited. Inland the ground rises quickly towards the base of the dramatic Law, so that modern developments have to be upwards. The burgh is a douce, well bred, well-doing and quite bustling little town stretching along two miles of scenic seaboard; but however varied and interesting its own shoreline of rocks, fine sands, skerries, low green headlands, and grassy cliffs rising to the east, it tends to be the magnificent seaward prospects which capture the attention; the reefs over which the tide boils whitely and further out the necklace of islands culminating in the soaring, spectacular column of the Bass, with far beyond, the white cliffs of the May Island, all backed by the Eàst Neuk of Fife coast. It is one of the finest seascapes on the east coast of Scotland, with craft, large and small adding interest and movement to the scene, pleasure-boats from North Berwick itself, fishing-vessels from Port Seton, cargo ships from Leith, Kirkcaldy and the other Forth ports, giant tankers from Grangemouth's refineries and the oil-terminal at Hound Point, naval warships from Rosyth and nowadays all the extraordinary tug-towed monsters connected with the North Sea oil developments, for which the Forth is a great maritime highway and haven of shelter.

North Berwick is the shopping-centre for a large area of rich farming country, so its long narrow main street is well provided with many good-quality establishments as well as the usual high-street stores. The east end of the street is the most characterful architecturally, for here is the picturesque little town-house of 1729, with its quaint ogee-roofed clock-tower; and close by, the tall and dignified, whitewashed mansion known as the Lodge, also of the eighteenth century, formerly the town-lodging of the Dalrymple family who have been lairds here since around 1690 but who now live at Leuchie, their estate a couple of miles to the south. It seems odd to have maintained so great a town-house so close to their country seat, but no doubt it was used as a dower-house. It is now divided into flats, and its delightful garden beautifully-kept and open to the public, its remaining grounds a recreation park.

Recreation is, of course, the main business of North Berwick, catering for the golfers – three more courses – the yachting fraternity, sea-anglers, the bathers and so on, along with the many who just come to picnic on the sands, explore the rocks and cliffs and soak in the lovely vistas. So all facilities abound, and hotels and guest-houses proliferate. Very large houses surround the town, indicative of its one-time drawing-power for the wealthy and the noble, including royalty itself;

and though many of these are now subdivided and some turned into homes for 'senior citizens', the aura of prosperity, even riches, remains. Many seaside resorts thrive exceedingly in the summer months but tend to become almost moribund in winter. Not so North Berwick, which has its own lively social activity. Some small industries have developed, but not to obtrude on the scene. Its high school is a quite well known establishment. Of great value is the local train service to Edinburgh, only retained after a struggle.

To look at it, then, one would not think that North Berwick had a blood-curdling history and background. But deep down, not necessarily entirely buried yet, there may be a different tale to tell, since in Scotland old notions die hard, in Lothian more particularly. Especially the sort of ongoings in which this community partook so vigorously. Of all things, it was the supernatural which really first made North Berwick famous, or otherwise – witchcraft. The celebrated witch-trials here, of 1591, involved James VI himself, and make extraordinary, macabre, if not pathetic reading. But even allowing for rampant superstition and King Jamie's preoccupation with demonology, there seems to have been more than the usual black-magic nonsense and diablery about here. The town was the acknowledged centre of a notorious witchcraft cult, led at this time apparently by the King's own cousin, Francis, Earl of Bothwell, from nearby Hailes Castle – Mary Queen of Scots' third husband's nephew and successor. The King claimed that the ship bringing himself and his Danish bride back to Scotland had been trapped in a private storm off the Bass Rock, engineered by these folk – but since he added that sundry of the ladies concerned had sailed round his vessel in a sieve, we perhaps need not take all his testimony too seriously. Nevertheless, the consequences were serious enough for all concerned, for the coven was duly stalked and captured one dark night, at the Auld Kirk out near the harbour, dancing in the kirkyard to the music of a Jew's Harp, and doing worse things, of which kissing the Devil's backside – presumably the Earl Francis himself – was not the most reprehensible. At the trial of the ninety-four witches and six wizards which followed – the Earl seems to have made good his escape – the King presiding, evidence given included this testimony:

... on his [the Devil's] command they openit up the graves, twa
within and ane without the kirk, and took off the joints of the
fingers, taes and knees, and partit them amang them; and Agnes
Simpson gat her ane winding-sheet and twa joints, whilk she tint
[mislaid] negligently.

That last phrase seems illuminating, evidence not forthcoming.
The interested monarch's methods of gaining confessions is
equally so – he ordered a rope to be tied round each accused's
forehead, and then twisted with an iron bar until the scalp
came off. By this means he extracted remarkable information –
and duly wrote a royal book on the subject. The Auld Kirk,
where it all took place, is still there, although only the small
whitewashed and vaulted south aisle remains intact, the rest of
the twelfth-century building represented only by foundations.
Its choice as a venue for such cantrips is not so strange when it
is realized that the site was really an island, known as the
Anchor Green, and linked to the town only by a causeway and
arch, which could be guarded – indeed, later, part of the
church and most of the graves were swept away in a storm.
The subsequent parish church, dating from 1670, situated near
the Lodge and the ancient St Andrew's Well, is also now a ruin
and replaced, but very attractive in its graveyard.

The link with the supernatural and the Church both started
early. No doubt the Picts, or Cruithne, performed their sun-
worship rites here, with their important fort on the Law, and
we know that human sacrifice went with it. Then the Celtic
missionaries came to Christianize them; but they themselves
seem to have got up to unchancy tricks hereabouts, with St
Cuthbert standing all night in the sea communing with seals,
and St Baldred arranging, when dying, to leave three distinct
corpses so that each of his three local churches could use his
remains for pilgrimage and relic purposes – to their multiple
profit. North Berwick was the southern terminus of the
MacDuff Earls of Fife's ferry – for they had lands here, at
Tantallon and elsewhere, of which more later. And prior to
1154 Duncan, fifth Earl, established a Cistercian nunnery at
North Berwick, apparently for select clients, mainly the
daughters of noble houses, who came to be known as the
White Ladies and of whom tales are told, not invariably
pietistic. Some were alleged to have graduated into wandering

ghosts, on account of their activities – although I have never met anyone who saw one. But one of the ladies *was* actually seen, no longer ago than last century when, excavating the railway-station site, a tomb opened. There lay a good-looking young fair-haired woman, her features and body preserved intact, until the fresh air turned all swiftly to dust. The nunnery – it was a priory not an abbey, as it is now called locally – stood near the station. As the Reformation loomed, it underwent the familiar process. The powerful Home family manoeuvred one of its daughters into the position of Prioress – and in due course the establishment was secularized, and her brother became Commendator-Prior, and in due course Sir John Home of North Berwick. That is how it was done, up and down the land. The present Home baronet of Blackadder still lives at North Berwick, although most of the barony was sold to the Dalrymples in the seventeenth century.

With North Berwick itself the Dalrymples gained the spectacular acquisition of the Craig of Bass, as the mighty rock used to be called, and have retained possession. It is situated three miles from the town, but because of its vast bulk looks closer, and less than two miles from the mainland at Tantallon. It is, of course, one of the most extraordinary physical features anywhere round the British coastline, a volcanic plug in the same geological system as Traprain and Berwick Laws. A book could be written about the Bass. Rising sheer from the sea to 350 feet, its guano-white cliffs tower to a grassy top of seven acres – on which, oddly, sheep used to graze, and to such satisfactory effect that Bass mutton was a notable and expensive delicacy as far away as London, where much that was sold as such must have come from much less romantic pastures. Up here too, grows a unique plant, the Bass Mallow. This rock was the inconvenient hermitage of the famous Celtic St Baldred, who died on the Bass in either 606 or 756 – like his triple corpse, his death seems to have been unusual. Though some say that there were two Baldreds of the Bass. Whatever the truth of it, his cell may still be traced half-way up on a terrace on the south side; it being succeeded, of all things, by a chapel which was a parish church – for the Bass actually became a parish on its own, surely the smallest and most inaccessible parish in all the land. It got secularized much earlier than most, coming into the hands of the Lauder family just after Bannockburn, who held it until the seventeenth century. The ruins of their eyrie-like castle cling to the rock not far from the chapel, and where is now also the lighthouse and the keepers' houses, perched between sea and sky. Here, in 1405, the young Prince James, second son of Robert III, was brought by Halyburton of Dirleton and the Earl of Orkney, on the first stage of his journey to France, to escape the clutches of his uncle Albany, who had already starved to death the prince's brother and heir to the throne. James was here on this dizzy rock for a month, safe – for there was no access save by hoist – until a French ship came to collect him. But Albany, in his spleen, sent word of the ship's passage to the Auld Enemy, Henry IV of England, and young James was duly captured off Flamborough Head and taken to London to begin his eighteen years of captivity. His father, a sick and feeble man died of heartbreak, and Albany ruled Scotland unopposed.

The Bass became a state prison in 1671, and during the Killing Times was the grim and secure gaol for many Covenanting divines. Peden, Traill, Blackadder – who died here – and many others were immured on this soaring rock, some for as long as six years. Later four Jacobites were imprisoned here, and managed to turn the tables on their persecutors by shutting out the garrison during a coal-importing operation at the only – and still very difficult – landing-place. The soldiers had to be rescued and taken off by boat. Thereafter, these young heroes held the Bass against all comers, and the powers of the state, for no less than four years, victualled by sympathetic French warships. They only capitulated on very good terms.

Today it is possible to visit the Bass, with the laird's permission, although landing is not always feasible because of the swell. But even a sail round it, by pleasure-boat from North Berwick, is an exciting experience, with the air above alive with thousands of soaring, plunging, diving gannets or solan geese, with their six-foot wing-span. As well as these there are vast numbers of other denizens, kittiwakes, guillemots, razorbills, fulmars, puffins, cormorants and others, clinging to every ledge and crevice; not to mention the seals resting on the tidal shelves. Well might the ancient poet write:

Rich East Lothian farmlands, with Fife beyond the Forth estuary

(*Left*) the seventeenth-century Mercat Cross at Preston, with Preston Tower behind, and (*below*) Gullane, one of the many fine East Lothian beaches.

(*Above*) North Berwick and Craigleith Island from Law Hill and (*below*) the west end of Haddington, with the Town House steeple.

Tantallon Castle and the Bass Rock with the Isle of May in the distance.

The Tyne at Preston Mill, East Linton

(*Above*) Dunbar, High Street, and (*below*) the hanging valley of Garleton, with North Berwick Law and the Bass Rock in the left background and Athelstaneford village on the right.

(*Above*) the East Lothian village of Athelstaneford and (*below*) Gifford village, its cross and parish church.

(*Above*) Garvald, one of the many East Lothian villages hidden in valleys and (*below*) the cloisters of Sancta Maria Abbey, Nunraw.

The air was dirkit with the fowlis, that cam with yammeris
and with yowlis,
With shrykking, screeking, skrymming scowlis, and meikle
noyis and showtes.

Facing the Bass from its own cliff-top is the great and
exciting ruin of Tantallon Castle. A small stronghold here was
the Lothian seat of the Celtic Earls of Fife, of Shakespeare's
MacDuff's line; but in the fourteenth century the rising house
of Douglas leased it – a curious arrangement I have not come
across elsewhere in early times – and in due course built up the
vast fortalice seen today. It is unique, in Scotland at least, in
that it consists basically of little more than a single huge
curtain-wall cutting off a triangle of thrusting headland, with
precipices to the sea, this wall surmounted by a parapet-walk
and embellished with a massive gatehouse-keep in the centre
and tall towers at each end, the whole protected by no fewer
than three widely-spaced moats or ditches, to keep siege-
engines, archers and early cannon out of range. It became the
seat of the Red Douglases, Earls of Angus, and here they could
safely cock a snook at all authority, for the place was impregnable and could be supplied from the sea; so that the old
saying was minted, "Ding doun Tantallon an' build a brig to
the Bass", meaning that one was as impossible as the other.
Until the mid-seventeenth century, that is, when General
Monk's more sophisticated artillery battered it into submission
to Cromwell. But during the 300 years of its independence
from all authority save that of its own earls, this stronghold
witnessed wild and extraordinary ongoings, even Scotland's
kings having to retire ignominiously before it. Now it makes
one of the most rewarding places to visit in all Lothian, with its
deep dungeons, its winding stairways, its dizzy battlements and
superb views.

Eastwards from Tantallon a mile is the picturesque cliff-girt
enclave of Auldhame and Scoughall (pronounced Scole) much
linked with St Baldred. Here is a most lovely hidden beach,
reached by a private road – which motorists may use by paying
a small fee. Above the beach on the cliff-top rises what is
known as the Priory of Auldhame, an establishment which
developed out of one of Baldred's personal parishes. But like

North Berwick's 'abbey', the building there now is really a ruined late-sixteenth-century tower-house, with turrets and shot-holes, built by the new owners at the Reformation land-grab. Below it nestles the tiniest, most secret harbour I know, on a half-tide islet called the Gegan, a place of delight. Even in East Lothian surprisingly few folk know of this attractive corner. The fine old farms of Auldhame and Scoughall still belong to the Dale family, to which R. L. Stevenson was related.

This is the end of the southern shore of the Firth of Forth estuary, with the land now swinging away southwards and facing the open North Sea. Beyond it here, Baldred's other two parishes, Prestonkirk and Tyninghame, are more conveniently dealt with in the next chapter which deals with the central vales of Tyne and Peffer.

II

EAST LOTHIAN – THE VALES OF TYNE AND PEFFER

EAST LOTHIAN divides conveniently into three roughly parallel and almost horizontal belts, for purposes of description, distinct in character as in topography – the coastal strip, the uplands of Lammermuir and the central vales of Tyne and Peffer. In the nature of things, this central area may not be the most dramatic and exciting scenically; but it is the richest single agricultural entity in Scotland, and looks it, with an aura of ancient peace – which may be misleading – obvious prosperity, and the care of centuries, but redeemed from any hint of tameness or even domesticity by the fact that it is flanked and overlooked so outstandingly by picturesque and vigorous heights, close enough on either hand always to challenge the eye. The combined Tyne and Peffer plain is really a sort of double strath, some fifteen miles long by only five wide, fair, fertile, felicitous, dotted with splendid farms, ancient mansions and parks, characterful villages, monuments of the past – and, of course, the three largest communities of the county, Haddington, Tranent and Dunbar.

The East Lothian Tyne rises actually deep in Midlothian, Tynehead being high on the Borthwick moors. As a growing burn it runs northwards for almost seven miles before it reaches the East Lothian border a mile or so from Ormiston. Until then it winds and bends modestly through woodland and estates and deep, sudden dens, with nothing like a vale. But once into East Lothian it straightens and widens to become a major feature of the county for its remaining twenty-mile course to the sea – although at Hailes, only four miles from salt-water, it again is narrowed into a deep defile by the upthrust of Traprain Law, a circumstance of which the Hepburn family took fullest advantage, as will emerge later.

At the head of the vale, then, lies the village of Ormiston, a pleasant place almost English in appearance, with its tree-lined, wide main street and air of quiet retirement. Yet for a time it was a mining community, which usually tends to leave its stark traces. That stage in its history did not last very long, and the disused pits here do not obtrude greatly. With a population of over 2000 it is quite large by Scots standards. The east end is the older part and most attractive, with its houses and gardens reaching down towards the Tyne's meadows. It was to the west that the mining houses proliferated. In the centre of the main street is a fifteenth-century mercat cross.

Ormiston's principal claim to fame undoubtedly is through the renown of the Cockburn family. The original Anglian incomers here who gave its name, the Orms, were succeeded by the Lindsays in the twelfth century, in David I's Norman colonization; and in 1368 a John Cockburn married the Lindsay heiress and commenced a long and notable line of lairds, who retained the estate until 1758. Ironically it was the last, who had to sell to the up-and-coming Hopes of Luffness and Hopetoun, who really made the name of Ormiston celebrated. For he was the greatest of the eighteenth-century Improvers, whose efforts and initiative heralded a revolution in farming practice, and to whom not only Scotland but the world owes an enormous debt. John Cockburn founded the Society of Improvers of Knowledge of Agriculture, who brought in a new age of drainage, tilling, enclosing, harvesting, tree-planting and marketing, and who introduced the potato and the turnip into Scotland.

Ormiston Hall, the Cockburn seat, lies a mile to the south, and still belongs to the Hopetoun family. The great mansion however, built in 1745 in the 'tea-caddy' style - an odd time to be erecting palaces, in the midst of the Jacobite troubles - is now only a shell, but with a modern house interestingly inserted within the walling. In fact there is a delightful enclave here, at the heart of the great estate, of modern houses developed out of the extensive range of domestic offices and walled gardens. But the more ancient fortified-house of the Cockburns is still there, recently excellently restored also. Here it was that George Wishart, one of the first martyrs of the Scottish Reformation, was arrested by the Earl of Bothwell in 1545, on the orders of Cardinal Beaton, whilst lodging with Alexander Cockburn, to go to his death at St Andrews. The fact that he was in the pay of Henry VIII, like sundry others of the Reformers, is sometimes forgotten; Henry, in his 'rough wooing' was making a determined effort to win Scotland, by hook or by crook, as we have seen at Luffness. He almost succeeded, too, for the Battle of Pinkie, a disaster for Scotland, was won by his invading army, only two years later, three miles north-west of Ormiston. The scanty ruins of the ancient church of Ormiston are still near the old fortalice – which probably means that the village was originally hereabouts also, but removed to improve the (laird's) amenity. Close by also is a tremendous yew-tree, which is known to have been old in 1474.

Not far away are two venerable defensive houses, Woodhall and Fountainhall, both dating from the sixteenth and seventeenth centuries. The latter, and larger, originally was called Woodhead; but when Sir John Lauder, of the Bass Rock family, bought it in 1681, he changed the name – for his son was about to be raised to the judiciary, and thought that a Senator of the College of Justice would sound better as Lord Fountainhall than as Lord Woodhead! The woods from which these two properties took their names are still very evident hereabouts.

A mile on the other side of Ormiston, on the long, high ridge of land which seals off the vale to the north, is the village of Elphinstone. This one is undeniably a mining community, and looks it. Nearby used to rise the mighty Elphinstone Tower, one of the most massive in the land. Unfortunately it was demolished about twenty years ago. It is from here that the well-known line of the Lords Elphinstone, related to the Queen Mother, take their title. And a little further along the same ridge, still standing fair and square thereon, is another fine ruined stronghold, Fawside Castle, overlooking the battlefield of Pinkie, happily about to be restored, privately. As well as Pinkie field, it overlooks one of the most magnificent prospects in all Lothian. The new and enterprising owners may have to complain about the wind, but never of the view, assuredly. This was for 500 years the seat of the family of Fawsyde of that Ilk – who seem to have played a less than glorious part in the famous battle. We read, from an English source admittedly, that before the fight the Fawsydes shot at the invaders ". . .

with hand-guns and hakbutts till the battle lost, when they pluct in their peces lyke a dog his taile, and couched themselfes within all muet; but by and by the hous was set on fyre and they, for their good will, brent and smoothered within." Stirring times.

Fawside or Falside is in the parish of Tranent; and the town of that name, the largest in the county – even though the population is only 6000-odd, but growing – lies at the eastern end of the aforementioned ridge. As with the other communities of this industrialized extreme western corner of East Lothian, Tranent lacks the picturesque aspect of the rest, with much of the humdrum and workaday about it. Yet its position is fine, on the high ground between the coastal plain at Prestonpans and the Vale of Tyne – its name, formerly Travernent or *Tref-nant*, means the homestead of the vale – and its background is far from humdrum, both resounding and grim. It was a Pictish religious settlement. Whether the Celtic monks there had any interest in the rich coal-seams we do not know. But the Roman Church which succeeded them certainly was concerned with developing material as well as spiritual wealth, and Tranent became important as a source of riches. Enough so for it to become a prize possession for the Norman incomers of the twelfth century. De Quincy was the family which got the rich barony of Tranent; and we have a charter of Seyr de Quincy in 1210, granting a coal-pit here to the monks of Newbotle. It is interesting that when the English invaded at the time of Pinkie battle, the local inhabitants were able to take refuge in these coal-pits, and so escape the ravages. Unfortunately the mining story was not all so felicitous. The details of employment conditions in these mines, of child and female labour, serfdom and the sale of workers, terrible punishments and general inhumanity on the part of the owners and management, make appalling reading. Children were actually arled, or sold, in their cradles, women hauled laden hutches on hands-and-knees along dark three-foot high tunnels and carried the coal on their backs up long ladders to the surface – and for the least infringement were savagely maltreated. No doubt other mining areas were as bad – but that does not make Tranent's story the prettier. Why the mining community was treated so much more inhumanly than other workers is not clear; but they seem to have been looked upon as the damned, partly on account of their underground work. They may have been, had to be, fairly tough customers, to be sure. Some indication of this is provided by the grim records of 1797, when the Tranent folk rose against the Scots Militia Ballot, protesting that it should not apply to them – which looks almost as though the men, at least, preferred the mines to being taken as soldiers. Anyway, the Cinque Ports Cavalry regiment was sent for – and greeted with sticks and stones. Whereupon the order to open fire was given, resulting in eleven dead, eight seriously wounded and thirty-six taken prisoner to Haddington gaol. Then the cavalry were ordered to clear the country around for two miles – and fifteen more corpses were found in the cornfields thereafter.

Other industries flourished here, of which we do not hear so much – brewing, candle-making, nail-forging, weaving and agricultural-machinery-making. All these have passed away, like the mining, although there is now quite a large industrial estate two miles to the east at Macmerry. But most of the development is now geared to the commuter, Edinburgh being only ten miles away and the A1 the link. However, open-cast coal-winning is now started at Tranent.

Actually that busy highway carries most travellers through Tranent without seeing the most interesting part of the town, which lies to the north and downhill, towards Prestonpans. Here is the original burgh, still with the parish church, traditional pantiled-roofed houses and quaint corners. In the midst rises the unusual small fortalice known as Tranent Tower, little-known, dating from the late sixteenth century, now surrounded by the litter of a contractor's yard. A family named de Wallange, latterly Vallance, held this directly of the King – why this small property was reserved for the Crown, surrounded by the great barony of the de Quincys and later the Setons, we are not told. What we are told is that the 'rental mail' was traditionally a snowball in summer and a rose in winter – if asked for. The King's feu collecter had to climb to the top of the tower to receive this rent. The snowball, of course, was produced from a permanent store of snow kept in the bowels of the earth, where the mineworkings could act as an ice-box.

The parish church is nearby. All that remains of the ancient edifice was converted into a mausoleum for the Cadell family of Cockenzie; and the present building dates only from 1800. Within it, somewhere, lies buried the famous Colonel Gardiner, hero of Prestonpans battle, his grave unmarked – rather extraordinary considering the number of odes, poems and memorial writings penned soon after his death. It was from the Tranent heights that Prince Charles Edward surveyed the field before the battle. Tranent looks forward to having the A1 by-pass it in 1981/82 when the open-cast mining should be finished.

The evocatively named Macmerry – the derivation is uncertain but might have been *Mag Mhairi*, St Mary's ridge – nowadays seems like a detached industrial suburb of Tranent. But it has long been a village in its own right and developed separately on this western edge of the large expanse of Gladsmuir. It had its own coal-pits and its quite large ironworks, with a blast-furnace, working local ironstone; but closed in 1874. Now it has a thriving local-authority industrial estate, with many small engineering and other factories and contractors' premises, built on part of a war-time airfield. Curiously enough, although there is notably little of antiquity to be seen about Macmerry today, one of the most famous names in Scottish history is connected with the place – that of Baliol. A family descended from the house which once briefly held the Scots throne, and later changed their name to Baillie, held the two properties of Hoprig and Penston, to north and south of Macmerry. Of this family came the Lords Lamington and many another distinguished line. In 1430 William Baillie of Hoprig and Penston married a Seton daughter and had four sons. The three eldest seem to have been almost too high-spirited even for those days. They mortally assaulted their clergyman tutor, and fled from Lothian. Oddly they seem to have split up, although so young. One went north to the Highlands and founded the line of Baillie of Dochfour, now Lord Burton; one went west, to Ireland; and one south, to Anglesey. All seem to have flourished. Their youngest brother carried on the line at home, which produced in due course Sir William Baillie, Master of the Wardrobe to Mary Queen of Scots, which must have been an onerous task. Also the Baillie-

Hamilton family, Earls of Haddington, still a power in the county. Both Hoprig and Penston are now only farms; but the latter was once quite a large village.

Just over two miles due south of Macmerry, on the Tyne itself, is the double village of Pencaitland, Easter and Wester, separated by the river and bridge. Both are quite attractive, the former more so, tree-girt and rural. Here is the old parish church, with its octagonal belfry and fine pre-Reformation aisle, possibly as early as the thirteenth century, although most of the building dates from the seventeenth century. A photograph and transcription of its fourteenth-century charter is displayed. Nearby was a row of cottages known locally as the College – which is an indication of how old links survive in country areas, for though Pencaitland never had a college, its church was collegiate before the Reformation.

At Wester Pencaitland the mercat cross still survives in the middle of the street, on its stepped plinth. Considerable modern housing development is taking place at this end. And a short distance to the west recently a vast new maltings has risen to dominate the scene less than graciously. Considering the profits made by the whisky business, it surely ought to have been possible to erect buildings less of an affront to the eye. Distilling itself has been part of the Pencaitland scene for long, however. At the Boggs, a mile to the north, now a smallholding community, was until the early nineteenth century a small family distillery which fitted well enough into the landscape. And on the Kinchie Burn a mile or so to the south, and remotely situated, another distillery was founded in 1824 and still operates, discreetly sited. It is now called Glenkinchie, as presumably sounding more 'Scotch'.

Facing the monstrous maltings across the Tyne is the important house or castle of Winton, within its parkland. Renowned as one of the finest examples of Renaissance architecture in the land, it was erected in 1620 on the foundations of an earlier dower-house of the Setons, by the famous master-mason William Wallace, the same who built the handsome George Heriot's School in Edinburgh. Constructed at the very end of the defensive period, it retains certain of the features of the fortified house in its L-shape, tall tower, turnpike stair-turrets and corbelling; but with its greater dimensions, ornamental stonework, decorative chimneys, handsome apartments and magnificent plaster ceilings, it pointed the way to a new age. The Setons lost it, as they had lost so much else, for supporting the Stewarts in 1715 – although their west-country female-line descendants still bear the title of Earls of Eglinton and Winton. The Hamiltons who were beginning to loom so large on the Lothian scene bought the forfeited estates and Winton has remained with their descendants, the present laird being Sir David Ogilvy, thirteenth baronet, who frequently opens his splendid home to the public. There used to be a village of Winton within the policies, or grounds; but as usual, later ideas of amenity ordained that this be removed out of sight of the mansion. So we have the rather pleasing small village of New Winton, built by Lady Ruthven, one of the Hamilton descendants, for employees and miners, in the middle of last century, she herself supervising the work, insisting on improvements and conveniences ahead of the times. She was greatly beloved, dying in 1885, aged ninety-six.

A mile down Tyne from Pencaitland, amongst the water-meadows, is Spilmersford, now only a picturesque scatter of cottages, but once another sizeable community, where local limestone was burned in kilns in a big way. Many fossilized sea-shells were found in this limestone although Spilmersford is now five miles back from the sea. There was also a waulk-mill, or fulling-mill here, where woollen cloth was scoured and thickened, a cornmill and a sawmill. It is interesting to note that in those days to avoid the hazards of Gladsmuir – see hereafter – the main road to Dunbar and Berwick and London came this way. And here was an inn, which became a noted resort of smugglers.

Obviously the river was crossed by a ford here formerly; but there has long been a bridge. Just beyond this are the lodge-gates to Saltoun Hall. This is another famous place, for long and until recently the home of the Fletcher family – although earlier giving title to a family of Abernethys, the seventh of whom became Lord Saltoun of Abernethy in 1445. This peerage passed through the female line to the Frasers, now based on Aberdeenshire, and in 1643 Andrew Fletcher, Lord Innerpeffer bought Saltoun. The name has nothing to do with salt, unlike Salt Preston and Saltcoats; it is thought to derive from Soulistoun, referring to the de Soulis family, once competitors with Bruce and Baliol for the Scots crown. There were many distinguished Fletchers, but undoubtedly the most famous was the patriot, Andrew, who fought so fervently against the Union of the Parliaments in 1707, and against the bribery and corruption of the statesmen and nobility which made it possible. Fletcher failed in that epic struggle, but succeeded in others - though not all. He opposed the Duke of York, during Charles II's reign, over his activities in Scotland, and was declared traitor and banished. He took part in Monmouth's rebellion, had to flee to the Continent, and on his return it is recorded "had the misfortune to shoot the Mayor of Lime". So back he went abroad. But he came into his own with the Glorious Revolution, and returned with the Prince of Orange. He was a voluminous writer. A contemporary description of him ends: "He hath wrote some very good things, but they are not published in his name. He hath a very good genius. A low, thin man, of a brown complexion, full of fire, with a stern, sour look and fifty years old." Along with his brother Henry, he was another of the agricultural improvers. They sent an emissary to Holland to learn the secret of making pot-barley - no doubt Andrew had learned of this during his exile there - and thereafter established the first barley-mill in Scotland. He founded a Young Scotland movement and a Home-Rule Party - oddly modern, this sounds. He is buried in the Fletcher crypt at the parish church in the pleasant village of East Saltoun, which climbs a gentle hill nearby. Here an annual commemoration ceremony is held each September. Saltoun Hall, a large and impressive rather than a beautiful mansion, incorporating the ancient tower of the Abernethys, is now divided into flats, but like its policies, well cared-for.

There is a pleasant village of West Saltoun also, hidden in the valley of the Birns Water a mile away, where the barley-mill was established, now converted into a delightful house. It is worth noting that the emissary sent from here to Holland was James Meikle, and it was his son, Andrew Meikle, who invented the threshing-machine. The first bleachfield formed by the renowned British Linen Company was also established here at West Saltoun. And there was a paper-mill and a starchworks. All these have gone now – but they started something which spread far and wide from East Lothian.

Down the Vale of Tyne again – for we were nearing the Lammermuir hillfoots area at Saltoun – on the way to the next bridge at Samuelston, lies the once highly important estate of Herdmanston or Hermandston, still a good farm but its glory long departed, its mansion only a site and its chapel only a neglected burial-vault. This was the seat of the great Norman-Scots family of St Clair, the Sinclairs, linked to the Earls of Orkney, Caithness and Rosslyn. Henry St Clair got a charter of Herdmanston as early as 1162. John St Clair erected the chapel in the thirteenth century. Sir Henry St Clair was companion-in-arms of Robert the Bruce, who after Bannockburn presented him with a sword inscribed: "*Le Roi me donne, St Clair me porte*". Descendants, in the late seventeenth century, inherited the title of Lord Sinclair, from the Orkney and Caithness line. There are still Lords Sinclair, but not at Herdmanston. It was here that one of the many murky incidents in the rise of the House of Stewart took place when, after the young Prince James had been safely conveyed to the Bass Rock in 1406, as described earlier, his uncle Albany's minions vented their master's spleen by attacking the group of nobles loyal to the sick King, who had escorted the boy. Henry St Clair, Earl of Orkney had remained with the prince, but his kinsman of Herdmanston, Sir David Fleming of Biggar and Cumbernauld, one of the monarch's closest friends, and others, were slain or taken prisoner, at Herdmanston. Now only pigeons and jackdaws haunt the lovely Tyne's bank here, where once there was a major castleton.

A mile on is the bridge at Begbie, leading over to Samuelston on the north side again. The place-names of East Lothian tell a fascinating story to those interested, helping to make the countryside 'three-dimensional', and represent the various layers of occupation, settlement and invasion of this desirable land – Pictish and Gaelic, both Celtic; Anglian, Saxon, Norse, Norman-French and English of the Braid Scots variety, a notable jumble. So that we have names like Pitcox and Pencaitland, Pictish or Brythonic; Dunbar and Aberlady and Garvald, Gaelic; this Begbie, Pogbie, Humbie and the like,

Anglian or Old English; Ormiston and Penston, Saxon; Luffness and Barnsness (Bjorn's), Norse; St Germains and Barney Mains (Barony), Norman-French; and Lammermuir and Gladsmuir, plain Scots. Many have become corrupted, of course, and are often mispronounced, especially by folk from the South, unsure where the accent comes. The local pronunciation is usually right. A fairly accurate and simple guide is to note where the accent is put. The Celtic (Pictish, Brythonic, Gaelic) names never put the accent on the first syllable. So it is not *Dun*-bar, as so many from England are apt to say, but Dun-*bar*. Whilst the non-Celtic and Norse do emphasize the first syllable; so we have *Hadd*ington and *Sal*toun and *Luff*ness.

A mile south of Begbie is Pilmuir, one of the most delightful small early-seventeenth-century laird's houses in all Scotland, standing within its old walled-garden and orchard, isolated amidst the great fields, its handsome doocot nearby.

Samuelston, across the bridge over Tyne, at least presents no pronunciation problem – although just who Samuel was is not clear. This is one of those picturesque, strangely hidden, and in this case decayed, villages, with resounding stories, in which Lothian is so rich. There is a theory for the placing of them, tucked in under a steep overhang of the land – even Haddington, the county town is so hidden, that the stranger is apt to be upon it before he knows it is there. It is suggested that these sites were deliberately chosen to be unseen from the coast, as security from raiders and invaders and Norsemen, all of whom were apt to come by sea. After all, there were plenty of more open and comfortable sites. Certainly, seen from the Forth, apart from the coastal havens, East Lothian rather gives the impression of being a lovely but uninhabited land, rising empty in green and gold folds to the hills.

Samuelston's secret site – it is safe to say that most East Lothian residents themselves have never seen it – well matches its story. For this was one of the major witch-centres of the land. Here no fewer than thirteen unfortunate women were burned in 1661. Samuelston's church of St Nicholas, now gone, must have been the scene of much thundering against the cult, for as late as 1705 its minister, the Reverend John Bell, went so far as to publish a book on the subject, entitled *An*

Ingenious and Scientific Discourse of Witchcraft. John Knox officiated in this church whilst still 'unreformed'.

Above Samuelston northwards the land lifts towards Gladsmuir. This, as its name implies – the gleds' or hawks' moor – is a large and wide place. It is a parish of its own and boasts a church and hamlet still, on the main A1 highway; but it used to be much more than that. It was the burgh muir or town common of Haddington, rather inconveniently situated, for the town is four miles to the east. It no longer gives the impression of a moor, having been tamed and drained and planted. But it was a wild enough place once, productive of many tales, in fact the haunt of robbers and sorners and the Scots equivalent of highwaymen. So much so that it used to be an occasion for prayers of thankfulness when unescorted travellers reached the safety of Haddington and Tranent.

There were more than hawks and highwaymen to Glads-muir, however. There was another coal-seam here, and Haddington folk used to mine it, not with consistent success. Latterly they used the coal to feed their gasworks. There was also a brickwork where the distinctive red pantiles for roofing were made; likewise a brewery. In the manse here was written Professor William Robertson's *History of Scotland,* published in 1759, highly thought of then, if less so nowadays. The parish church for a wide farming area is still here, its predecessor of 1692 standing roofless in the kirkyard. There is a saying that lightning never strikes twice in the same place. Gladsmuir can disprove this. Twice in the nineteenth century was it struck. On the first occasion the school was wrecked and no fewer that a dozen boys died, the master and others injured – or so we are assured. It would certainly tax Gladsmuir to raise a dozen schoolboys today. And on the second occasion it was the manse itself which was struck, and a maid died.

On the north side of Gladsmuir, the tract not the hamlet, the land is much more fertile; and here is a cluster of old estates stretching eastwards from Hoprig – Elvingston, Trabroun, Huntington and Alderston. Trabroun is especially interesting, although now only a farm. This was the seat of the Heriot family for centuries, of which came the famous George, goldsmith, banker and friend to James VI, who called him Jinglin' Geordie and took him to London with him in 1603, when he ascended the throne of the United Kingdom. Geordie was a notable character, and made a great fortune out of the English. He left a large sum to found the well-known school in Edinburgh, modelled on Christ's Hospital in London which he greatly admired. It was opened in 1647, built by the aforementioned William Wallace, and is still one of the most admired buildings in Edinburgh. Nevertheless, Wallace at least did not seem to do so well out of it, for when he died, soon afterwards, his widow petitioned the Governors for help for her needs on account of her "great burding of many small young babies". The school however has achieved renown far outwith Scotland; the present writer had the privilege of attending. There has been some confusion about the name Trabroun. In 1633 or thereabouts, with the prosperous George away in London with his master, his cousin sold the property to another cousin, the King's right-hand-man left in Scotland, the new Earl of Haddington, and moved away to another estate, fifteen miles to the south, Collielaw in Lauderdale, Berwickshire. He took the old name with him – only here, in time, they spelt it in the more genteel form of Trabrown. Today there is a farm and hill of that name two miles north-west of Lauder, and close to the hill of Collielaw.

At Alderston, two miles to the east of Trabroun, its Georgian mansion now used for local government offices, we are just above the all-but-hidden county town of Haddington. Before it is reached there is what still manages to remain the separate hamlet of St Lawrence. This was the medieval town's leper hospice, well outwith the walls, as necessary by parliamentary edict. The name is interesting. There are other St Lawrences in Scotland, often just outside towns, which could also have been leper-houses. If so, it seems likely that the name is merely a Scots form of St Lazarus; for this was the usual saint connected with leprosy-relief – whence came the terms lazar-house and lazaretto. This was because of the ancient Order of Chivalry, the Military and Hospitaller Order of St Lazarus of Jerusalem, which from crusading times has devoted itself to this cause, and still does.

An entire book should be written about the delightful and historic royal burgh of Haddington; but space here permits

only the briefest references. Far enough removed from Edinburgh, sixteen miles, and in the midst of its own rich farming
area, it has retained its true character of a country town,
market and shopping hub, cultural and social institutions and
above all, independent outlook, even though commuters inevitably increase. Its population is under 6000. I once heard it
described as a sleepy little place; but this is a complete
misjudgement. It is a busy, bustling, lively community, architecturally and scenically very pleasing, with the Tyne running
through it. Because of its narrow, valley-floor site, mercifully,
expansion has been limited, and such new housing development as there is has had to be at either end, where it is not
obtrusive.

A few years ago a most admirable 'face-lift' programme was
instigated by the town council and other public bodies and the
citizens and shopkeepers responded nobly – they had excellent
material to work on, admittedly. As a result, the streets are
bright with varied colour-wash, paintwork is freshened and
plaster renewed, the many intriguing wynds and lanes invite
inspection, and humbler buildings set off the more handsome –
of which there are not a few. Fortunately the A1 traffic no
longer roars through the town – although many travellers
may well tear along the by-pass unaware of what they are
missing so nearby.

Like many another old Scots burgh, what has been the
original wide market-place has been divided down the centre
by an island-sited tolbooth or town-house and later rows of
houses and shops, to form two main central streets, now High
Street and Market Street. The Haddington town-house is now
no tolbooth but a very fine Adam building of 1748, with a tall
church-like steeple and clock added in 1831 – which still
strikes the hour of curfew at 10 p.m. and 7 a.m., 103 chimes.
Internally it is very handsome and in great demand for local
functions. The burgh's most notable building, however, is the
great cathedral-like parish church of St Mary, sited on the
bank of Tyne some distance from the town-centre. This
impressive and splendid edifice, cruciform in design and dating
in the main from the late fourteenth century probably, seems
really too large to be the parish church for a comparatively
small town – and there are other Established churches too; but

it is an indication of the early importance of Haddington and the wealth of its hinterland. The square tower at the crossing, 90 feet high, although it has lost its original open-work crown similar to that of St Giles, in Edinburgh, is magnificent; and the great west doorway surmounted by a beautifully-worked mullioned and arched window 18 feet wide, is equally handsome. It is often referred to as the Lamp of Lothian, *lucerna Laudoniae*; but this name originally applied to the Abbey of Haddington, a proud and renowned nunnery of the Franciscans which lay almost a mile to the east of the town, where is a hamlet still known as the Abbey and a fine, old bridge. This establishment, now wholly gone, had a stirring story. Another misapprehension is that the church got its by-name from being so often alight, set on fire by successive English invading armies, which came this way *en route* to Edinburgh. Haddington, and no doubt its church and abbey, were indeed frequently in flames; but in fact the phrase referred to the Abbey's reputation as a lamp of learning and spirituality – although some of the tales relating thereto scarcely convey that impression. It was founded in 1178 by the Countess Ada, mother of Malcolm IV and his brother William the Lyon; and a parliament was held in it in 1548, when the decision was taken to send the infant Mary Queen of Scots to France for safety from Henry VIII's 'rough wooing'. As to the great St Mary's Church, however, if it was not the Lamp of Lothian it was sufficiently important in its own right. Prior to the Reformation it had no fewer than eleven chapels within it, some oddly named, such as the Three Kings of Cologne and St Towbart's. Herein was buried Jane Welsh, a Haddington woman and Thomas Carlyle's wife; also in the underground Maitland crypt, amongst others, the notorious John Maitland, Duke of Lauderdale, who ruled Scotland, and badly, for King Charles II. It used to be of great local interest how the Devil did not allow the wretched Duke to sleep in peace in his vault, the coffin frequently changing position; actually this was caused by the waters of the Tyne flooding in, and then receding again. The Tyne floods are still a hazard at Haddington. In 1775 the water rose 17 feet above normal and the entire town was awash as high as the third step of the High Street's mercat cross.

Today there is a most praiseworthy movement known as the Lamp of Lothian Collegiate Trust, connected with St Mary's Church, which has set itself most ambitious and varied tasks in the rehabilitation and enhancement both of the great church building and in aspects of the spiritual and cultural life of the town. Active and dedicated efforts by supporters from all walks of life, known as the Friends of St Mary's, with the Queen Mother as patron, help to keep going the organization started by the Duchess of Hamilton and the former Town Clerk, and sundry others, in 1967. Great things have been achieved and Haddington is to be congratulated; not many modestly sized communities such as this have attempted and achieved so much - even though some of the cherished projects have yet to be fulfilled.

One of the efforts which has borne fruit is the excellent restoration of the fine late-seventeenth-century Haddington House, in Sidegate, a tall, commodious and dignified Scots laird's town-house in the vernacular style, of L-plan, stair-tower, steep roofing, crow-stepped gables and gleaming white walling. It is now an asset to the townsfolk both in its appearance and its accommodation. A subsidiary trust has more recently been set up to create a seventeenth-century garden here. And not far away is another success, the Poldrate Mill complex, in which an old riverside water-mill, with its storehouses and barns, has been imaginatively converted into halls and work-rooms and premises for a variety of youth and other community activities which require space and less-than-formal surroundings. The most costly efforts, of course, have been in the re-roofing of one transept of St Mary's, and other restoration works in the great church.

From all this it will be perceived that the county town suffers no lack of facilities for the fuller cultural and social life, with groups and societies, literary, artistic, musical, educational and sporting, well to the fore - rather extraordinary, really, for a place of such relatively small population; again, it is the rich agricultural hinterland which greatly helps.

There was a royal palace here once, on the site of the former County Buildings. William the Lyon was often here; and indeed his son, Alexander II was actually born here. Margaret Tudor, Henry VIII's sister, came here, at the age of fourteen, on her way to wed James IV. And John Knox was allegedly born in the Giffordgate of Haddington – although claims have also been made for Morham not far away. At least he practised here as notary around 1540; and when George Wishart preached his last sermon in St Mary's, before being apprehended at Ormiston, Knox went as his bodyguard, carrying a great two-handed sword before and complaining at the smallness of the congregation. Many other famous folk have been natives of the town, including the renowned Samuel Smiles.

A part of Haddington beloved of artists and photographers especially, is the Nungate, a sort of suburb east of the Tyne, on the way, as its name suggests, to the former Abbey, the old hump-backed bridge to it highly scenic, with a carriageway only 12 feet wide and extraordinarily steep approaches. Malefactors used to be hanged from the arch at the west end. The ruined ancient church of St Martin's, has a vaulted roof, still in part evident. For a church of this period – it is older than anything in St Mary's – it is peculiarly high and narrow, the choir or chancel being only 12 feet wide. It is surrounded by one-time riverside mills and tanneries, typical of an agricultural community, with many old houses and cottages, all in the authentic sturdy stonework and red pantiled roofing of old Scotland, almost like a separate village with its lanes and closes. Much of the modern council-housing has had to be in this area, but it has been placed fairly well apart and behind. Beyond Nungate lies the Amisfield estate, once belonging to the Charteris family, who brought the name from their old lands of Amisfield in Dumriesshire. It is now Haddington's golf-course.

Other ancient and renowned estates ring the town – Lennoxlove, Coalstoun, Letham, Stevenston and others, still in private hands. Lennoxlove, the seat of Elizabeth, Duchess of Hamilton, barely a mile to the south, is particularly interesting. This was anciently Lethington, and the massive fifteenth-century, thick-walled tower still forms the dominant part of the mansion, with its magnificent Great Hall, Scottish Baronial architecture at its finest. This must have been part of a much older castle, for the hall has three holes or hatches in its lofty vaulted ceiling for the escape of smoke from an early central fireplace – before flues and chimneys were thought of – although now there are two storeys above this. The historic apartments are open to the public in the season, and full of treasures including a death-mask of Mary Queen of Scots; and a silver toilet service presented to La Belle Stuart by Charles II – and thereby hangs a tale. The lovely Frances Teresa Stuart, Duchess of Lennox, was a reigning beauty of Charles's Restoration Court – she is said to be the model for the effigy of Britannia on the pre-decimal coinage. A favourite with the monarch, naturally, she was also fond of her cousin, another and impoverished Stewart, the Lord Blantyre. He was very eager to possess Lethington, which the objectionable Duke of Lauderdale seems to have been prepared to dispose of – he had other properties galore. But Blantyre could not afford the price, and the fair Frances came to his rescue and sent the necessary cash in a casket still preserved in the house, with her love. So Lennoxlove Lethington became. There is a less romantic story that when the Duchess of Lennox died in 1702 she left the bulk of her fortune to Lord Blantyre's son, for the purchase of property to be called after her. You can take your choice. Originally there was a family of Lethington or Levington of that Ilk, here – no doubt the same who went to Saltcoats near Gullane: but the Maitlands of Lauderdale came in the fourteenth century. The twelfth of the line was a renowned poet of the early sixteenth century, who appears to have been, like others since, distressed by the flightiness of the other sex in that day and age. Haddington's ladies in especial seem to have offended his susceptibilities:

> Sum wyfis of the burrows-toun sa wondir vane ar, and wantoun,
> In warld thay watt not quhat to weir.
> On clathis they waist mony a croun, and all for newfangilnes of geir.
> Sumtimes they will beir up thayre gown, to shaw thayre wilicoat hing-and doun,
> And sumtimes baith thay will upbeir, to shaw thayre hose of black or broun;
> And all for newfanglines of geir.

This Sir Richard Maitland was also impressed by the massiveness of the house he had inherited:

Greit wes the wark to houke the grounde and thy foundation
    cast;
But greiter it wes tan to found and end thee at the last.
I marvel that he did not feir wha raisit thee on hicht,
That no foundation should thee beir but thou should sink for
    wecht.

The sons of this poetic laird were still more famous.
William, the eldest, was the well-known Secretary Maitland
of Lethington, to Mary Queen of Scots, a man dexterous if not
consistently reliable; and his brother John became for a time
the power behind the young James VI, Mary's son, and in due
course Chancellor of Scotland and first Lord Maitland of
Thirlstane. So that Scotland could be said to have been ruled
largely from this house twice, in the late sixteenth and late
seventeenth centuries.

The adjoining estate of Coalstoun – or Cumbercolstoun as
it was called in the earliest charters – has been in the possession
of a family of the good Scots name of Broun since the
thirteenth century, not a few of whom seem to have been
notable characters. The Coalstoun Pear is a cherished relic, a
wizened fossilized fruit, alleged to have been plucked from a
tree by Sir Hugo de Gifford, known as the Wizard, in the
thirteenth century, during the wedding procession of his
daughter, and given to the bride. Whether she or one of her
descendants married a Broun is not clear; but it came into the
Coalstoun family early on, and is supposed to ensure that
Brouns will remain in possession so long as they cherish the
said pear. There are still Broun-Lindsays there.

Letham is a particularly attractive mansion lying a mile
west of Haddington, deep in the valley, a long whitewashed
late-seventeenth-century house of the same period and style as
Haddington House but larger. At one time it belonged to the
Hepburns. And Stevenston, two miles to the east, at a former
ford of the Tyne, amidst woodlands, shows less signs of
antiquity but is a most pleasing property, formerly belonging
to the Sinclairs, like Herdmanston.

Here, east of Haddington, under the Garleton Hills to the
north, the great productive fields of the vale are abruptly
interrupted and upheaved by the isolated, towering volcanic
hill of Dunpender or Traprain Law, which for a mile or two

changes the entire character of the land, and not only scenically. Instead of sweeping broad acres of cornland we have
whin-clad slopes and rough pasture, outcropping rock and
thorn-scrub. The river changes too, from a wide and fairly
placid stream to a fast-moving torrent surging through a
narrow defile. And in the centre of this defile, rearing on a
rock above the river stands the castle of Hailes, darkly impressive and long ruinous but now well cared-for by the Department of the Environment. Although deep in this gloomy den,
its site was well chosen by the acquisitive Hepburns. For the
old main road, indeed the only one, used to run through here,
not climb over Pencraik Hill to the north as the A1 does
now; and no traveller could pass Hailes Castle unless he paid
toll or was sufficiently strongly escorted. These old barons
were apt to have a keen eye for financial advantage – just as
many of their successors still have in the board-rooms of the
City of London. The Hepburns rose to great power in East
Lothian, becoming Earls of Bothwell, the fourth Earl and
seventh Lord Hailes marrying Mary Queen of Scots as her
third husband and coming to a sorry end in Denmark, after a
highly adventurous career – where his embalmed body is still
the source of controversy. His nephew and successor was the
witch-master of North Berwick and bane of Mary's son James
VI's existence. A very constricted battle was fought here in the
defile in the early fifteenth century between Hotspur Percy
and his invading English and the Scots under Douglas leader-
ship, the latter triumphing on this occasion. The Percys of
Northumberland and the Douglases were at famous feud for
centuries of course; and it is good to point out that the present
Dowager Duchess of Hamilton, at Lennoxlove, was the Lady
Elizabeth Percy, who surely ended the feud at last by marrying Douglas Douglas-Hamilton, premier duke of Scotland and
Earl of Angus, in 1937.

High above Hailes towers Traprain which, as I have indicated, could be called the true heart of Lothian in that here
was the greatest early centre of population for the entire
seaboard, in Pictish times, strange as this may seem. Although
not so strange when the extraordinarily strong defensive
nature of the site is considered, the tremendous view-point,
the rich land around and the fact that invasion and attack was

all apt to come by sea and Traprain was able to overlook the entire southern mouth of the Forth or Scottish Sea. So here grew up the garrison-town and capital of the Votadini or southern Pictish nation. No doubt they did not all dwell, in their thousands, on the top of this soaring hill, even though it covers quite a large acreage, but would have their cabins and dwellings scattered over a wide area around of pastureland and tilth, only retiring to the mighty hilltop fort in time of danger. Traces of their occupation of the lower ground survive. A standing-stone, all that remains of a stone-circle for sun-worship, is to be found below the steep south escarpment. And the present writer remembers the elation with which he found some years ago a small souterrain or Pictish earth-house, on a shelf of the lower slope to the west, a stone-lined, underground little corridor, less than three feet high and about eight feet long. These constructions, typical of the Picts, were not really houses, of course, except in the sense of storehouses for the safe-keeping of grain and perishable meats, which could remain cool and also hidden. It seems strange indeed that no full-scale exploration and excavation of the entire site has been put in hand. Especially as, in 1919, some excavation was started on the summit of the hill, and here was found the tremendously exciting 'treasure of Traprain', a hoard of Roman silver now kept in the National Museum of Antiquities in Edinburgh. This, of course, was nothing to do with the Pictish Votadini but thought to be a pirate's hoard buried up here at a later date. But it is a pity that further digging is not pursued, for the ramparts and foundations are clearly visible. An even greater pity that the local authority stone-quarrying operations at the east end of the hill are permitted to continue year after year, gouging out a vast bite of the site. I would hazard a guess that if it had been a private quarrying venture, this defacement of one of the most historic sites in all Scotland, would have been stopped by the said local authority's planning committee long ago.

Where the Tyne's valley begins to open out again after the constriction of the Hailes-Traprain defile, the quaint little town of East Linton nestles in the river's hollow, another of Lothian's hidden communities. Although small, with under 1000 of population, it was a burgh with its own provost and

town-council until the recent unfortunate municipal revolution imposed by far-off politicians. Actually, despite its modest
dimensions, it is in the nature of a double-town, two communities half-a-mile apart. The northerly section is not North
Linton or even West Linton however – there is a West Linton
thirty miles away in Peeblesshire – but Prestonkirk. Altogether
the name situation is odd here. One might expect the place to
be called Tinton rather than Linton, or Tyne-ton. But the
Tyne here, rushing out of its gorge, surges over a series of rock
shelves and scoops, forming cataracts and waterfalls, hence the
word Linn, as in the famous Linn o' Dee and elsewhere. But
why the East? It did not used to be so distinguished, a charter
of 1127 referring to it only as Linton. And why not Prestonkirk, the parish name, for it all? There is the parish church.
The fine old bridge, however, is at the Linton end.

Because of the great rush of water-power, this has always
been a great place for mills. Possibly the monks of the nearby
Red Friars or Trinitarian monastery of Houston, across the
river, first established their mill here in the haugh, hence the
names Preston Haugh and Prestonkirk. The successor of that
mill still functions as a working water-wheel mill, a famous
and picturesque landmark beloved of artists and visitors
generally, now in the cars of the National Trust for Scotland,
complete with its old mill-lade and duck-pond. But the
others, clinging to the waterside at East Linton itself, are now
converted to other uses. The parish church on its knoll is
interesting. It was rebuilt in 1770 but retains the fine chancel
of the earlier building dedicated to St Baldred. Baldred has left
his name very much in evidence all around here. There are St
Baldred's Bed, Cradle, Buss (a sunken rock), Boat, Well and
even an eddy on the Tyne called St Baldred's Whirl. Saxon
chronicles refer to this church as "*Prestoni Baldridi Espiscopi*".

If East Linton's situation is not apt to be perceived until one
is upon it, seemingly lost amongst the rolling fields, yet
strangely the main A1 road to the South thunders past it only
a hundred or two yards away, and the main Edinburgh-
London railway-line crosses Tyne here also. Yet a comparatively sleepy atmosphere seems to prevail. Or is that only an
outsider's impression?

A short distance east of the town lies the fine farm of

Phantassie, an odd name – although there is another of the same near Haddington – no doubt a corruption of something ancient, *fan* in Gaelic meaning a slope. This was the birthplace of the brothers George and John Rennie in the 1760s. George, the elder, was another of the East Lothian agricultural improvers and inventors of farm machinery – also he was claimed as her first love by Jane Welsh, of Haddington, before she married Thomas Carlyle. But his brother John was still more famous, best known now as the designer of Waterloo Bridge, in London, and buried in Westminster Abbey. He started out by designing improvements to mill machinery, started early, for by the age of ten he had made working models of windmills, a steam-engine and a pile-engine. By eighteen he had erected three corn-mills along the Tyne and others elsewhere. Then he turned his hand to bridges and canals, to become one of the best-known civil engineers in Britain. He built harbours and docks and the enormous mile-long breakwater at Plymouth. Of his fine and graceful bridge at Musselburgh, which still carries the A1, it was so different from most bridges of the time that a passing carter, when asked how he liked the new bridge, said: "Brig? Yon's nae brig ava. Ye neither ken when ye're on't, nor whan ye're off't."

The Tyne beyond this meanders widely and more placidly, its journey to the sea nearly over, its final miles rich as ever. Just over a mile north-east of Prestonkirk, but well away from the main road, the attractive little village of Tyninghame lies west of the river, one of the prettiest in Scotland. Also one of the most ancient, for with Preston and Auldhame it was a St Baldred's parish, to which he left his useful corpse in triplicate, as it were. In time Whitekirk superseded it as the parish, and now there is no church at Tyninghame; indeed it is more or less an estate village for the great property of the same name, seat of the Earl of Haddington, nearby. The ruins of St Baldred's Church, or its medieval successor, lie within the grounds, in twelfth-century Romanesque architecture, now the Haddington family burial-place. It used to have the privilege of sanctuary for wrong-doers or fugitives.

Tyninghame estate is a fine place by any standards, held by the Baillie-Hamilton family since Tam o' the Coogate, Sir

Thomas Hamilton of Binning, James the VI and I's Lord Advocate and crony, bought it in 1628. Like Geordie Heriot, another of the Wisest Fool in Christendom's intimates, he became very rich and, in due course, first Earl of Haddington. We shall hear a deal more of him hereafter. The present and popular Earl is the twelfth. His estate stretches along this quiet and lovely coastline – quiet save in an easterly gale – for miles, and includes the mouth of the Tyne area which, with the agreement of Lord Haddington, is now designated the John Muir Country Park, along with much of the Dunbar coastal fringe. Here a variety of activities are available for the public, over 1667 acres of very attractive country and seaboard, including nature trails, horse-riding, sea-fishing and simple walking and observing birds. There are picnic areas and special events, with a resident warden who tends to cover the ground on horseback. Tynemouth itself is a most scenic and interesting place, of green saltings, red rocks, golden sands and the white breakers of the long bar – for this is the open North Sea now, no longer the Forth estuary – all backed by dark old pine-forest and fine parkland, a haunt of wildfowl and waders. The mansion of Tyningham is a huge and rambling red-stone pile, largely rebuilt in 1829 but incorporating older work and full of treasures. Its gardens are a delight, frequently open to the public, its great and ancient holly-trees notable. Binning Woods nearby used to be one of the largest and most renowned beech-plantations in Scotland, planted by the sixth Earl in 1705 and covering 400 acres, with thirteen rides or avenues leading to a central hub. Unfortunately all this was cut down for timber in the national need during the last war; it has however been largely replanted.

At the other side of Tynemouth estuary Belhaven Bay opens, a wide and shallow indentation, with two communities at its head, Belhaven itself and Westbarns. The name should really be Beilhaven, for this is where the quite major Beil Water or Burn reaches the sea. Its village is another delightful, old-world community of vernacular architecture, white-washed walling and red roofing, narrow lanes and gardens. It has quite a well-known brewery, but this is tucked away unobtrusively. Also a hospital. Pantiles used to be manufactured here. The name of Belhaven almost rivals that of

Fletcher of Saltoun in the annals of Scotland's fight to retain national identity. John, third Lord Belhaven and Stenton, one more Hamilton, was another stalwart in the struggle against the incorporating Union of 1707, and suffered imprisonment in the Tower of London for his views. He lived at Biel House, a couple of miles up the secluded valley of the Biel Water, a huge and handsome mansion incorporating an ancient tower, as so often, set amongst fine hanging gardens. He built a Latin inscription over his front door - "TRADITIONIS SCO. ANNO PRIMO 1707" - *traditionis* here meaning betrayal or surrender.

West Barns, which lies near the outfall of the Biel Water into the bay, lacks the charm of Belhaven, being neither ancient nor characterful; but it has its own attraction, and the industry, although less discreetly sited, is equally authentic of the soil, an agricultural machinery depot. A former maltings is now a racing stable.

Belhaven has managed to maintain its separate identity despite Dunbar's encroachments - for they are only a mile apart. The Dunbar golf-course, along the coast, helps. Dunbar is the last of the seven East Lothian burghs and the third-largest, with a population of almost 4000. It is very much a place by itself, in distinct isolation, facing out to the North Sea, Edinburgh twenty-eight miles away, Eyemouth, the next town, twenty two-miles to the south-east. The Lammermuirs come close to the sea here, adding to the cut-off impression. So it is another self-sufficient sort of community, quite attractive of appearance and full of individuality. Famous too, for all sorts of things; its magnificent rich red soil, almost startlingly red, which has for long been productive of the finest potatoes, known wherever such crops are grown; its climate, for next to the Isle of Tiree this is the driest place in Scotland, with considerably lower rainfall and higher sunshine averages than all rivals. This does not make it the warmest, for it is very much exposed to easterly winds off the sea. It is of course a favoured holiday-place, with a great deal to offer the discerning, unspoiled by such as promenades, amusement-parks and the like but with ample to keep the visitor happy including a picturesquely-sited open-air pool under a cliff. It is still a fishing-port and a notable yachting-centre, with its twin harbours, these spared the estuarian drawbacks of drying out at low-water.

Historically Dunbar is famous also. When in 1072 William the Conqueror ejected Cospatrick, Earl of Northumbria from that great inheritance, Malcolm Canmore, his cousin, made him Earl of Dunbar in compensation – he being of the Celtic royal line – with most of Lothian and the Berwickshire Merse as well, whence presently came the title of March to add to that of Dunbar. So commenced a period of great power and influence in Scotland emanating from Dunbar, which was not terminated until 1435 when, by a murky intrigue, the Douglases in conjunction with the Crown which saw the house of Dunbar as too powerful altogether, brought them low and ensured that their successors did not rise again. Oddly, however, the record has been put straight twice; once, when Sir George Home, a direct descendant, and one more minion of James VI and I, Chancellor of the Exchequer in England and Lord High Treasurer of Scotland – a notable combination – ruled Scotland for his master, and was appointed Earl of Dunbar of a new creation in 1605; and again in recent times when Sir Alec Cospatrick Douglas-Home, descendant of both the Dunbar and Douglas earls, became first Foreign Secretary and then Prime Minister of Great Britain. In the thirteenth century the grandson of the third Earl of Dunbar married the Home heiress, in the Merse, and their descendants took that name, for the Celtic royal line did not demean themselves with surnames. The Homes still flourish in the Merse, just over Lammermuir from Dunbar.

The earls' castle of Dunbar, now represented only by an enduring fang of red-stone masonry overhanging the old harbour, was an extraordinary fortress, one of the so-called 'keys of the kingdom', in its own way as unusual as Tantallon of the Douglases, ten miles away, and almost as impregnable. Today, its size, strength and curious construction are seldom appreciated, for harbour-works have cleared away most of its site. The fact was that its builders utilized the rugged coastal rock buttresses and stacks here, in highly dramatic fashion, linking them together with bridging masonry, covering them with towers and bartisans and creating an astonishingly out-spread and extensive citadel, much of which was necessarily suspended over salt-water. One of the linking vaulted corridors was no less than 69 feet long. And the harbour, busy and important, could not be entered save by permission of the earl, who charged his tolls naturally. This castle withstood many sieges, both from Scots and English monarchs – for the Dunbars looked upon themselves as almost independent princes and sided with whichever best suited their book at any given time. The most famous siege, probably, was that of 1339, sustained by Black Agnes, Countess of Dunbar, a lady of spirit. She was a daughter of the famous Randolph, Earl of Moray, Bruce's nephew and companion-in-arms. Montague, Earl of Salisbury came here on his way to attack the dead Bruce's infant son's regime, and Black Agnes held him up for nineteen weeks. Salisbury brought up a great siege-engine, called a Sow; but Agnes shouted scoffingly: "Beware, Montagow, for farrow shall thy Sow!"

Also, she and her ladies mockingly wiped with their ker-chiefs the walling where the Sow's stones hit. Wyntoun the chronicler describes it thus:

> Schyre William Montague, that sua, had tane the siege in hy gret ma,
> A mekil and richt stalwart engine, and up smertly gert dress it;
> Syne they warpit at the wall great stanes, baith hard and heavy,
> But that nane merrying to them made, and alsua when they castyne had,
> With a towel a damiselle arrayed jollily and well, wippit the wall,
> That they micht see to gere them mair annoyed be.

The long poem ends thus:

> The English oysid to make karping: "I vow to God she makes gret stere,
> The Scottische wenche ploddere,
> Come I aire or come I late, I fand Annot [Agnes] at the yate!"

Because it was situated on the direct route north from the Border at Berwick-on-Tweed for invading armies, Dunbar was inevitably much involved in turmoil and war. Out of the innumerable encounters fought here, two were important enough to be referred to in our history as the Battle of Dunbar

- one, in 1296, in the early stages of the Wars of Independence; the other in 1650, in Cromwell's campaigns. Both were disasters for Scotland. Here is no place to go into details. Suffice it to say that it was folly, not inferior numbers or lack of bravery, which lost the day in both.

Dunbar still has its battles, of a different sort. The siting of a great cement-works here a few years ago was strongly contested by some, supported by others. One school of thought said that it would ruin the amenity of an otherwise unspoiled coastline, and stick out like a sore thumb – as indeed it does, as well as coating the immediate vicinity under a film of white dust. Also that it would ruin excellent farmland. Those in favour declared that it would bring much-needed employment to Dunbar. Great deposits of the necessary limestone were available here, a mile or two east of the town. Anyway, the objectors failed, the lime being mined in vast open-cast pits reminiscent of the infernal regions; but the famous red topsoil is carefully scraped aside and then replaced on top of the infilling. Whether this will burgeon again as highest-quality tilth remains to be proved. But nothing will lessen the impact of the huge, gaunt, grey concrete constructions rising starkly out of the level fields, their tall chimney-stacks emitting plumes of dusty-white smoke visible ten and more miles away. Now a noted archaeological site, a Pictish fort and settlement, is in the way of the excavations and seemingly must go.

There is a new controversy. The electricity authorities propose to erect a mighty nuclear generating-station at Torness in the same area, a monster capable of producing unheard-of quantities of power. Needless to say there has been a still greater outcry against this, not only the amenity and conservation but the anti-nuclear and safety interests protesting their horror. The issue seems to be now decided, to build; any delay is more on account of technical problems and second-thoughts than persuasion by the objectors. The juggernaut of so-called progress is hard to halt where power is concerned. The balance between nature, beauty, amenity and the rights of small communities, on the one hand, and of industry and employment on the other, is difficult indeed.

Dunbar itself as a town remains fairly unspoiled. Most of its architecture is typical Lowland Scots burghal, but there are some distinctive buildings. The most distinguished undoubtedly is the large mansion, almost a palace, built by Robert Adam for the Earls of Lauderdale, converting an earlier house of the Fall family, a notable merchant line descending allegedly from the gipsy Faa 'royal family' of Yetholm. Oddly, it was a Provost Fall who in 1781 held off an American privateer also called Fall, two years after Paul Jones himself had made a raid here. This mansion, variously called Dunbar House, Lauderdale House and the Barracks – for it was so used in later years – blocks the north end of the wide High Street and is now used as a local-authority hostel and flats, part of the barrack-block turned into a seafood factory. Midway along the street is the attractive seventeenth-century tolbooth, with its crow-stepped gables, six-sided stair-tower with two clocks and two sundials, and steeple roof, the highly unusual burgh cross, with four mask-gargoyles, standing nearby.

The excellence of some of the council housing down near the harbour is worth mentioning, designed by Sir Basil Spence and a lesson in what can be done in this sphere. Behind the town-centre, in the area still known as Friars' Croft, is the peculiar-looking tower of the former Red Friars' monastery, resembling a doocot. And the parish church is interesting, a notably large building seating no fewer than 1800, when it was rehabilitated in 1820 by the well-known Gillespie Graham, who converted an ancient cruciform collegiate church which, when the ninth Earl (Black Agnes's husband) founded it, had no fewer than a dean, a vice-dean and eight prependary priests. Remaining within, from the earlier building, is one of the most elaborate and extraordinary monuments in stone and marble to be seen anywhere in Scotland, to the memory of the aforementioned George Home, Earl of Dunbar, so created in 1605. It is 26 feet high and 12 feet broad with, apart from the life-size effigy of the earl himself, in his Garter robes, kneeling before an open Bible, female figures representing Justice, Wisdom, Fame and Peace, with an inscription sufficiently adulatory to conceal the fact that this was one of the most-hated individuals in Scotland, on whom Jamie depended for the imposition of prelacy in his northern kingdom, and who died in London in 1611 "not without suspicion of poison" – some suggested administered by King Jamie's own command.

The Vale of Tyne could be said to end at Dunbar, for the narrow coastal strip south-eastwards is really only the final shelf of the Lammermuirs, which here come to within a mile or so of the sea. This seven-mile stretch will therefore be dealt with under Lammermuir.

The Vale of Peffer lies parallel to that of Tyne, to the north, and separated from it by the modest heights of the Pencraik, Garleton and Kilduff Hills. Compared with the other, it is a modest valley, indeed not always to be recognizable as such, only some ten miles in length and averaging three to four in width, with a peculiar and much higher hanging-valley of Garleton forming a sort of horn to the south-west. But though very much the junior partner in this central belt, its lands are fully as rich. And it has a distinction denied to Tyne – in fact, I know of no other such phenomenon in all Scotland; for the Peffer Burn succeeds in flowing both east and west, so that the vale has no head but two mouths. There are indeed two Peffer Burns, whose headwaters rise within a short distance of each other, one flowing six miles to the east to fall into the open sea between Auldhame and Tyninghame; the other six and a half miles, to reach Aberlady Bay on the Forth estuary. Both are called Peffer, without distinction and both are fairly sluggish and uninspiring rivers, with a fall of no more than twenty-five or thirty feet in all their lengths. Yet between them they have formed this extraordinary and fertile vale which, considering its size is probably worth more per acre than any other agricultural terrain in the land, for spaced out here is an uninterrupted succession of the richest farms in Lothian. Indeed, to stand on one or other of the gentle heights on either side and look out over the Vale of Peffer in harvest-time is an experience hardly to be rivalled or forgotten.

When describing the Aberlady-Gullane area of the coastal belt we dealt with Luffness and Saltcoats and Fentoun, near the western mouth of Peffer. Proceeding eastwards from there, across the vale is one of its only three villages, Drem, a small and pleasant place on the main railway-line, where the minor branch to North Berwick turns off. A strange name, it might derive from *druim*, a ridge – only there is no very evident ridge around. It was quite important once, a barony in the hands of the Knights Templar, a mere fragment of whose chapel remains between the farmhouse and the road. During the last war it came back into prominence for a while when its fine level fields were turned into an airfield, with hidden dispersal points far and wide around. Somewhere to the east of it was probably fought the great semi-legendary battle which influenced Scotland in a way no other has done. The exact date, site and even the identity of the leaders are not known for certain. But allegedly, in the mid-eighth century, an invading Northumbrian army of great size was challenged here, in the Vale of Peffer, by an unusual alliance of Picts and Scots. The story goes that Hungus or Angus mac Fergus, King of the Southern Picts and Achaius, King of Scots (there was no Achaius reigning then, but there was a succession of Eochaid, Aedh and Eochaid again, which Latin scribes might well so translate) not normally prepared to co-operate, prayed God to be given the victory; and thereafter a peculiar cloud-formation in the blue sky, of a white diagonal cross, greatly cheered them. Taken to be the cross of St Andrew, the two kings vowed, when victory was indeed theirs, that thereafter St Andrew should be the patron saint of their two realms, and his white cross on blue the national flag. This is far from factual history, of course, for it was not until a century later that Kenneth MacAlpin united Picts and Scots; and there could not have been a joint banner at that time. But the tradition is strong and enduring. The Northumbrian leader who was slain was named Athelstan – not the well-known king of that name, whose period and death are otherwise; but it was a common Saxon name. It is perpetuated in the village of Athelstaneford, up in the hanging valley two miles to the south; and most folk assume that the battle was fought there. But this is clearly mistaken. For one thing, there could be no ford there, with only the tiny Cogtail Burn, which any child could jump over. For another, the village was moved up there only in the eighteenth century from the lower Pefferside area, in another case of improving the laird's amenity. The ford must have been over the Peffer itself, and its marshy margins, in those drainless days, a favourite position for defensive battles.

At the farm of Prora, a mile eastwards, is the shaft of a Pictish cross, with typical Celtic ornamentation, locally known as the Bore-stane. A field on this farm bears the name of Bloody Lands or Bloodyside, and this may represent the site of the battle.

Further east, still beside the river, lies Congalton. There is no village here now, only fine farms and the high walls of an enormous garden, the largest the present writer has ever seen. There must once have been another important community here, for the Congaltons of that Ilk cut a wide swathe in old Scotland, members of the family holding eminent positions in church and state. Usually, these ancient families, even if they fall from power and influence - as East Lothian ones seldom seem to do - leave many of the name and clan scattered up and down the land. Not so the Congaltons. I have never heard of anyone of the name - there are one or two Congletons, but that is an English family from Cheshire. Only this huge garden in the Vale of Peffer remains to hint at the great castle which must have borne their proud name.

South a mile is East Fortune, scarcely a village but the site of quite a large hospital. Also of another war-time airfield, some of which survives in a private capacity - and is used at weekends as the scene of a large open-air market, to which folk flock from far and near. The name has nothing to do with fortunes, being derived from fort-toun, the fort probably being the Chesters on the north flank of Kilduff Hill. There are other Fortune names around, one indeed still spelt Fortoun. It has become a not uncommon local surname - and when the telephone-exchange at Aberlady was manually operated, the name of the lady in charge, Miss Fortune, used to intrigue the youngsters.

Across the vale from here is the farm, formerly the large property, of Waughton, with its ruined castle and circular doocot. Presumably this is where the family of Waugh originated. But the earliest recorded lairds were De Airths and then Ramsays. One of the latter slew John Bickerton, son of the keeper of Luffness Castle at his own door, in revenge for the murder of the Earl of Douglas - so presumably they were

vassals of Douglas. That was in 1388 and soon thereafter
Waughton passed, probably through marriage, to the Hepburns, who in due course acquired Luffness also, making it
their main seat. Waughton Castle was besieged in 1568,
strangely enough by Hepburns, and Lord Home went to the
rescue – as reported to Queen Elizabeth by her ambassador.
This was, of course, during Mary Queen of Scots' troubled
reign.

Newbyth, a mile or so to the east and on the bank of the
east-flowing Peffer, is an Adam mansion in the Gothic,
sham-castle style of the late eighteenth century, now divided
into flats. It was the seat of the Bairds, an Aberdeenshire
family, from the seventeenth century, one of whom was
created Lord Doveran by Charles I but died before the title
could be ratified and sealed. But the most famous of the line
was General Sir David Baird, the hero of Seringapatam, born
here in 1757. He also was commander-in-chief at the capture
of the Cape of Good Hope and lost an arm at Corunna. He
seems to have been a lively character from his earliest days,
and when, during his Indian adventures, he was captured by
Hyder Ali and chained to a fellow prisoner, and his mother
heard of it her alarm was not for her son but for the other
man. "Lord peety the lad that's cheenied to oor Davie!" she
exclaimed. It was to this family that the Lord Blantyre's lands
eventually descended, including Lennoxlove.

Nearby we come to the renowned and remarkable place of
Whitekirk, properly the White Kirk of Hamer, a small village
set under a green ridge crowned by an ancient burial cairn,
with a most splendid old church and story enough to fill a
volume. Whitekirk's fame is wholly ecclesiastical, but
sufficiently dramatic nevertheless, from St Baldred's time right
down to the present century, when supporters of the
Suffragette movement burned the church to draw attention to
their claims, extraordinary as this may seem. Happily the
ancient and lovely building has been handsomely restored, and
both internally and externally it is a delight. The age of the
oldest work is not known, but this was one of St Baldred's
churches, and from the twelfth century belonged to the monks
of Holyrood. In the fourteenth century Black Agnes of Dunbar was cured by an alleged miraculous spring here, and added

a chantry to the church, which became a noted place of pilgrimage – indeed no fewer than 15,653 pilgrims are recorded as having visited Hamer Church and the holy well in 1413. And a few years later, no less than Aeneas Sylvius Piccolomini came, when as Papal Legate he visited James I, before he became Pope Pius II; as far as is known, the only occupant of the Holy See ever to visit Scotland. He walked from his ship at Dunbar barefooted – the approach had to be made thus, for maximum benefit – and being in winter and the ground frosty, he complained of rheumatism in his feet, not benefit, for ever after. The great square, parapeted tower in rose-red mellow stone is particularly fine, as is the fifteenth-century vaulted choir, built by Adam Hepburn of Hailes in 1439. James I often came, and his widow, Queen Joan Beaufort, managed by a ruse to smuggle the infant James II here and out of the clutches of usurping forces.

Behind the church is an unusual building, often called the only tithe-barn remaining in Scotland. This is obviously not so, for it is constructed out of a late-sixteenth-century peel-tower, and by the time of its conversion tithes were no longer being paid in Reformed Scotland. It is on the side of the ridge, which has its own name of Fairknowe. And here, in 1681 the Covenanting divine John Blackadder held his last conventicle. Unfortunately the dragoons arrived, roughly handled him and confined him on the Bass Rock, where after four years he died.

Two miles east of Whitekirk this Peffer enters the sea at the fine beach known as Peffer Sands, between Scoughall and Tyninghame.

There remains only the hanging valley of Garleton back some eight miles at the other end of the vale. This peculiar topographical feature lies between 200 and 300 feet higher than the Peffer levels, forming a most attractive and secluded enclave between the Garleton and Kilduff ridges, rising from east to west, about three miles in length. Towards the east end lies the village of Athelstaneford, unspoiled, retired, on the road to nowhere in particular. It was another Hepburn barony and one of its lairds, Sir John Hepburn (1598-1636), was one of Gustavus Adolphus's companions-in-arms, a Marshal of France and the founder of the Royal Scots regiment. His castle is gone but his father's initials, G.H., and the date 1583 appear on the doocot which stands behind the present church.

It is another castle altogether which dominates Athelstaneford from an out-thrust ridge of the Garleton Hills to the south. This is known locally as the Vaults, but its real name was to be Barnes Castle – and had it ever been finished it would have made a magnificent and, in more ways than one, an outstanding sight up there on its skyline. It was commenced by one of the Setons and never got beyond the extensive series of vaulted basements, before Sir John died, in 1594, and of course the fortunes of the family went steeply into decline. Over 200 feet long and 150 broad, if completed it would have been as palatial as Seton Palace and other lordly houses of that illustrious line. Sir John was Treasurer of the Household, and brother of the sixth Lord and of the Chancellor, the Earl of Dunfermline.

But it is in things literary that Athelstaneford is most renowned. For the parish had a succession of very distinguished ministers and, possibly because of its remote and out-of-this-world situation they seem to have turned to writing. Robert Blair was ordained minister in 1731, and here wrote "The Grave" a poetic work which, we are assured, was esteemed one of the standard classics of English poetical literature. Sadly, I have never met anyone who has read it. His son became the renowned Lord President Blair of Avontoun. Blair was succeeded by a still greater celebrity, John Home, a kinsman of the Earl of Home, who here wrote seven plays including the tragedies *Douglas* and *Agis*. The former was immensely popular, performed both in Edinburgh and at Drury Lane, London. The famous Mrs Siddons acted in *Douglas*. Burns compared it with Shakespeare's work, and Scott declared that *Douglas* had no equal in modern and scarcely a superior in ancient drama. Home got into trouble with the Kirk for such ungodly success however, and had to resign the Athelstaneford charge. However, he did not go far away, but built for himself a house, which now forms the nucleus of Kilduff House, further up the valley, where he continued to write. But it was not all literary activity at a manse desk. A direct descendant of the ancient Celtic Earls of Dunbar, he supported their Stewart successors sufficiently to be captured at the Battle of Falkirk in 1746, but made a dramatic escape from captivity at Doune Castle thereafter.

In 1777 the next minister, Thomas Hepburn, was joint author of a book called *Magofico*, a farce about a ridiculous parish minister of somewhere called Muchtiwharrack. The next incumbent, George Goldie, only managed to write the original parish account in the first *Statistical Account of Scotland* – but then he was a very busy man, begetting no fewer than sixteen children and building a new manse. In 1846 John M. Whitelaw came to Athelstaneford and kept up the tradition by producing many volumes of general literature plus poems and hymns. Finally, Thomas Duncan, who came in 1912, published in 1934 an excellent parish history. Surely few rural parishes could produce such a record. In recent times, the Reverend A. Downie Thomson, now retired, was the prime mover and sustainer in the excellent project whereby a plaque commemorating the battle of so long ago, and its consequences, was raised in the kirkyard; and above it a tall flagpole bears the blue-and-white saltire of St Andrew and Scotland, always flying, and floodlit on occasion.

West of the village the very lovely valley rises gently to its head in a quite scenic corrie of the Garleton Hills, where a steeply climbing road soars and twists over to Haddington, and where the vista is superb. Facing this, on the north side, Kilduff House, which grew out of Home's retreat to become the dower-house of the Gilmerton estate, near East Fortune, sits most serenely on its terrace, quite a large mansion, now, whitewashed and fair. The name Kilduff implies a chapel or hermitage of a Celtic saint called Duff or Dubh, meaning dark, as in the Clan MacDuff; but no trace of such now remains. On a spur of the north side of the hill is the early Pictish fort known as the Chesters – which gives it a mistakenly Roman sound.

The Garleton Hills opposite are higher and longer, extending for almost three miles and rising to almost 600 feet, with more rugged outlines. The westmost summit is crowned by a very tall, slender monument, rather like a factory-chimney if the truth be told, which stands out as one of the best-known landmarks in the county. It commemorates one of the Luffness Hopes, John, fourth Earl of Hopetoun, who was another distinguished soldier contemporary with Sir David Baird - indeed at the Battle of Corunna, when the latter lost his arm and Sir John Moore died, the command devolved on the Earl. According to the inscription, it was erected by his affectionate and grateful tenantry. Oddly enough, equally and similarly grateful tenantry erected an almost identical chimney-like memorial just across the Forth, in Fife, where the Hopes had, and still have, other lands. Collusion, emulation - or instructions from aloft?

Garleton, or Garmylton as it was originally, however, is most renownedly linked with the earlier ownership of Luffness, the Lindsays, their two castles of Garleton itself, and of the Byres, being sited a bare mile apart on the north slopes of the hill. Quite a lot survives of Garleton Castle, now part of East Garleton farm, below the steeply-climbing road over to Haddington; in fact one of its wings is still intact and roofed. Here was born the famous Sir David Lindsay of the Mount, Lord Lyon King of Arms to James V, of whom he was a personal friend. He is best known as the author of the famed *Ane Satyre of the Thrie Estaitis*, performed with acclaim at one of the early Edinburgh International Festivals - in which he certainly does not pull his punches. But he wrote much else, including *The Dream* and *The Complaynt*, both much thought of. As well as being the Court herald and playwright, he was a notable poet and something of an early reformer, to boot, with a lusty wit and an edge to his tongue. It is recounted that, before all the Court, he once asked James for the office of Master Tailor to the King, recently vacant. Astonished, the monarch asked why such an office should be bestowed on a man who could neither shape nor sew. He answered: "I have servit Your Grace lang, and luik to be rewardit as others are. That I can naither shape nor sew maks no matter, for you have given bishoprics and benefices to mony standing here about you, and yet they can naither teach nor preach; and why not I as weill be your tailor?" James is said greatly to have appreciated this sally, even if the courtly clerics did not. Other similar stories are told. The priests tried to get their own back, when James was dead, by getting his widow, Mary of Guise, to have Sir David's books officially burned. But presently came the Reformation, and Sir David lived just long enough, until 1567, to laugh last. He was the son of the Laird of Garleton, and in due course became that himself; but because he was Lord Lyon before his father's death, he took the title 'of the Mount', a subsidiary property in Fife, and that name has always stuck to him.

The other Lindsay castle here has only its former walled garden and a small vaulted tower remaining, at the present large farm of the Byres. Despite its distinctly humdrum name – originally Byres of Garleton, of course – this odd linking with cow-houses does not seem to have worried these Lindsays, for they incorporated the name in their title. This was, in fact, the seat of the second-most-important branch of that powerful house, linked to royalty. In 1445 Sir John became the first Lord Lindsay of the Byres. He was Justiciar of all Scotland north of the Forth. His son brought no fewer than 1,000 horse and 3,000 foot to fight for James III at Sauchieburn, and presented the King with the 'great grey horse' which was to figure in that monarch's grim death. They kept that peculiar title of the Byres until, in 1633, the tenth Lord became first Earl of Lindsay, which title still subsists. Perhaps it was a suitable enough name for a line with roots so deep in the farmlands of East Lothian.

West Garleton House, formerly a farm, standing high and overlooking a glorious prospect, ends the hanging valley 400 feet above the Peffer's mouth.

III

EAST LOTHIAN – LAMMERMUIR

THIS stretch of high country and its foothills is not just a convenient division for a description of Lothian; it has always been a distinct and separate entity on the Scottish scene, with its own character, far from typical of the rest. Only the northern third of it all is in East Lothian, the southern part being in Berwickshire, reaching down to the Merse and Lauderdale. A corner even projects into Midlothian, in the Fala and Soutra area. Nevertheless, nine-tenths of its population probably is in East Lothian, in its north-facing valleys – and an attractive and intriguing terrain it makes.

The area stretches from the Midlothian border in the west, to the sea at Dunbar and Cockburnspath and Eyemouth, some twenty-four miles on average and perhaps fifteen in general width; so that it comprises a large territory of almost 350 square miles. But we are concerned here with only some 100 square miles, in a belt five or six miles wide, with the Lothian border running along the summit-ridge of the highest of the ranges of rounded grass and heather hills, which average around 1,400 feet in height. Lammerlaw, the largest and most prominent from the north, is usually spoken of as the highest, at 1,730 feet; but in fact Meikle Says Law, three miles to the east, is 25 feet higher. The name Lammer is almost certainly from the word lamb; and other sheep-connected names include two Wedder Laws and two Wether Laws, two Wedderlies and the Wedder Lairs – wedder or wether being a castrated ram; Hogs Law and Hogs Rig – hogs being yearlings; Lamb Rig, Lamb Hill and Lamblair; Ewelairs Hill and Ewiesside Hill, Rammer and Sheeppath Glen. And so on. Sheep have always been all-important on these high pastures, and still are. There could be as many as 200 sheep-farms in Lammermuir. Cattle are also grazed on the lower slopes. And grouse share the heights with the sheep, to produce additional revenue from the shooting tenants. East Lothian's agricultural initiative and know-how reach up here also, however, and some of the hills are ploughed and raise corn at quite extraordinary heights, so that one can see oats and heather marching side-by-side over the lofty skylines.

The hills are full of secret valleys and cleughs, nursery of streams innumerable. But most of the water finds its way southwards, eventually into the Tweed, via the Rivers Whitadder and Blackadder – these have nothing to do with snakes, the adder being merely a corruption of water – and also the Leader; the Eye Water, which drains the eastern heights, reaches the sea at Eyemouth in Berwickshire also. This lack of major north-flowing streams is because the highest ridges are on this side, with the steepest slopes, so that the burns are comparatively short. It is odd that the Tyne gets comparatively little water from the Lammermuirs, which flank it all the way. Another oddity is that there are practically no true lochs in all this hilly area. There are artificial reservoirs. The Hopes, above Gifford, has long supplied the county with water; and there are many smaller reservoirs. Fairly recently the headwaters of the Whitadder were tapped by East Lothian County Council, to collect a large storage-lake in the Penshiel-Gamelshiel area – and thereafter came the reform of local government, to take the benefit of this water for Edinburgh, much to the offence of local rate-payers.

It is difficult today to realize the peculiar significance of this great tract of Lammermuir in old Scotland. It was a barrier, a more or less empty frontier area, almost roadless – it still is, to a large extent – and what went on thein, and beyond it, scarcely the business of the authorities centred at Scone and Perth, Stirling and Dunfermline. It was only when, comparatively late in time, Edinburgh became the capital and administrative centre, in the sixteenth century, that this stretch of hill country began to become more than a sort of no-man's-land. On this east side of southern Scotland two names were more or less accepted as covering all – Lammermuir and the Forest. The latter, more properly Ettrick Forest, was used to describe almost the entire upland Border area from the headstreams of the Clyde to the Tweed's mouth, another territory apt to be left to its own devices. Which, in the case of Lammermuir, explains why the Earls of Dunbar and March, and then their successors and descendants the Homes, were able to act like independent princes, a law only to themselves; and why the Borderland had its own official code of laws. The Homes became known as the Kings of the Merse, hidden away from the rest of Scotland behind Lammermuir. So, for centuries, it was not so much the Tweed which bounded Scotland on the south-east, as Lammermuir - and the Merse, beyond, was a sort of *terra incognita*. This also explains why the English found it so comparatively easy to steal the important seaport of Berwick-upon-Tweed from Scotland, and to keep it.

The northern foothills contain within their green folds a fascinating series of villages, as well as many famous lands and properties. At the western limits, near the foot of that former traffic-hazard of the A68, Soutra Hill, lies Humbie. This admittedly is not really a village but a wide-scattered com-muvity - although it happens to contain an excellent institu-tion called the Children's Village, a pleasant group of residential holiday-cottages for children, on a terrace above the Humbie Water. There are a few houses nearby and post-office and school, but that is all. Humbie House, another former lairdship of the Hepburns, is a mile away to the north-east, noted now for its extensive and meticulously trimmed beech-hedges. And nearby, deep in the den of the burn, is Humbie Mill, most picturesque. Half-a-mile on, down the deep wooden cleft, is the parish church and manse, not to be found without exploration, and highly inconveniently placed - for all but the laird, of course.

Soon after this, the Keith Water joins the Humbie Water in the depths of Humbie Wood - the name incidentally used to be Hundeby, probably connected with hounds. Nearby, in the Keith valley, is an ancient estate which sounds loud in Scotland's story once more - Keith Marischal. This is where the name of Keith comes from, quite common both as a family and a Christian name. There is, of course, quite a large town called Keith in Banffshire, but this was formerly Geth, then Ketmalruif; the surname originated here in Lothian, although the family of the name, in time, moved north. The first Keiths seem to have been another of David I's Norman importations. In the early twelfth century that king granted to Hervey son of Waren the lands of Keith; and his son became Knight Marischal under David's grandson, an office Bruce made hereditary, as one of the great officers of state. In 1458, the tenth in succession rose to be Earl Marischal, possible to be upsides with the Howards, Earls Marshal of England. They left Keith in Lammermuir and moved up to the great castle of Dunottar in the Mearns, oddly enough exchanging it with Lord Lindsay of the Byres, who seems to have 'married it'. But the name of Marishal still remains attached to the Keith estate, a late-sixteenth-century tower-house being part of the present mansion. This was erected in 1589 by George Keith, fifth Earl Marischal, who had gone to Denmark as ambassador to negotiate James VI's marriage to Anne of Denmark – and in gratitude the King of Denmark sent the earl a shipload of timber to be used in building this house. Another link with the Danish match was Agnes Sampson, the Witch of Keith, who was burned for being the main instigator of the storm off North Berwick, which so alarmed James and his bride on their way home. There is a ruined chapel, dating from the thirteenth century, near the mansion. It is of much interest architecturally and historically, and should be better preserved. Here were buried a succession of the Knights Marischal of Scotland.

We are fairly near the Saltoun area here. But in this foothill terrain communities tend to be quite far apart and hidden in their separate valleys. East of Humbie and Keith it is more than five miles before another village is reached – with farms all the way, of course. Then we come to Gifford, one of the most delightful in the land, highly popular with visitors and residentially favoured. It is another planned village, an early one, dating from the seventeenth century – the earlier community having been at Bothans, close to the mansion-house of Yester, were still is the former church, now the Tweeddale family burial-place. Although by East Lothian standards, Gifford village is not very ancient it has an aura of old-world peace and charm, with its mercat cross, broad village street, tree-lined avenue and attractive parish church. This last, whitewashed and substantial, with a tall tower, dates only from 1708 but looks older. Amongst other refinements it has a fireplace in the laird's loft or gallery. It is notable as having been the birthplace of the Reverend John Witherspoon, born in the manse here in 1723, who emigrated to America, became Principal of Princeton College, New Jersey, and a power in American affairs, being the only clergyman to sign the American Declaration of Independence. Strangely, not long afterwards, another native, Charles Nisbet, son of the school-master at Longyester, became the Principal of Dickinson (Methodist) College, Pennsylvania. The inns and hotels of Gifford are popular eating-places, and antiques are sold – it is that sort of place today – the largest of the hillfoot villages.

The great estate of Yester has long dominated Gifford, although its present mansion stands at the end of a mile-long driveway, starting at the village. The original castle's ruins stand almost another mile further up the Hopes or Gifford Water, and are now commonly known as the Goblin Ha' – although stand is perhaps scarcely the apt word, for most of what remains is in fact underground. It is fairly common for Scots castles to have a subterranean pit, prison or well-chamber; but this one is unique in having a great vaulted hall, reached down twenty-four steps, 37 by 13 feet and 19 feet high, a gloomy, impressive place indeed. The reasons for its construction are not clear; but inevitably for those days, whether from cause or effect, its builder, Sir Hugo de Gifford, was known as the Wizard and endowed with dread and supernatural qualities – hence the by-name of Hobgoblin or Bo' Hall. He built it in 1267, so he may indeed have been the first of the East Lothian witchcraft practitioners. Walter Scott goes to town on this:

A wiser never at the hour of midnight spoke the word of
    Power,
The same whom ancient records call the founder of the Goblin
    Hall;
Of lofty roof and ample size, beneath the castle deep it lies.

This from *Marmion*, with much more.

The de Giffords were more of King David's Normans, a Walter Gifard being one of the Conqueror's original com-panions. The second to settle in Scotland was given the lands of Yester, or *Ystrad*, the Cymric word for the Gaelic strath or

open valley. The line ended in an heiress in the fourteenth
century, who married Sir William Hay of-Locherwart, later
renamed Borthwick, in Midlothian. So commenced the long
connection with the Hays of Tweeddale, who had owned
Neidpath Castle on the Tweed before that, and who chose to
take the title of Tweeddale when created earls in 1599 – before
that they had been Lords Hay of Yester. John, fourth Marquis
of Tweeddale erected the fine classical William Adam
mansion in 1745; but on the death of the eleventh Marquis
a few years ago, the estate was sold. However, the twelfth
Marquis has recently come to live at Gifford again, though
not in Yester.

Beside the mansion is the old Gifford parish church of
Bothans, called after St Baithen, one of Columba's disciples. It
is a small but massive building, with a heavy stone-slab roof.
The village used to be here, but on the mansion being built,
was removed well out-of-sight, in the usual fashion.

The Hopes reservoir lies deep in the hills due south of
Gifford, near the foot of Lammerlaw, a scenic feature, roughly
star-shaped, flooding the rugged Hopes Glen and surrounded
by a cluster of prehistoric forts and settlements. It is strange
that there are so many hereabouts, for this is probably the
most rough and steep portion of the northern escarpment –
but perhaps this is indicative of the defensive nature of the
sites, for folk under pressure. Between Lammerlaw itself and
the hamlet of Longyester is a fort-site known as the Witches
Knowe, probably taken over in the medieval period for
witchcraft practices.

It is four miles north-eastwards to the next community, at
Garvald. But before that is reached, some way to the north, is
the *site* of another village, Morham, still the name of a civil
parish. The old church still survives, although much rebuilt,
and there was a school with accommodation for fifty-four
children ninety years ago. Why this village, in its rather pretty
little glen, should have disappeared so completely is something
of a mystery. It claimed to be the birthplace of John Knox,
counter-claimed by Giffordgate in Haddington, and elsewhere;
but certain it is that the Knox family farmed Mainshill here
for generations, and many of the family are buried in the
Morham kirkyard. Morham belonged to the Giffords in the

early days, before passing to the Bothwell Hepburns.

Garvald – the name is pure Gaelic, *garbh-allt,* the rough burn – is another favourite for the visitor, and the epitome of these hidden East Lothian communities, in that one can be within two or three hundred yards of the village, tucked into its deep, steep valley, before knowing of its existence. It is much smaller than Gifford, but a place of character and charm, with some pleasing housing, both old and very recent, and a venerable burnside church which has to be searched for also, at the far east end. The said rough burn has the strange name of the Papana Water – which might come from *penn enaich,* the hunting heights. The church contains Norman traces. There is a piscina in the west wall and, outside, a sundial dated 1633. The famous Countess Ada, David I's daughter-in-law, gave the church of Garvald to the nuns of Haddington in the 1150s. Presumably these nuns dwelt uphill to the south nearly a mile at Nunraw, which was a grange or farm of Holy Church, James II giving an unusual charter to the ladies to "fortifie the nunnery and to have guns aye loaded to shoot at our aulden enemies of England".

It is up here that Garvald is probably best-known today, for its Abbey of Sancta Maria, the only new abbey to have been founded in Scotland for many a long day. It is sited on a high terrace of the hillside about a mile south of the village, up a twisting minor road, on the estate of Nunraw – so that, although the abbey may be new, Holy Church has been there for a long time. At first the present Cistercian monks, a very friendly community, used the mansion of the estate as their monastery; and while some worked the fields and gardens – for it was to be a true and self-sufficient working establishment in the old tradition – others quarried and dressed the stone and gathered the materials and dug the foundations of the abbey-to-be. For years the work has gone on and it is not completed yet; but enough is established to bring it into full use, a splendid seat of activity and worship amongst these sheep-strewn braes. The new buildings are extensive and substantial, but far from ornate, indeed starkly simple and practical, but none the worse for that – although I have heard the criticism that from a distance the place looks more like a factory than an abbey. Whatever one's religious persuasion, it all must make a heartening development in the long story of Lammermuir.

The mansion itself, within its wooded policies, is now used mainly for charitable works and the benefit of visitors. It is a massive, castellated pile, the original part of which is the mid-fifteenth-century square tower which James II allowed the nuns to erect, complete with parapet, stair-tower, massive walls and gun-loops. Additions were made later and in 1864, to turn the whole into a large Z-plan castle, in the same style of architecture – very handsome. There is a most interesting painted ceiling in a first-floor chamber, dated 1461, with a great variety of ornament, including the fanciful coats-of-arms of a score of ancient kingdoms. Nunraw passed out of the nuns' hands at the Reformation, and into those of the acquisitive Hepburns. It passed through many other hands until 1946 when the white-habited Cistercians acquired it.

Across the deep valley of the Thorters Burn from Nunraw stands the red-stone ruin of Stoneypath Tower, an early sixteenth-century stronghold of the Douglases. Presumably there was an earlier tower on the site, for Stoneypath was one of the lairdships given to Sir James Douglas of Aberdour and Baldwinsgill by his father, the Lord of Dalkeith, about 1406. The father, ancestor of the Earls of Morton, was one of the wealthiest nobles in the kingdom in the reigns of Robert II and III, and left the oldest recorded will in Scotland, a quite fascinating document which will be dealt with under Dalkeith, in Midlothian. Stoneypath he gave to his eldest illegitimate son, who led an adventurous life which the present author used in his novels on the rise of the House of Stewart. This remote hillfoots tower must have seen some stirring scenes.

A couple of miles to the north, with Traprain Law once again dominating the skyline, is another well-known name, Whittinghame. This is a district, a parish and an ancient estate, not a village, although there is a small hamlet. The hills are very close here. It also was a Douglas place, and their sturdy old tower of the fifteenth century still stands intact and occupied, a stocky, L-shaped fortalice of three storeys and a garret, with parapet and wall-walk and some modernizations. In its garden is a great and very old yew tree, its branches curving over to re-enter the ground and reroot themselves, as at Ormiston Hall; and in this secret cover traditionally the plotters met to arrange the murder of King Henry Darnley, Mary Queen of Scots' husband, at Kirk o' Field in Edinburgh, in December 1566 – Archibald Douglas of Whittinghame, his chief the Earl of Morton, Secretary Maitland and Mary's third-husband-to-be, the Earl of Bothwell, being the conspirators. In 1817 the property was sold to one of the Balfours of Balbirnie in Fife, and the large classical-style mansion built by him almost half-a-mile to the east. Of this line came the statesman A. J. Balfour, Prime Minister in 1902. An earldom was created in 1922. The present fourth Earl of Balfour lives again in the old tower, a much more manageable entity, in modern conditions, than the vast mansion, which is now the Holt public school for boys.

Whittinghame Church, standing amongst old trees, is comparatively modern, dating from 1722. Its parish is the largest in East Lothian, covering no less than 15,500 acres, with the lowest population, of less than 500. The farm of White-law, to the south, with its pleasing eighteenth-century small laird's house, was once much more important, the seat of a family of that name, quite prominent in Scotland's story – and still apt to be in the news.

Just over a mile north-east is the village of Stenton, above the wooded valley of the Whittinghame Water. This is a pleasant place of no great size, which once used to be namely for its weavers. Also for its witches. It is recorded that in 1659 Bessie Knox and four other Stenton women, who had confessed to witchcraft, were strangled and burned. The old church here had an unusual gabled tower, which still survives, succeeded by a large and handsome building of 1829, to seat 400 – which seldom can have been filled to capacity even in those days. Nearby is a quaint old canopied well of pre-Reformation days; its real name is the Rood Well but is locally called the Cardinal's Hat. The Hamiltons of Beil – the Lords Belhaven and Stention – are buried in the old ruined church. The tradition was that so long as they kept the Rood Well in good condition they would retain their fine estate – but this does not seem to have worked.

To the north is the old lairdship of Ruchlaw, with an

attractive late seventeenth-century mansion of medium size, long in the lands of a minor but ancient family called Sydserff. Sydserff itself, now a farm, lies next to Congalton, nine miles to the north-west; but it is long since any of the name lived there, whereas a Miss Buchan-Sydserff was still resident at Ruchlaw until comparatively recently. This name presumably has something to do with the Celtic St Serf, Abbot of Culross and Loch Leven, St Mungo's benefactor.

To the south of Stenton a mile, and some 300 feet higher – for the hills rise steeply here – is the property of Pressmennan, a farming estate of note, long in the hands of the Hamilton of Beil family, one of whom was a Senator of the College of Justice with the title of Lord Pressmennan. He was father of the second Lord Belhaven and Stenton, and together they petitioned the King and Parliament to grant the right to hold two yearly fairs and a weekly market at Stenton, for cattle, sheep and wool. These fairs continued to be quoted as extant as late as 1862. A long wooded hanging valley up here at Presmennan was dammed in 1819, to form an artificial loch a mile-and-a-half long, but very narrow, a picturesque feature and noted haunt of wildfowl.

Out of Pressmennan Loch drains the headwaters of the Spott Burn, which runs five or six miles to the sea near Dunbar, through a deep, romantic and scenic valley, in a succession of twisting, wooded dens. There is a village of Spott, Spott House estate, Spott Mill, two farms of the name, Spott Dod, a hill, and the amusingly named farm of Little Spott. However odd, the name is very old, and this Spott valley featured with some importance in both Battles of Dunbar, its position being strategically vital.

The village, four miles east of Stenton, but on another and minor road, is still smaller, and likewise narrow. The church is small but ancient and very plain. It had tragic links with some of its incumbents. In 1544 its priest was assassinated; his successor, John Hamilton, became Archbishop of St Andrews and was hanged in 1570; the next one was also executed. John Kello murdered his wife in the manse on the Sabbath day, and thereafter went into church and preached an unusually eloquent sermon. Spott is said to have been the scene of the last witch-burning in Scotland. This seems to have been a not-uncommon occurrence here. The parish records for 1705, for instance, say laconically: "Many witches burnt on the top of Spot Loan".

Spott House stands in an almost cliffside position, with formerly a burn plunging down at the front door, crossed by a drawbridge, so that the place was all but impregnable. Although much added to and altered, it contains very old work. It had the distinction of giving shelter to General Leslie before the Battle of Dunbar, of 1650, and the following night the victor, Cromwell, occupied it instead. Originally a stronghold of the Dunbar earls, it was long held by a branch of the Hays of Yester. Below it, across the Spott Burn, is the site of the 1296 battle, the defeat which led to the grim eighteen years of the Wars of Independence, until Bruce freed the country in 1314 at Bannockburn.

Here we come down to the coastal plain near the Dunbar cement-works again. The hills bend away sharply southwards, as does the coast to a lesser extent; and in the foothills there are two more attractive villages hidden away, before we finish with East Lothian's part of Lammermuir. But first there is the district of Pinkerton, a name which has become well-known in other connections but which stems from here. There are farms of Meikle Pinkerton, Easter Meikle Pinkerton, Little Pinkerton, Easter Pinkerton, and a Pinkerton Hill of 577 feet – but no hamlet. This area was where the 1650 battle was actually fought, as tragic a business as the other, through the folly of the Scottish divines with Leslie's Covenanting army, practically religious commissars in those Kirk-ridden days. They urged, indeed commanded, the reluctant general to abandon his strong position on the Doon Hill here, and to fling his troops down towards Pinkerton, to smite the heretics hip and thigh. Cromwell watched this unexpected move from a hillock on Broxmouth estate, to the north. He had grimly anticipated defeat for his weary and discouraged force. But seeing this, he cried out that God had delivered the enemy into his hands. 3,000 Scots died and 10,000 were taken prisoner, for a loss of only thirty of the English. So much for ecclesiastical strategists. Scotland was incorporated in Cromwell's Commonwealth until the Restoration.

Two miles to the south-east is the village of Innerwick, a

peculiar name, part Gaelic, part Norse, which gives the impression that it is at the mouth of a river beside a bay; whereas it is neither, being two miles inland on a terrace 250 feet above sea-level, with only a tiny burn. Innerwick Castle, from which probably it took its name, is on a larger burn over a mile away, but still not near its mouth or at a wick or bay. One of those mysteries. The village is typically unobtrusive, and rather unusual in that it is square-shaped and compact, not elongated as these hillside places tend to be, in the local rich red stone and pantiles, with its road running along its southern edge. The parish church is plain, dating from 1784. Innerwick, so far as I know, has no reputation for witches; but in place of them it had an unusual parish minister, who published a chapbook entitled *The Laird of Cool's Ghost,* in which he describes his several meetings and discussions with the ghost of Mr Maxwell of Cool, in Dumfriesshire. His first meeting with the apparition took place on 3rd February 1722, at Thurstan, an estate nearby. The next one whilst riding at Elmscleuch, deep in the hills – this on 5th March. One wonders about this, especially when he informs that the ghostly laird told him, at the second meeting, that he was in fact riding on one of his own tenants, by name Andrew Johnson, who had died forty-eight hours before him and was transformed into a horse.

Innerwick Castle's ruins, set on the western edge of the deep ravine of the Thornton Burn, in a very strong position, makes an arresting scene. It was the stronghold of that branch of the Hamiltons from which descend the Earls of Haddington. It was defended, during the invasion of 1548, by the Master of Hamilton and "eight other gentlemen". Somerset's hagbutters killed eight of them, however, and the ninth, having jumped from the high walls, was killed in the water of the burn. One wonders what happened to the non-gentle staff? Directly across the ravine was another similarly placed hold, Thornton Castle, belonging to the Homes of Dunglass. Somerset captured it at the same time, and made a better job of demolishing it for nothing now remains. Innerwick Castle seems to have been restored, for there is building later than mid-sixteenth century here, with much intricate vaulting.

This Thornton Burn enters the sea at Thorntonloch, with

the main A1 highway passing close by. There was a village here once, now only a farm and cottages, plus a large caravan-park, for there is a splendid beach on to which the great North Sea rollers pound majestically – and sometimes dangerously. On to this beach in 1950 a school of whales, over a hundred strong, stranded themselves, and could not be refloated – a dire problem. People came from far and near to see the sight. They had to be killed. Disposing of the carcases was a major operation. Presumably there was a loch here, to account for the name; probably it was more in the nature of a tidal basin. Just to the north is Torness Point, where the proposed nuclear plant is to be sited; and beyond it, the one-time fishing-station of Skateraw, with its natural harbour and boat-strand. Much limestone used to be quarried here – the same deposits as are used today by the cement works – and the harbour at Skateraw was improved for the export of the material. There was a suggestion that the harbour should be further improved to become a haven-of-refuge, for this coast is a savage one and productive of many wrecks.

The last village of the county is quite hard to find, even map-in-hand, Oldhamstocks – the accent on the ham – not only being hidden behind the usual ridge but tucked away in a side-valley beyond a network of narrow roads and twisting byways, about four miles south of Innerwick. But it is worth searching out, one of the most delightful in Lothian; and unusual too, set on a south-facing terrace above the Dunglass Burn, with a great feeling of light and space about it and nothing of the narrow village street. It is not large, but no doubt was larger once, for it extends for quite a distance, with a lot of green grass and garden evident. It had its own village green and once possessed large common lands; also two churches, two smiths and a colony of weavers. One of the smithy families was called Broadwood, a member of which went to London and founded the famous piano firm of that name. The shaft of the mercat cross still subsists. Oldham-stocks is reached by road only from the east end, the valley to the west petering out roadless amongst the hills.

The parish church is situated pleasantly amongst old trees in an interesting kirkyard at the top end of the village. Much of the building is ancient, with the chancel dating probably from the fifteenth century. The date 1701, which appears above the door refers only to an alteration. One of the incumbents here, Thomas Hepburn, whose initials appear on the walling, was made Master of Requests to Mary Queen of Scots immediately after her marriage to his chief, Bothwell. He was one of those who aided Mary to escape from Lochleven Castle. His son went much further afield, ending up as librarian to the Vatican and writing many books himself, including a Hebrew dictionary. He is said to have learned every known language.

Cromwell spent the night on his way north, a few days before the Battle of Dunbar, in a house here. Asked how he had slept, he declared: "As sweetly as though I had lain in Abraham's bosom". The term stuck to the house, which became an inn.

The valleys beyond, branching off and probing deep into the Lammermuir heights, make splendid walking country – riding also, although not motoring – full of cleughs and scarps and deans, more steep and sudden than the general run of these hills, the outcropping limestone producing quite spectacular formations. The names of the ridges reflect this – Monynut Edge, Lothian Edge, Spartleton Edge and so on. It should be better known by the walking fraternity, only some thirty miles from Edinburgh.

Seawards of Oldhamstocks its valley drops dramatically down a wooded defile for three miles and almost 500 feet, the Dunglass Burn here forming the Berwickshire boundary. Half-a-mile back from the mouth, above the dean, is Dunglass itself, one more renowned name in the long tale of this land. There is an ancient estate, a very fine former collegiate church in the policies, no longer used but now kept in fair repair – although it was not always – and an estate hamlet. All this hidden away from the A1 road by the railway embankment and the tree-clad banks of the dean. The present classical-style mansion stands on the foundations of the original castle of Dunglass, incorporating its vaulted basements. This was long a stronghold of the Earls of Dunbar and their descendants, the Homes – although the original owners seem to have been one more of those families which have almost completely died out, the Pepdies. It was ancient in 1380, and the Homes still incorporate the Pepdie achievement of three

green popinjays in their coat-of-arms. This castle came to a
sorry end. In 1640, during the Covenant wars, it was blown
up by the English page of the Earl of Haddington, who,
resenting some taunt of the Earl anent his countrymen, thrust
a red-hot poker into a powder-barrel in the magazine, killing
himself, the Earl, and many of the East Lothian gentry.
Thirty-seven years before, James VI had spent the night here
on his way south to take over Queen Elizabeth's throne. Later
that century the property passed to Sir John Hall, a Lord
Provost of Edinburgh who had married a Home daughter.
This line continued at Dunglass until comparatively recently.
One of them was a notable philistine, however, who shamefully desecrated the splendid church, built by Sir Thomas
Home at the end of the fourteenth century, a cruciform
building with a low tower and considerable architectural
virtue and imagination. Unfortunately, in 1712, the second
baronet, Sir James Hall, decided that it would make an
excellent stable and coach-house, even though his own first
wife, another Home, and his only son, were buried therein. He
dug up centuries of graves and threw away the bones; used the
gravestones to make paving for the stables; broke down the
east wall to allow his coaches to enter; and so on. It is
astonishing that so much has survived this treatment. The
place was very substantially-built, of course, with thick walls
and a stone-slabbed roof. Even though the Homes lost the
estate in the seventeenth century, they retained the title of
Lord Dunglass, for the heir to the earldom; and this was the
name by which Sir Alec was known for most of his political
career.

Dunglass Dean, with its near neighbours Bilsdean and Pease
Dean, presented major hazards and ambush-places for invaders; so that much happened here over the centuries, much
bloodshed. The bridging of these very deep defiles also
provided serious problems for the road and rail builders.

This, then, is the end of East Lothian, with Berwickshire
immediately to the south, the North Sea pounding the cliffs to
the east, and the Borderline only twenty-five miles away as
the crow flies.

All lands are equally ancient; but only the very un-
imaginative and wholly unperceptive would deny that some

demonstrate their antiquity more than others, just as some are more colourful than others. In both of these East Lothian surely ranks high. If this brief survey reads repetitiously or wearisomely, blame the writer, not the land. If it seems over-concerned with the past, and the families which made that past, then consider that the present is too close – and there has been a lot of past in this knuckle end of Scotland.

IV

MIDLOTHIAN - THE ESK VALLEY

IF IT was convenient, indeed almost necessary, to describe East Lothian laterally, in three divisions horizontal to the coast, it is easiest to deal with Midlothian as it were vertically, in separate sections from north to south. For two reasons. This is the true axis of the land here, the way the rivers run, dictated by the hill formations; and because the city of Edinburgh, not to be included in this survey, sits in the midst, separating the divisions, which are in themselves fairly distinctive. It will be noted that Midlothian is one word, where the others use two. It is strange that the three contiguous counties which form the recognizable entity of Lothian should be so very different one from another, in character and history as well as in physical feature. Midlothian is the largest in acreage, though not by much. And it has much the largest population, over twice that of East Lothian - larger even when Musselburgh is subtracted and then added to East Lothian, as the busy bureaucrats have recently ordained. No part of East Lothian is more than a dozen miles from the sea; whereas Midlothian's most southerly point, actually in the Borderland near Galashiels, is nearly thirty miles from salt-water. The average altitude is higher, with loftier and more extensive hill areas. Inevitably there is less good agricultural land, although there are many excellent farms in Midlothian also. There is more mineral wealth however; and the lower-lying parts and river-valleys are fairly heavily industrialized. There are larger towns and fewer picturesque villages.

Yet this kind of comparison must not give the impression that Midlothian lacks attractiveness scenically. It has its less-inspiring areas, in the wake of mining and decayed industry; but basically it is a county of varied and pleasing scenery, with numerous beauty-spots and always the challenging hill vista at the end of every prospect. Some folk might even claim that

East Lothian, with all its rich farmlands, is tame by comparison.

As a county it is as uneven in outline as it is in character and topography, and does not fall into fairly simple sections as do its neighbours - presenting problems in delineation. But a glance at a map will reveal the salient features - the two great hill masses of Moorfoot and Pentland, the valley of the Esk between, and the area drained by the Water of Leith and the Almond, north-west of the Pentlands. A closer glance will show that by far the greater part of the population, with most of the towns and large villages, are in the Esk valley. And then there is Edinburgh, and Leith its port, on the north-central lip of it all. So we shall deal with these divisions of Esk, Moorfoot, Pentland and Almondell. Edinburgh already has a volume to itself in this series of Portrait books.

Nevertheless, a brief word about Edinburgh in relation to Midlothian is called for. Heart of Midlothian as it has been so often called, a title still given currency as the name of the famous football-team. Edinburgh was in fact, until recently, the county-town of Midlothian, the seat of its county buildings, sheriff-courts and so on; and it is still the administrative headquarters of the Lothian region. Inevitably therefore the city has sapped some of the life's-blood and importance from the other Midlothian towns; and as it expanded has absorbed more and more of the countryside, as well as establishing its commuting communities throughout the areas. Every great city does this. The fact that Edinburgh is one of the most beautiful, famous and characterful cities in the world, in its magnificent setting of spectacular hills on the edge of the scenic Forth, has much overshadowed its neighbouring communities. As has been said, Musselburgh, for one, has fought vigorously and fairly successfully against this absorbing tendency; but the pull is always there, especially in these modern and centralizing times when large units everywhere are swallowing smaller ones.

We shall start with the Esk valley, where the population is greatest. The name itself is significant. There are many Esks, or derivatives of the word such as Usk and Ex and Axe, all over Britain, reminders that all these islands were Celtic once, although so few English folk appear to think of themselves as having a Celtic background, preferring to believe that they are Anglo-Saxon or even Norman. The name is merely the Pictish-Gaelic word for water, *uisge*. Whisky, the water-of-life, comes from the same source. It is worth noting, perhaps, that the river which bounds Midlothian on the west is the Almond, another similar name which comes from the Gaelic *abhainn*, a stream, more usually spelt as Avon – and all know how many Avons there are south of the Border also. Actually there is another Avon even in West Lothian. Rivers are useful as the features of any country apt to retain their original names for longest.

The Midlothian Esk has two main headstreams, the North and South Esks, rising many miles apart, the first in the Pentland Hills at the Bore Stane pass below the Cairn Hill, not very far from the Water of Leith, which flows in the other direction. Within a couple of miles the stripling river has been dammed, to form the North Esk Reservoir; and thereafter it flows, in the main north-eastwards, for another sixteen miles, to Dalkeith Park, where the South Esk joins it. This has risen high on the side of Blackhope Scar, 2,136 feet, at the Peeblesshire border, in the Moorfoots, and after five miles has been dammed to form the Gladhouse Reservoir, a very large sheet of water. Thereafter it flows almost due northwards for some fourteen miles, to the confluence. From this joining, five miles more brings the united and quite major river to the sea. Although the total course therefore is not much more than twenty miles, the Esks have carved for themselves very deep troughs, in some places dramatically so; and they can bring down a great volume of water, despite the reservoirs.

At the mouth sits Musselburgh – which indeed at one time was called Eskmouth and is in the civil parish of Inveresk, which means the same. This was always an important place, strategically and otherwise. Because of the deep, steep defile of the Esk and the marshy nature of its estuary formerly, this was the only point where the river could be bridged – and the ancient narrow, hump-backed bridge is still a feature of the town, although Rennie's 1807 wider bridge now replaces it nearby, carrying the A1 traffic. This bridging situation, which was in fact the reason for Musselburgh's existence, is now the town's major problem; for because of the difficulty in finding another crossing, all the tremendous weight of traffic has to come grinding through the streets, causing great hold-ups and much damaging Musselburgh's amenity. It should have been by-passed long ago, of course, whatever the engineering difficulties; but this has been held up for an unconscionable time by Edinburgh's failure to decide upon the exact routing for its own projected by-passing ring-route to the south, into which the A1 traffic would be fed – much to the resentment of Musselburgh folk. Crossing the High Street here can be one of life's hazards.

The Romans recognized the importance of this position and established a settlement and camp-fort at Inveresk, with their port at what became the fishing-haven of Fisherrow. Many Roman relics have been found, including the site of a hypo-caust or heated bath-house. The Celtic Church followed, with St Modwenna building one of her seven churches in Scotland here, this dedicated to St Michael. She died in 529, so there has been a church on this site for 1450 years, for the parish church of Inveresk still rears itself proudly on this high site well above the town. However, that is only a minor proportion of the period of settlement here, for evidence has been uncovered of Bronze Age occupation of 5000 years ago. When Simeon of Durham refers to the place in the seventeenth century he calls it Eskmouth, but that may be only a translation of Inveresk. When the town, as distinct from the parish and kirkton, became Musselburgh is not clear; but in 1020 the *Ecclesia de Muskilburgh* is mentioned, thought to take its name from the large mussel-beds or scaups at the mouth of the river. This is still a great coast for mussels, even though modern sewage has not improved them. Malcolm Canmore in the 1070s gave the revenues of the Celtic cashel or monastery here to the great new Romish church of the Holy Trinity at Dunfermline, which his wife, the beautiful and determined Queen Margaret, was building in her successful efforts to change the Celtic Church over to her own Roman Catholic model.

Musselburgh's proudest hour came in 1332 when it gave succour and shelter to Thomas Randolph, Earl of Moray, the good and popular Regent. Bruce had died three years before, leaving the five-years-old David II as King, and his nephew Randolph as Regent. The hero-king gone, the English were using every effort, and their puppet Edward Baliol, to bring Scotland under thrall again; and Randolph was resisting them with all his might. He took unaccountably ill in the Musselburgh vicinity, not without suspicion of poison by the Baliol faction, and was brought to a house near the east gate of the town – this building remaining standing until 1809. He was cherished, and both himself and the town stoutly guarded by the citizens – for in those days it was a defensive walled place. He lingered for some time but eventually died. It was his successor as Regent, the Earl of Mar, not Moray as is often alleged, who declared the Musselburgh folk to be honest and their burgh an 'honest toun', over this incident, and promised them certain privileges. The Honest Toun Musselburgh has remained – honest here having the original meaning of honourable and trustworthy. Each year the Honest Toun celebrations are held in July, with much fervour, after the fashion of a Border common-riding, with processions, decorated streets festivities, ridings-of-the-marches and civic junketings. The Honest Lad and his Lass, elected each year, are the town's mounted standard-bearers. And 'Honesty' remains the burgh's motto. Two tall pillars still stand at the east end of the High Street, to mark the place where stood the town gate – the other to the west was in the middle of the old narrow bridge. This east end of the High Street used not to be so broad as it is today; for down the centre used to be the Mid Raw, as at Haddington and other towns.

Being, again like Haddington and Dunbar, on the direct invasion route to the capital, Musselburgh suffered badly at English hands, being burned and destroyed at least twice. But somehow it grew and prospered. Milling and fishing were natural industries here, and ancillary trades grew from these, in especial net-making and paper-milling. The net-works at one time employed 700 people, using 450 net machines. And the paper-making developed into the internationally-known Inveresk Paper Company, which still exists, but not at Musselburgh. Bruntons Wire Works grew into a very large establishment, and happily still flourishes; and a more recent success story is the major building company of Crudens, at Fisherrow. Salt pans, pottery and tile works, and brewing, were long staple industries; and in the seventeenth century was established a cloth manufactory making a strong coarse woollen check material which became known far and wide as 'Musselburgh Stuff', much in demand in America. Add to all this Musselburgh's preoccupation with keeping Edinburgh at bay. And golf. For the town was from early times one of the game's major centres, played on the Links here – one of James VI's favourite ploys. Musselburgh Links are now more namely for their well-known race-course, where great crowds flock to the race-meetings; and the Royal Musselburgh Golf Club has removed to Prestongrange, the former Grant-Suttie estate near Prestonpans. Great land-reclamations are going on seaward of the Links, with the help of the waste from the Cockenzie Power Station, valuable if less than scenic. The Musselburgh Links were where Cromwell stationed his troops, for two months after his victory at Dunbar, while he 'set Scotland to rights'. The Links are also renowned for being the site of an annual shoot for the Musselburgh Silver Arrow of the Royal Company of Archers, the Queen's Bodyguard for Scotland, the prize for which, much sought after, is a 'riddle of claret' presented by the town. This custom has been going on since the sixteenth century.

Despite all this, the town retains no great aspect of antiquity, save for the old town-house and tolbooth at the east end of the High Street, with the mercat cross nearby. It is an attractive parapeted building, even though once the town goal, with an unusual sixteenth-century tower topped by an octagonal, tiered steeple, Dutch in style. The major part of the structure dates only from 1762, but the tower was erected in 1590 out of materials taken from the Chapel of Our Lady of Loretto, demolished at the Reformation. This chapel had an unusual story, founded by an eccentric hermit called Thomas Douchtie in 1533, who enjoyed a reputation for miraculous powers. His chapel became a great resort of the sick and disabled, as the present-day Lourdes is; and Sir David Lindsay made it the target of his satire, and other highly-placed characters seem to have looked down their noses at it. Not so the Vatican, however, for when the Reformers dinged it doun and Musselburgh used its stones to build their tolbooth, the Honest Toun was excommunicated by the Holy See for two centuries no less. Which is odd, considering how much

demolition and down-casting was going on throughout the
land at that time. Today, the well-known public school of
Loretto occupies the site and lands of the chapel and makes its
own quite substantial impact on Musselburgh life.

Across the road from Loretto and now used by the school
also, is the important, large and very splendid mansion of
Pinkie House. This was another of the palaces built by the
illustrious Seton family, who had acquired the Church lands at
the Reformation. Alexander Seton, Chancellor or chief
minister of Scotland, and first Earl of Dunfermline, was
brother of the Sir John who started to build Barnes Castle at
Athelstaneford and of Robert, sixth Lord Seton and first Earl
of Winton, who built Winton Castle. At Pinkie he intended
to outdo his brothers, taking the older L-shaped fortalice of
the Abbots of Dunfermline and erecting to the south of it the
extensive and ambitious range, also L-planned but three times
as large, which turned it into one of the finest seventeenth-
century houses in Scotland. There are a number of especially
notable features, including the massive row of chimney-stacks
along the wallhead of the east front, the two unusual squared
angle-turrets of the north gable, the magnificent three-
storeyed oriel window in the south gable, and the outstanding
Painted Gallery on the first floor, 85 feet long and the full
width of the house, containing a most wonderful coved and
painted timber ceiling in tempera, done by Italian artists.
Pinkie came into the Hopes' hands in 1788 and remained the
seat of the baronet branch of that family until recent times.
Pinkie Pans salt works lay to the north, at the coast.

The other end of the High Street finishes at John Rennie of
Phantassie's handsome bridge. And down Bridge Street is the
very modern and rather extraordinary Brunton Hall complex,
a vast new building of composite character containing town
and district offices, a theatre, halls and chambers, gifted to
Musselburgh by members of the wire-works family, a most
notable acquisition although not everyone's taste in architecture. Otherwise this end of the town tends to be rather
undistinguished, save for the harbour area of Fisherrow. The
Eskside residential district is attractive however. The 19-acre
site of the former Inveresk Paper Company here is to be
turned into an industrial estate.

On the south side of the town is the 'suburb' of New-bigging, once a separate hamlet on the way to Inveresk, where is now sited the quite major educational establishment of Musselburgh Grammar School, dating from the sixteenth century.

Inveresk itself, the village not the parish, is a remarkable place by any standards. If Musselburgh has managed to keep Edinburgh at arm's-length. Inveresk has achieved the same with Musselburgh. I know of no similar community in all Scotland, a village composed almost entirely of mansion-houses – like the Grand Army of Mexico, more generals than privates. Why this should be so is unclear; but Inveresk consists of a succession of great houses of the seventeenth and eighteenth centuries in the main, the latest building being dated 1820, set in their extensive walled gardens amidst fine old trees, along a gentle spine or ridge. Not a few of these houses are architectural gems, with notably few cottage-type buildings. There is a great air of quiet reserve about the place, much aided by the fact that it is served by a road which leads nowhere very vital. Two centuries ago the village was thus described: "... beautiful Inveresk which from its situation, houses and salubrity of air, is justly reckoned the finest village and most healthy place in Scotland". It is remarkable how little has changed. Admittedly there is the terrace of sub-stantial villas at the extreme south end, nineteenth-century incomers, but these are well round the corner, out-of-sight of the lordly ones. The oldest of the mansions, Inveresk Lodge is a quite splendid example of late seventeenth-century Scots style, just outwith the fortified period – although there may be an older nucleus – but retaining many of the typical defensive features, vaults, thick whitewashed walling, steep roofs, crow-stepped gables, conical-roofed stair-tower and the distinctive L-plan. The gardens are now the property of the National Trust for Scotland. It was once the seat of a family called Colt who produced two seventeenth-century ministers of Inveresk, one of whom, Adam, was a notable fighter against James VI's efforts to bring down Presbyterianism, his grandson Sir Robert, becoming Solicitor-General of Scotland. The gardens of this, and other west-side houses, are most lovely, slanting down to the river. Unfortunately a disastrous flood of the Esk

(*Above*) Rolling, sheep-strewn Lammermuir, with the modern Whitadder reservoir in the distance and (*below*) Musselburgh, Town House and old Tolbooth, looking west.

(*Above*) Pinkie House, Musselburgh, now part of Loretto School and (*below*) Dalkeith Palace, a former seat of the Dukes of Buccleuch.

(*Above*) Newbattle Abbey, now a college, once seat of the Marquis of Lothian and (*below*) Roslin Chapel.

Interior of Roslin Chapel. The famous Prentice Pillar is third from the right.

Hawthornden Castle in the valley of the North Esk, where the poet William Drummond lived and wrote.

(*Above*) the burgh of Penicuik from the south-east, the Pentland Hills beyond and (*below*) the castle and parish church of Borthwick. Mary Queen of Scots made a romantic escape from here.

(*Above*) Rosebery, one of the Moorfoot reservoirs, looking south to the Moorfoot Hills and (*below*) Stow-in-Wedale, almost in the Borderland. The pack-horse bridge and Gala Water.

in 1948 actually swept away acres of formal rose-gardens. The gardens of Inveresk Gate are famous amongst botanists. Here too is established the important research station of Inveresk Research International.

St Michael's Church stands apart, at the north end, on a commanding site amongst trees also, a square and hipped-roofed building of 1803, with a tall steeple which can be seen from afar, large enough reputedly to seat 2,400, although this surely would be on the ambitious side. It is unusual in having two galleries, both extending round three sides of the church, although the secondary one, known as the Fishermen's Loft, has been reduced in size. The picturesque kirkyard has many interesting monuments. Of Inveresk's many distinguished ministers, the most famous is probably Dr 'Jupiter' Carlyle, who was incumbent here for no less than fifty-seven years. He was a great character, a friend of John Home of Athelstaneford, who wrote the plays, and himself a regular playgoer, which drew the censure of many in those days (1748–1805) – although Carlyle himself wrote that when the famous Mrs Siddons was appearing in Edinburgh in 1784, at the time of the General Assembly of the Church of Scotland, the Kirk had to put their business on to the alternate days when she was not appearing on the stage, to avoid absenteeism by the younger ministers. He was a son of the minister of Prestonpans, and watched the famous battle there from the belfry of his father's church – although he had previously enrolled as volunteer to defend Edinburgh against Prince Charles. Scott wrote of him that he was "the greatest demigod he ever saw ... and a shrewd clever old carle was he".

This road, A6124, after leaving Inveresk, heads southwards eventually to reach little-visited places like Cousland and Fordel and Cranstoun, on the plateau-lands which are a westwards extension of the Fawside ridge. On the way, it passes through the market-gardening terrain around Sweet-hope and Pinkie Mains and Goshen, which deserves some mention. This area, and eastwards well into the Prestonpans vicinity, occupies what is called the Hundred-Foot Beach, a belt of particularly fertile soil which was in some past age the shore of a wider Scotswater or Forth estuary. This has been intensively cultivated for centuries, more horticulture than

agriculture, to provide vegetables for the Edinburgh market –
and was, by way of suitable return, long manured by the
so-called night-soil of the city, brought down here by a
regular system. Our modern sensibilities may shudder a little
at this arrangement – although it is not so very different from
much present-day sewage treatment – but the results were
highly satisfactory, some of the finest vegetable-crops being
produced on a great scale. A number of old Musselburgh
families have been involved in this market-gardening for
generations. It was on this territory, below Fawside Hill, that
the Battle of Pinkie was fought. Edenhall Hospital now covers
some of the site.

A mile or so further south is a famous place, the estate of
Carberry. Here was fought, in 1567, the battle which more or
less ended Mary Queen of Scot's troubled reign, and at which
she took her final leave of Bothwell. The Queen's Mount is
still pointed out, on the slope of Carberry Hill, where she
watched the victory of the Confederate Lords. The castle of
Carberry Tower, was, until fairly recent times, the seat of the
Lords Elphinstone, kin of the Queen Mother; but in fact they
only gained this property by marriage in the late eighteenth
century, before which they had been seated at the nearby
Elphinstone Tower, shamefully demolished a few years ago.
Carberry is a splendid house, extending from a massive early
sixteenth century square keep of rather unusual design, with
flat roof and heavy parapet. This parapet is supported on a
corbel-course consisting of innumerable cherubs' heads which
have brought a kind of immortality to the builder, one Hugh
Rigg, in 1543:

> Auld Hugh Rig was very big, but a bigger man was he,
> When his cherubs chirped upon his new toure of Carbere!

The house was extended at various times to become a large
mansion, and was presented by the late Lord Elphinstone to
the Youth Committee of the Church of Scotland as a
conference-centre. The estate is beautiful, but the land around,
which begins to rise quite sharply above the coastal plain, has
been much scarred by mining. Indeed the sole remaining
coal-pit in this area is located a little way to the west, at
Smeaton – not to be confused with Smeaton-Hepburn in East

Lothian – drawing its miners, by bus nowadays, from the many old mining communities round about.

Smeaton has more to offer than coal, however. For hidden away behind the high wall which bounds the great ducal park of Dalkeith Palace here, is Smeaton Castle, a little-known fortalice of much character, still occupied as a fine house but today generally referred to as Dalkeith Home Farm. It has been a large-scale courtyard-style stronghold in a quite strong position where the Smeaton Burn joins the Esk, one of its massive circular angle-towers surviving to four storeys, where unfortunately it has been finished with an unsuitable modern roof. Another of the round towers has been much reduced in height. But internally much remains of interest, vaulted basements, mural cupboards and garderobes, turnpike-stairs and gunloops. Mary Queen of Scots granted a charter of Smetoun to Master Robert Richardson, Prior of St Mary's Isle, Treasurer of Scotland in 1563; but the castle is older than this. In 1604 Mark Acheson, of Acheson's Haven, had to find security not to harm James Richardson of Smeaton or his son – while the following year the situation was reversed, and the Richardsons had to find caution for 2000 merks not to assault Acheson. Those were the days.

The high walls surrounding Dalkeith Park are a very prominent feature hereabouts, running for miles in a southerly direction, with a busy A road twisting and curving to fit their blank contours, and known locally as the Duke's Dykes. The park of Dalkeith Palace flanks the Esk for three miles, a large demesne in an industrialized area. But though still belonging to the Dukes of Buccleuch and Queensberry – and Monmouth too, although they do not use that title – it is long since they lived at the palace, a large and scarcely beautiful mansion built for the Duchess Anne by Vanbrugh in the early eighteenth century, modelled on the Loo Palace in Holland. Anne, who had been Countess of Buccleuch in her own right, heiress of the Scotts who had bought Dalkeith in 1642, was the young widow of the ill-fated Duke of Monmouth, illegitimate son of Charles II, but now believed to be legitimate, in that Charles had actually married Lucy Walters – a situation which could have altered history in a big way. There was, of course, an earlier castle here, the seat of the second line of the Douglas family, Lords of Dalkeith and Earls of Morton. From it General Monk governed Scotland for Cromwell for five years – with grave suspicions on the part of the Lord Protector; and with reason, evidently, for Monk is believed to have largely planned the Restoration from Dalkeith. Prince Charlie spent two nights here in 1745. The great house is now let to a computer firm, but the estate surrounding still remains with the Duke. Near its gates is the Episcopal church of St Mary's, with the Buccleuch side-aisle, and crypt below. The public are allowed to walk in the policies – indeed there is a most attractive and imaginative children's adventure playground, with tree-houses, climbing-nets, chutes and so on. Also nature trails.

It was in the earlier castle that Sir James Douglas, second Lord of Dalkeith, made his famous will of 1390, mentioned briefly under Stoneypath in East Lothian, the oldest known will preserved in Scotland. It reveals much of the life-style, interests and priorities of a great Scots noble of the medieval period and makes fascinating reading; but is too long to set down here. Some of it is surprising indeed. For instance, referring to his library. Sir James instructed that all books he had borrowed should be returned by his executors to their owners. And he details his own books, including romances – novels – which he wants back from *his* friends. It certainly came as an eye-opener to me that folk were borrowing books – and forgetting to return them – as early as the fourteenth century, and that romances were being read and borrowed likewise. Another clause refers to his foundation of the collegiate church of St Nicholas at Dalkeith, giving it funds for the support of a provost and five prebendaries, with suitable manses – these to reside there continually, decently dressed in gowns and black hoods furred with lamb's wool. Incidentally there is a telling reference regarding the grant, that should the chaplain of one of the chaplainries keep a concubine publicly, and refuse to dismiss her upon being asked to do so, he should vacate his charge. Sir James left half of all his free goods to pay for the funeral expenses; the Vicar of Lasswade's funeral fee was to be his lord's best horse – the stipulation written in that he was not to get any more than this. Presumably Sir James knew his Vicar. St Nicholas Church itself got his robes of cloth-of-gold to make vestments of; also chalices, missals and so on; whilst another of the chaplainries, Newlands, was honoured with "a robe with a fetterlock, which John Gibson last bought in Flanders", whatever that might mean. Sir James's widow didn't do too well. She was the Princess Egidia, sister of Robert II. She got back only an "owche" presumably a brooch, which she herself had given to her spouse – provided that she did not lay claim to other jewels. He must have found marrying into the royal family less than rewarding. His earlier wife, Agnes, had been a daughter of the famous Black Agnes, Countess of Dunbar; and it was through her and her dowry lands of Whittinghame that he was able to give his illegitimate son Stoneypath Tower aforementioned. There is a great deal more, including the fact that his eldest legitimate son, as well as heiring the principal landed estates, got his second-best horse, some armour and a silver reliquary containing some hairs of Mary Magdalene – perhaps there was a moral here? Sir James died of "the quhew", or as we would say, the 'flu, in 1420, actually some thirty years after making his will.

St Nicholas' Church still stands in Dalkeith's High Street, the most ancient part ruined, or at least roofless, and containing the Douglas monuments and recumbent effigies. The more modern portion, restored in 1852, is now the East Parish Church. This east end of the High Street is spacious, 85 feet wide as against only 30 feet elsewhere, and acts as an approach for the palace gates, with some quite pleasing architecture, including the Old Tolbooth, a fairly plain low building, dated 1648, decorated with the Buccleuch initials and coronets – built six years after the Scotts purchased the barony. The rest of the town is fairly undistinguished, but with a modern shopping-centre grouped round an open court, where the wide and narrow sections join, and the main A68 highway strikes southwards for Lauderdale and the Border.

Dalkeith, with a population of around 9000, half the size of Musselburgh, is another traffic-hub, and for the same reason, the lack of crossings of the Esk, there being no road-bridge between. It is a busy place and fairly compact, with more air of a country-town than has Musselburgh. It has its own industrial estates at Thornybank and Newbattle, but these are well-detached to north-east and south-east. There are now two Esks in their valleys through the town, and this has tended to restrict development into the compact form and at the same time mean that the suburbs are indeed detached, beyond the rivers. One such is Lugton, across the North Esk to the west, off the Edinburgh road; but there is nothing industrial about this one, an attractive place on a south-facing terrace of the deep valley, with its own history as a separate village and barony, although belonging originally also to the Douglases. Detached and residential likewise is Eskbank, half-a-mile to the south-west, a quite extensive community of mainly large and substantial houses and villas, set in their gardens, with more traffic tending to spoil it unfortunately; for here the A7 from Edinburgh comes in over another bridge, at Elginhaugh, on its way to the mid-Border area, and sends off spokes in four other directions. So Dalkeith has two major highways to cope with, not very far apart.

Despite all this, the more rural atmosphere manages to persist, partly accounted for no doubt by the deep wooded Esk valleys on either side; and also by the presence of three great estates which still press close – even though they no longer rank as noblemen's seats. For, complementing Dalkeith Palace, here at the other end of the town, Melville Castle occupies the North Esk valley and Newbattle Abbey the South Esk. The former is now a hotel, standing in policies which stretch for over a mile along the valley-floor to Lasswade. Wherein grow some of the finest old beech-trees in Scotland, mentioned by Scott: "Who knows not Melville's beechy grove and Roslin's rocky glen!"

Melville Castle, although incorporating older foundations, is typical of the late eighteenth-century romantic castellated style, of proliferating sham towers and spurious crenellations. It was built by Playfair in 1786 for the famous, or otherwise, Henry Dundas, first Viscount Melville, modelled on the English idea of a castle, not the authentic and very different Scots tradition. It is strange that the two styles should be so distinct; but history had a lot to do with it, the sturdy and entirely practical native style being notably enhanced in the sixteenth century by the more decorative French *château* flourish introduced by Mary of Guise's and Mary Queen of

Scots' artists and architects brought from the Continent, something England never experienced. Melville Castle is a fine example of its kind, however, its magnificent open staircase soaring in spirals towards a loftly painted ceiling. The late eighteenth century was the North British period, of course, when the eyes of the enlightenment – of which Henry Dundas was no mean member – turned ever southwards. The older Melville Castle, whence sprang that well-known family name, from the Norman de Malevilles, had seen some stirring times, even though it does not feature largely in Scottish history. The ballad, "Willie's Gaun to Melville Castle" is renowned.

Newbattle, in the other valley, has a very different story. This was the site of the great and powerful abbey, founded in 1140 by David I, which pioneered the developments of the Lothian coalfields and the salt industry. It likewise led the way in agricultural improvement, so that it became one of the richest establishments in the land, and its proud mitred abbots immensely powerful. Here, in this green and sequestered valley, they lived in tremendous style amidst fine gardens and orchards – and, as has been indicated, when at length the Reformation overtook them, Abbot Mark Kerr had so carefully arranged things that he stayed on as temporal instead of spiritual lord, with an annual income from the abbey of no less than £1413, an enormous sum for those days. His son became first Earl of Lothian. Newbattle remained the seat of the family – in time they became marquises – until fairly recent days, when they returned to their calf-country in the Borders and the Abbey became an important residential college of further education.

There is a pretty hamlet of Newbattle, deep in the valley, wherein stands the parish church, of 1727, notable as having been the charge of the venerable Robert Leighton from 1641 to 1653. He became thereafter Bishop of Dunblane and later Archbishop of Glasgow, also Principal of Edinburgh University, a man of singular piety and humility in an age of religious intolerance. The old manse adjoining is attractive, with work at least as old as the seventeenth century. And nearby, in marked contrast to the tiny old-world village, is a large modern private housing estate in the parklike grounds. On this same side-road, nearer to Eskbank, is another educational establishment, the new Esk Valley College.

Since the Esks now diverge rapidly, we shall follow the shorter but more populous valley of the North Esk first. One of the radial roads from Eskbank flanks the Melville estate, above the riverside, to Lasswade, a former milling village hidden in the glen. Paper-milling became the staple industry of the Esk valley, and the first paper-mill here was opened in 1750. It is now defunct however, and the whole industry fallen on evil days – of which more hereafter. There have been many and elaborate attempts to explain away the name Lasswade, usually ignoring the almost certain Gaelic derivation and fastening on this character or that who either urged his mare or his lady-companion to wade the river. It is to be feared that place-names never arose thus, not in Scotland anyway. The most likely origin appears to me to be from *lios aodann*, the garden on the face of the slope although Johnston suggests the Old English *loes woed*, the meadow-ford. To the west, on the way to Loanhead, is the former hamlet of Wadingburn; and this of course has encouraged the wading enthusiasts although no burn here is large enough to wade and it is half-a-mile from the river. At Wadingburn is the picturesque house, which has had various names, in which Sir Walter Scott spent the six years from 1798 to 1804, where he wrote his *The Grey Brother* and other works. Lasswade is thought to be the Gandercleugh in his *Tales of My Landlord*. Here he was visited by the Wordsworths. In the kirkyard of the ruined Norman church of Lasswade lie the bones of Henry Dundas, Viscount Melville, who ruled Scotland virtually from 1775 till 1805. Also of Drummond of Hawthornden, of whom more later.

Lasswade, until the recent municipal upheaval, was part of the burgh of Bonnyrigg and Lasswade. Bonnyrigg, a larger place occupying the higher ground above the deep valley, is reached by a steep road. It is not a particularly attractive place to look at, despite its name, although it has a pleasant residential area called Broomieknowe, on the braeside. It is a comparatively modern town, now spreading in proliferating modern housing to east and south, away from the river. Standing quite high, it rather lacks trees, always a great help to a landscape. But it has views.

Across the river from Bonnyrigg, not much more than a mile, is Loanhead, another industrial and mining town. To reach it requires a considerable detour on account of the valley and bridge situation, either north-about by Lasswade or south-about by Polton. This latter, another former paper-milling village deep in the valley-bottom, on a twisting and very steep sideroad, must be one of the least-known Mid-lothian communities, so hidden and so daunting the road. Yet it has its claims to attention. Oddly, it was formerly the terminus of a branch railway. And Thomas De Quincy, author of *Confessions of an English Opium Eater* lived at the former Man's Bush cottage here from 1840 until his death in 1859. His curious ongoings made a big impact on the district. The former paper-mill is now a small industrial estate.

Loanhead, immediately above Polton via a one-in-five gradient, might be in a different land, open and rather bare instead of deep-sequestered and overhung with woodlands. It is the same sort of place as Bonnyrigg, industrialized with widespread council housing. As well as the mining there is a long-established engineering works here and an industrial estate. In the Loanhead area there are said to have been no fewer than twenty-five individual coal-seams, for long worked. Indeed in 1770, a pit went on fire accidentally and despite all efforts to extinguish it, burned for over twenty years. There is still a large colliery at Bilston Glen about a mile to the west of Loanhead, with sundry National Coal Board satellite departments.

Up the main river from the Polton-Loanhead area another mile is the estate and castle of Hawthornden. The early seventeenth-century poet, William Drummond of Hawthorn-den has made this name renowned – which is rather strange considering how comparatively little-known are his works today. Nor did he achieve any special fame in other fields, living a life of 'learned leisure' in his beloved glen. He first became noted for the elegy he wrote on the untimely death of James VI and I's eldest son, Prince Henry, in 1613. One of his later books of poems had the unlikely title of *Poems – Amorous, Funeral, Divine, Pastoral.* He also wrote a *History of Scotland* published in 1655. More quoted is his actual in-scription carved on the east wall of his castle, in Latin, translated thus: "By the Divine gift, William Drummond, son of the gilded knight John, in order that he might live in honourable ease, restored me for himself and his successors in the year 1638." The father, Sir John Drummond, had bought Hawthornden from the Douglases, so there is much older work than 1638 here. The building is romantically perched on the beetling edge of the precipitous den amongst hanging woodlands and consists of a ruinous fifteenth-century tower and older foundations, to which has been added the early seventeenth-century L-planned house with later extensions. Directly beneath are a number of caves, one of which has been turned into an unpleasant underground pit or prison, reachable only by a hatch from above – although, in turn, this was transformed into a secret oratory or chapel. These caves are famous, and are thought possibly originally to have been an underground Pictish fort, part natural, part artificial, linked by passages carved in the soft rock. They are traditionally associated with Bruce, as a hiding-place during the Wars of Independence, three being known as the King's Diningroom, Bedchamber and Gallery. One is, extraordinarily, a doocot, with its access in the cliff, square nest-boxes cut in the stone. Scott wrote of "cavern'd Hawthornden". The Abernethy family, from Saltoun in East Lothian, were early lairds, descended from a Celtic Church Abbot of Abernethy. Sir Lawrence thereof changed sides frequently during the Wars of Independence. Mary Queen of Scots is said to have spent three nights here. Queen Victoria also came but did not stay. Both Ben Jonson and Samuel Johnson visited Hawthornden, the former having walked all the way from London. He stayed three weeks, and Drummond became slightly disenchanted. John Knox preached from a flat rock overlooking the steep gorge, able to address a crowd on the opposite bank, which gives some idea of the nature of the site. After years of part-neglect the castle has recently passed into hands suitably appreciative.

One mile further upstream, on the other side, is a still more famous place; the castle and chapel of Roslin, with village nearby. Roslin's story goes far back. There was a battle, when a Scots force under the Red Comyn and Sir Simon Fraser, defeated three English forces in one day, slaughtering the

prisoners taken in the first two, as it were, to free their hands.
The castle, larger but less picturesque than Hawthornden, was
built by successive generations of the "lordly line of high St
Clair", which came over with the Conqueror from Normandy
and settled here with much success in the reign of David I, in
the early twelfth century. In the main, the building as we see
it today dates from 1452; for just previously the castle had
been largely destroyed by fire – not siege or war in this case
but through the fondness of the Countess Elizabeth for her
dogs, which she kept in her bedroom and even allowed to
whelp there, which, for some unexplained reason was the
cause of the fire. She was a Douglas, wife of the princely third
Earl of Orkney, who called himself Prince thereof, and was
also Duke of Oldenburg, Earl of Caithness, and with other
titles. Many tales are told of his magnificence; that he had
three Scots lords as his Master of Household, Cup-Bearer and
Carver, and his lady seventy-five gentlewomen, and so on.
We may take all this with a pinch of salt; but William St
Clair has left tangible proof of his magnificence in Roslin
Chapel. What remains of the castle, to be sure, is only a small
part of the original, five storeys high to the east and only three
to the west, owing to the steep drop in the ground-level, the
three lower storeys all having four vaulted chambers, semi-
subterranean. The upper floors were altered in the seventeenth
century. The castle was largely destroyed in Hertford's invasion in the sixteenth century and again by General Monk in
the seventeenth; so it is not to be wondered at if it does not
reflect all its pristine grandeur. There is still an earldom of
Rosslyn – which is the more accurate spelling, a ross or
headland at the lynn or waterfall; but the present family,
called St Clair-Erskine, is somewhat detached from the main
line, of which the Lords Sinclair, mentioned under Herdmanston in East Lothian, are more direct. The castle is no
longer occupied as a mansion but kept in repair and open to
visitors.

The chapel, nearby, is one of the architectural wonders of
Scotland, an extraordinary place, still in occasional use for
worship and a magnet for tourists. It was erected in 1501 by
the aforementioned William St Clair, Prince and Earl, as
recorded on the wall of the north clerestory, thus: "William

Lord St. Clair fundit yis college ye zeir of God MCCCCI". It will be noted that he calls it a college; and it was indeed intended to be a great and most ambitious collegiate church, but the earl's death intervened and it was never completed as such. What resulted however was sufficiently dramatic, the choir and chancel turned into a private chapel and burial crypt, in the most elaborate and luxuriant decorative architecture in the land, almost overpowering in its effect – but it must be remembered that this would not seem so crowded with detail and design if the large nave had been added as planned. The stone-carving is almost unbelievably fine, the pillars and vaulted roofing patterned and intricate, like the richest foliage. Pride of place goes, of course, to the famous Prentice Pillar, magnificent in its craftsmanship. The usual story told is that the Prince-Earl, who actually designed all this himself, ordered his master-mason to execute his drawings, based on something he had seen on the Continent. The master just could not cope with it, and was sent by the Earl to Europe to study the original for himself – and whilst he was away, his apprentice mason took it upon himself to execute the design on his own, with this result. When his master returned, the story goes, he was so jealous and infuriated that he slew the apprentice. This kind of story has been related for other places; but it looks as though there might be some truth in it, for the Archbishop of St Andrews, Primate, refused consecration of the building until an act of reconciliation was performed, because of blood having been shed in it. And there are three carved heads high at the west of the chapel, said to represent the master-mason, the murdered youth and his weeping mother.

The village of Roslin seems rather tame after all this, an open and now residential community, although with a mining background also. But it was important as the castleton of the St Clairs, of course, long before the coal days; and in 1456 it actually received from James II a charter erecting it into a burgh of barony, with all the rights of such, these rights being confirmed by both James VI and Charles I. There was a gunpowder factory here which blew up in 1872. And the inn, dating from 1662, had many famous visitors, coming to see the chapel, including Boswell and Johnson, Burns, Scott, the

Wordsworths and Edward VII, when Prince of Wales – who, like the others, fulfilled the tradition of scratching his name on a window-pane. One last reference to Roslin. The youth George Meikle Kemp came to the chapel, to wonder at what he saw. He was the son of a humble shepherd in the Pentland Hills. This revelation of what man could design and create, at the age of ten so impressed him that it fired him to become one of the great architects of his age; and of his works, the Scott Monument in Edinburgh's Princes Street, is perhaps the best known. He died in 1844, only in his forties, falling into the canal-basin at Fountainbridge and drowning.

A steep and winding road plunges eastwards from Roslin down into the gut of the dean, with mill premises now used otherwise, passing St Matthew's Well – it is noteworthy that Roslin Chapel was dedicated to St Matthew – and climbing out to the former mining village of Rosewell beyond. Set on the edge of lovely and unspoiled country, Rosewell, despite its pleasing name, like Bonnyrigg, is no beauty-spot, with its uniform rows of former colliers' cottages. Of all industries, the mining one seems to have had the least concern with amenity, or its work-force's living conditions, being interested only in immediate profit, leaving behind almost everywhere an un-lovely heritage for future generations. Rosewell is no excep-tion. Its pit is now closed down. There is a large St Joseph's Roman Catholic hospital and establishment here, in pale brick which is also less than beauteous, but its good works more than compensate.

The very different type of country south of Rosewell falls to be described under Moorfoot.

Following the North Esk upwards above Roslin, still in the wooded glen, we come to Auchendinny in over a mile, a small paper-making village on a side-road largely hidden in the valley. Built on a fairly steep hill, it is quite a pleasant place, although lacking any vistas. Auchendinny House, to the south is interesting. It is a medium-sized mansion, the last work of the famous architect Sir William Bruce, builder of Hopetoun Palace and other great houses. Auchendinny he designed for an Edinburgh lawyer in 1707, a great house in miniature, but with nothing of the new classical lines, a return to the vernacular style of harled walls, without ornament, yet having a hipped and slated roof, not crow-stepped gables. It has an oblong central block linked to pavilions at each side by curving walls, very attractive. It was later the home of a very well known character Henry Mackenzie (1745 - 1831), author of *The Man of Feeling,* one of Scotland's literati.

Up-river from here we are into the Penicuik area. Penicuik, a name which has inevitably given rise to witticisms, but which is generally accepted as being derived from *pen-y-cog,* the hill of the cuckoo, is the third largest town in Midlothian, and still growing, with a now quite large commuter element, ten miles only from Edinburgh. It has now overflowed from the Esk valley, where it began, quite considerably, on the higher ground to the south-west, not all to its scenic advantage. But its position is fine and it is the gateway to splendid country. It has been for long the main paper-making town of Midlothian, and although the industry has fallen on evil days hereabouts, owing to the trade getting into the hands of the great multi-national corporations, with wood-pulp becoming all important, the Valleyfield Mills here functioned until recently. Valleyfield had the unusual experience of being taken over and used as a barracks for French prisoners of war, in 1810–4, 300 of whom died here. Their graves are marked by a monument, erected by local people, inscribed in Latin which may be translated thus: "Certain inhabitants of this parish, desiring to remember that all men are brethren, caused this monument to be erected." A rather nice touch. Other paper-making establishments also have gone, including the Bank Mill, which used to manufacture bank-note paper. Edinburgh was, and still is, a great centre for printing, book-binding and publishing, and thus Esk paper used to find a large local market. Sad that it should be otherwise now.

The town has a quite attractive centre, on a south-facing slope, fairly wide and open, even if it is not particularly distinguished architecturally, with little of the ancient or authentically vernacular about it. The parish church of St Mungo, sited at the top of the High Street, has a notable Doric portico at the front, but as notably plain and uninspiring a back. It dates from 1771. But nearby is the ruin of the older predecessor, with a good Romanesque tower, the former nave now used as a burial-place. One of the memorials is graced by the carving of a dog's head; and here is interred the Howgate carrier and his wife immortalized in *Rab and His Friends* by Dr John Brown. Penicuik's links with the past tend to be literary, what with Henry Mackenzie at Auchendinny and R. L. Stevenson at Glencorse. But Allan Ramsay is the main pride of the place. Born in Lanarkshire in 1689, his roots were nevertheless in the Esk valley, for he came of the Ramsays of Cockpen and Dalhousie. He became a wig-maker in Edinburgh, but gradually began to emerge as a notable poet, to become the most popular versifier in Scotland since Sir David Lindsay of the Mount. His most famous work is undoubtedly *The Gentle Shepherd*, published in 1725, an immediate success. His popularity brought envy and enmity from some rivals, however, and one published a diatribe entitled: *The Flight of Religious Piety from Scotland upon the account of Ramsay's lewd Books and the Hell-Bred Playhouse Comedians who Debauch all the Faculties of the Souls of the Rising Generation*. Ramsay did not live at Penicuik – the house he built for himself in Edinburgh, on the north-east slope of the Castle Rock, is now the nucleus of the attractive Ramsay Garden enclave – but he seems to have been very fond of this Esk area and was a frequent visitor at Penicuik House. Also at Newhall, a smaller estate on the Esk to the south-west, in the vicinity of which is the dell he immortalized as Habbie's Howe. His son, of the same name, was an almost equally celebrated portrait-painter.

Penicuik estate, very extensive, lies to the west of the town, with the Esk running through its beautiful grounds. There is an obelisk erected here to Allan Ramsay. The mansion was a splendid Grecian edifice built to his own designs in 1761 by Sir James Clerk, third baronet; but unfortunately it was badly burned some time ago, and the present baronet and his family live in the converted stables. But these in themselves make a splendid house of considerable interest, the centre-piece of which is an extraordinary doocot with a lofty dome built in the style of a Roman temple, copy of the famous building on the Carron, near Falkirk, known as Arthur's O'on, or Oven. The Clerks came to Penicuik in 1646, the first of this line having amassed a great fortune in Paris and buying the estate from Penicuik of that Ilk. Apart from the ruined mansion, there are two ruined castles on the property, one at Uttershill to the east, overlooking the main road to Peebles; the other, Brunstane, three miles up-river to the west, a former seat of the Crichton family, who became Lords Crichton and later Earls of Dumfries, now merged with the Crichton-Stuarts, Marquises of Bute.

Around Penicuik a number of localities deserve mention. Just over a mile to the north-east is the great army establishment of Glencorse Barracks, the headquarters of the First Regiment of Foot, the Royal Scots – founded, it will be recollected, by Sir John Hepburn of Athelstaneford, out of the famous Scots Brigade of Gustavus Adolphus. This large depot, with its offshoots and training areas, inevitably makes a big impact on the neighbourhood. The name of Glencorse, the valley of the corpse, is given to three localities some miles apart – the barracks complex; the old estate with its mansion and ruined church; and the actual Pentland valley with its large and picturesque reservoir out of which the Glencorse Burn flows. Since we have to draw our lines somewhere, these latter are better dealt with under Pentland.

The other south and east side of Penicuik quickly ascends towards the empty higher ground of the extensive Auchencorth Moss, across which runs the Peebles-shire border. Right on that border, out in the midst, is the little crossroads community of Leadburn, with its inn, an exposed spot indeed. Three miles to the north, over high open country, and nearer Penicuik across the Esk, is another inn, on the Rosewell road, at the small village of Howgate, renowned as the base of the principals in *Rab and His Friends,* the carriers who daily made the journey to Edinburgh, taking the dog with them. Today it is better-known for its popular eating-house in the former inn. The Peebles border comes close.

The North Esk goes on for some six miles above Brunstane Castle, to its source in the hills; but this is very much in the Pentlands area and is moreover very different and mainly unoccupied country. So we return to the Dalkeith area and the *South* Esk.

After Newbattle, the South Esk, in a mile or so, flows past the vicinity of the mining village of Newtongrange, quite extensive if typically industrialized and without beauty, founded in 1830. The word grange, of course, refers to the farm of a monastery or abbey; and this originally was one of New-battle's farmeries. Part is still called Monkswood, although both monks and woodland have long been missing. Newton-grange is half a mile from the Esk on the east side; and a similar distance on the west side is another, Dalhousie Grange, on the tributary Dalhousie Burn. Dalhousie is one more of those names of small and in themselves unimportant places in which Lothian abounds, which have become celebrated, even world-famous, on account of the families which arose there, in this case the Ramsays of Dalhousie Castle. This castle still stands entire but very drastically altered and remodelled, although retaining its ancient nucleus, with even the old drawbridge gatehouse and portcullis-chain grooves. For some time it was a public school, but it is now in use as a hotel. The Ramsays were another of the Anglo-Norman families intro-duced into Scotland in the early twelfth century – David I brought them in not only because he preferred their company to that of the native Celtic lords but because of their military prowess, to guard his southern counties from invasion. The Ramsays cut a wide swathe in the land over the centuries, one signing the famous Declaration of Independence at Arbroath in 1320, another being starved to death in Hermitage Castle by that so-called Flower of Chivalry, the Douglas Knight of Liddesdale, another falling at Flodden, and so on. The fourteenth in line, was created first Lord Ramsay of Dalhousie – previous to that they had called their property Dalwolsey – and his son, in 1633 created Earl of Dalhousie and Lord Kerington (Carrington). In time one of the line married the heiress of the extinct earldom of Panmure in Angus and the family became Maule-Ramsays and made the great estates in Angus their main seat. One of them in 1849 was created Marquis of Dalhousie and was very famous as the Governor-General of India at the time of the Mutiny. He is buried at nearby Cockpen Church. He left no direct heir and the earldom went to a cousin. Queen Victoria visiting here in 1842 was "much impressed".

Cockpen lies across the Dalhousie Burn near the Grange, a name familiar to most Scots because of the fine old ballad "The Laird o' Cockpen," by Lady Nairne. That laird's house is now gone, but the parish church is still here, standing isolated, a rather fine cruciform edifice in the Perpendicular style, of 1820, with a tower seen for miles around. There is no village; Bonnyrigg is only a mile away.

Above Dalhousie, over a mile, the quite major Gore Water joins the Esk on the east; and now there are two deep, wooded valleys. We shall come back to the Gore Water hereafter. The South Esk itself now winds through very lovely and unspoiled country for the remainder of its course of ten miles or so. Its valley in the main is less deep and abrupt than that of the North Esk, its surroundings more gentle and rurally pleasing, much less populous. The Carrington area is reached, a delightful and sequestered village which, being on the road to nowhere in especial, has retained its character and sturdy identity notably - but not by being merely a sleepy hollow, for it has won prizes as the best-kept village in the land. The village used to be called Primrose and gave name to the family which became Earls of Rosebery - of which more hereafter. The former parish church is attractive, simple, but with good, authentic lines, of cruciform shape with an ogee-roofed tower, dating from 1710. Why the change of name from Primrose to Carrington, is not clear. It probably had something to do with the Ramsays ousting the Primroses of that Ilk. The earliest reference to 'Keryntoun' I have found was in the fourteenth century. Even then it was a Ramsay possession.

Further up-river from this area is the great estate of Arniston, seat of another branch of the Dundas family, descending from Sir James Dundas of Arniston, Governor of Berwick in the wars of Charles I, son of Dundas of Dundas in West Lothian. His son was a Senator of the College of Justice who resigned his seat on the Bench rather than abjure the Covenant. He was called Lord Arniston; and so was his son, another Senator, for no less than thirty-seven years. Indeed there was a long line of eminent lawyers, for the next son was also Lord Arniston of Session; and so was *his* son, so that the thing became almost hereditary. When his son likewise became Lord President of the Court of Session, and the fifth in succession, supreme head of the country's judiciary, it was without parallel. His uncle was Henry Dundas the famous Viscount Melville. The Dundas line is one of the oldest in

Scotland, of Celtic origin. Arniston House is a large Palladian mansion, much added to. Coal was discovered on the eastern fringes of the estate, in the Gorebridge area, which garnered much wealth. The Emily Pit here, at 160 fathoms, used to be considered the deepest worked in the east of Scotland. But the main part of the property, extending far to the west, is not affected by this industrialization, and is very attractive, with fine parklands as well as the Esk's wooded valley.

Two miles up is another delightful and sequestered place, Temple village, so named after the Knights Templar establishment at what was then called Balantradoch, their chief seat in Scotland, the Order being established here by David I, that busy monarch. The Order was suppressed in 1312, and the lands given by Pope Clement V to the Knights of St John. The old preceptory, roofless but otherwise entire, is still to be seen in the kirkyard of the present parish church, down in the steep dip of the glen, a simple but pleasing building, long and narrow, with lancet windows, a piscina and an Easter sepulchre. There is a strange inscription on the east gable which long puzzled antiquaries, "VAESAC MIHM". This is now thought to be the initial letters of *Vienne Sacrum Concilium Militibus Johannis Hierosolymitani Melitensibus* (The Sacred Council of Vienna, of the Knights of St John of Jerusalem and of Malta). This building was used as the parish church until the building of the present one, close by, in 1832. There is a very odd gravestone in the kirkyard, relating to the Reverend James Goldie who died in 1847, his will and testament carved here in stone, at great length, detailing all his bequests. The village, now becoming a favoured retreat for discerning folk appreciative of scenic quiet, is on the higher ground to the south-east, consisting of a single climbing street of cottages.

Above Temple the river winds through a further couple of miles of sylvan valley, this growing ever shallower now as it nears the Rosebery Reservoir, its passage making a delightful walk. The reservoir is merely a mile-long dammed-up flooding of the Esk's course, the trees which have clung to its banks all the way from Musselburgh left behind at last and the Moorfoot Hills closing in. The Rosebery estate here is where the Primrose family takes its title of Earl of Rosebery, although they no longer live at the small mansion-house but at Dalmeny in West Lothian. The first Primrose of note to emerge after their departure from Primrose-Carrington was a Fife laird, James, whom James VI appointed Clerk to the Scots Privy Council in 1602 and who held that office for forty years and produced nineteen children, the eldest of whom, Alison, married the famous George Heriot, as his second wife, in 1609, being aged sixteen. She was a maid-in-waiting to Queen Anne of Denmark. His son became Clerk to the Privy Council after him and it is perhaps interesting to note that when, at the Restoration, he became a Senator of the College of Justice, he took the title of Lord Carrington. So there was a Lord Carrington and a Lord Keringtoun at the same time, taking their titles from the same village. His son became first Earl of Rosebery in 1703. The fifth Earl became Prime Minister in 1894 – not a very notable one perhaps – and created Earl of Midlothian also. His son, the famous racehorse-owner and very popular character, died fairly recently, and the sale of his great English seat of Mentmore Towers, for death duties, created a sensation.

The Rosebery estate is now wedged between two reservoirs, for just to the west the Esk's tributary the Fullarton Water, has been dammed to form the Edgelaw Reservoir, Edinburgh's need for water ever growing. It is long and narrow, with wooded banks. Up this Fullarton Water a couple of miles is Fullarton itself, now only a farm but once greater, with the site of an ancient St Mary's Chapel, and nearby, at a lonely crossroads, the property called Mount Lothian. This last name is a bit of a mystery. It stands only 850 feet above sea-level and there is much higher ground not far away, going up to 2,000 feet; moreover it is not a hill. Yet it was once a parish on its own – and presumably the St Mary's Chapel was its church. There are old quarries in the neighbourhood.

The Esk itself has only a mile of course between the Rosebery and Gladhouse Reservoirs. The latter is many times as large, a great sheet of water nearly two miles long by half that in width, with two wooded islets. Edinburgh used to draw a quarter of its water-supply from this one source. It still takes much more water from the Moorfoots than from the nearer Pentlands, rather strangely. Above Gladhouse the South

Esk, only a stripling stream now, comes down from its high cradle near the summit of Blackhope Scar (2,137 feet) in a swift rushing descent of 1,200 feet in 3 miles. It passes near its foot the scanty ruins of Hirendean Castle, a remote tower which can never have been large. The remains of a chapel and the farm of Moorfoot itself are nearby. This was formerly another grange of Newbattle Abbey. David I granted these lands to the abbey about 1120, and they were still in its possession at the Reformation. So presumably the little castle, which has not very thick walls and looks like sixteenth-century construction, would be built by the fortunate Mark Kerr or one of his nominees. There would be quite a sizeable community here in those days, accounting for the fact that it gave its name to the whole range of hills.

Back to the Dalhousie area and the Gore Water's confluence, for the final stretches of this description of the Esk valleys. Only a mile up is the small town of Gorebridge, occupying the valley-floor and climbing out beyond, of less than 2,000 population. Although the site is picturesque the town is hardly so, mining once again having cast its blight – although there are bright spots, for Gorebridge had its own character before the coal-owners made their mark. The ruins of Newbyres Castle stand at the riverside, in the town. It was a sixteenth-century L-planned fortalice, with the usual vaulted basements, stair-tower, mural chambers and gunloops. Also a heraldic stone with the Borthwick arms. It was one more Newbattle property, which was granted away to Michael Borthwick of Glengelt in 1543, who no doubt built the castle. It was sold to the Dundases of Arniston in 1624 and was used as their dower- or jointure-house. Across the Gore Water, in 1793, was erected the first gunpowder works in Scotland, at Stobs Mills. There were collieries all the way from Gorebridge to Newtongrange.

Up-stream another mile is Fushiebridge, a former milling hamlet where the A7 enters the Gore valley having skirted Gorebridge to the west. On the Harvieston estate here are the small remains of the ancient castle of Catcune, said to have been the first seat of the Borthwick family before they built the magnificent keep bearing their name further up the river.

Hereafter the entire character of the country changes, rising and becoming more bare and wild and much less populous. River and road share the twisting valley but separate after a mile of so, the latter to climb southwards to the bleak heights of Middleton Moor, where there is the small crossroads village of North Middleton, formerly an important coaching stage occasional meeting-place of Walter Scott and Lord Cockburn. Middleton village proper, a mile to the south beyond the grounds of Middleton House, a mansion of 1710, now used for institutional purposes, was once a gipsy centre.

The Gore Water swings away to the east, however, as it were through a green gateway into a secluded and very pleasing stretch of valley, hidden amongst grassy braes and dominated by the proud and thrusting keep of Borthwick Castle. There is a parish church here too, with a steeple, but this is quite dwarfed by the castle, one of the finest of its kind in all Scotland. Dating from 1430, it is a massive E-shaped tower, soaring to no less than 110 feet in height, with parapet-walk and stone-flagged roof, the walling being no less than 14 feet thick at the base, the masonry honeycombed with mural chambers and passages. The great hall, stone-vaulted, is 51 by 24 feet, and 30 feet high. It is still intact and entire and still belongs to the Borthwicks, although no longer used as their seat. Strangely, the name is an importation, for Borthwick is really a district of Teviotdale in the Middle March of the Borders. But sometime before 1430, Sir William, the first Lord Borthwick, a great man of his day, bought part of the Hay estate of Locherworth or Loquhariot here – there is still a farm of the name not far away – and brought his Border name with him to give to this great fortalice. A long line of Lords Borthwick followed, and a lively lot they were, taking a prominent part in most of the stirring activities of centuries. An amusing story is told of the genesis of this great castle. The William de Hay who had sold Borthwick the land, still owned ground close on the other side of the Gore Water. Green with envy as he saw the magnificent stronghold rising on his former territory he constructed his own mill immediately beneath the knoll on which the castle rose, declaring that the Lord Borthwick, for all his pride, should never be out of hearing of the clack of his neighbour's mill. The present Borthwick of Borthwick, who was born in the castle, now lives at Crookston House in Moorfoot, some ten miles away, but retains an interest. The title lapsed for a considerable period, but Major Borthwick is in process of claiming it again. Much of note naturally happened here. Perhaps the most dramatic incident was when Mary and Bothwell were here for four days in 1567, and the Confederate Lords approached to trap them – or at least, Bothwell, whom Mary had created Duke of Orkney on their marriage. The bridegroom made his escape alone, in due time, for some reason leaving the Queen behind – which seems less than gallant, but presumably there was some excuse. He hurried over the moors three miles eastwards to Cakemuir Castle. Later, with the lords besieging Borthwick, Mary, dressed as a page, made her own daring escape by night, being lowered on a rope from an upper window, to make her own way to rejoin Bothwell at Cakemuir and thence to flee to Dunbar – a most extraordinary exploit for any woman, much less a queen. But Mary was no shrinking flower. The present writer had the notable experience, a few years ago, of watching Miss Margaret Hope of Luffness herself a descendant of Mary on both her mother's and father's side, re-enacting this incident, climbing out of the same castle-window and climbing down the sheer walling on a swaying rope. Who says that Scotswomen are not what they were? Eighty-three years after that escape, Borthwick Castle held out against Cromwell; but like Tantallon, the Lord Protector's cannon were too much for it and it was battered into submission. The damage of the cannonballs to the massive masonry is still visible on the east walling.

The church of Borthwick was burned down in 1775 but later rebuilt, incorporating part of the original, which was dedicated to St Mungo or Kentigern with the recumbent effigies of the first Lord Borthwick and his lady, now the south transept.

We are nearing the county boundary with both East Lothian and Berwickshire here, on Fala Moor, and also the source of the River Tyne, at Tynehead. Here is the aforementioned Cakemuir Castle, a sturdy and substantial mid-sixteenth-century tower – which meant that it must have been fairly new when Mary and Bothwell were here – with eighteenth-century additions. It has a quite massive square keep with a parapet and circular stair-tower, with gunloops. The basement, curiously, is not vaulted. A pine-panelled chamber is still pointed out as the Queen's room. The builder was Adam Wauchope, oddly enough a lawyer, not the usual free-booting baron, who successfully defended Bothwell against the accusation that he was one of the assassins of King Henry Darnley at Kirk o' Field.

A narrow ridge of high ground which looks like an enormous railway embankment – and it indeed has a railway-line running along the top – divides the Gore Water valley from that of the stripling Tyne here, a curious formation. The east-running and unexpectedly major-seeming Tyne valley is very attractive. It is as though a mirror had been held up to that of the Gore Water, for here is an almost identical situation, a hidden, all-but-empty glen, with a castle and a church in the middle but no village. This side it is Crichton, another famous name in Scotland's story – pronounced Cry-ton. This castle, although now a ruin in the care of the Department of the Environment, is as celebrated as that of Borthwick and even larger. It is suggested that Borthwick was in fact built so high in order that from its parapet Crichton could be seen over the ridge. Growing from the original small square fourteenth-century tower of the Crichton family, it was added to a century later by the famous Sir William Crichton, Chancellor of Scotland for James II, a ruthless character. Another addition was made the same century, and then between 1581 and 1591 were erected the notable extensions by Bothwell's nephew, and successor, the aforementioned witchcraft-loving Francis Stewart, the bane of James VI's early life, that half-crazy but cultured ruffian, who had travelled widely in Italy and elsewhere and built this splendid memento of his travels, with its extraordinary piazza-like courtyard and Italianate portico, unlike anything else in Scotland. Mary is reputed to have spent part of her honeymoon with Darnley at Crichton.

The collegiate church of Crichton, with manse adjoining, stands nearby, a fine substantial building of 1449, dedicated to St Mary and Kentigern – the latter of whom seems to have been very popular hereabouts – with a massive, square saddle-backed tower, distinctly unusual. It was staffed by a provost, a sacristan, eight prebendary priests and two singing boys. Intended to be cruciform, its nave was never completed, so that it consists only of chancel and transepts. It must have been an ambitious intention, since the chancel, now used as the parish church, contains seating for no less than 500.

The Crichton area is open and genial, with a sequestered and quite pretty hamlet; and once out of the actual valley of Tyne, slants gently up towards the Fala and Soutra ridges. Just below the church is the site of an Iron Age fort; and a mile to the east, on higher farmlands, is a souterrain or Pictish earth-house, set within a fence in a field, in good order, and at about four feet high, considerably larger than the one mentioned at Traprain in East Lothian. Crichton House, which might be described as the successor of the castle, stands just to the north of the souterrain, nearer Pathhead, a delightful, tall, whitewashed building of the later seventeenth century, typical in the L-plan with steep roofing and octagonal stair-tower.

The quite large village of Pathhead climbs a long hill from the Tyne, almost a mile in length but only a single street, carrying the A68 on its way to Soutra Hill and Lauderdale. It has no especial character but is pleasant enough, save for the traffic. The path it takes its name from led up from the older village of Ford, down in the dip of the Tyne, now largely gone, with the road and ford replaced by the great Lothian Bridge designed by Thomas Telford, five-arched and 80 feet in height – this now bearing the highway. Ford House, however, still remains down by the waterside in its walled garden, another late seventeenth-century small mansion of great charm, of similar architectural style to Crichton but not so tall.

The Tyne valley winds south-eastwards, flanked by two fine estates, before it reaches the East Lothian border – Preston Hall and Oxenfoord Castle. The former, a handsome classical mansion of 1794, was built by William Adam for Lord Adam Gordon. It has magnificent gardens. Oxenfoord, belonging to the Earls of Stair, who bear the subsidiary title of Lord Oxenfoord, has for some time been run as a private school, by members of that family. The castle dates from various periods, the original nucleus of great age, but this was rebuilt in the reign of Charles II by the Makgill Viscount of Oxfuird, as it was then called; then again remodelled by its new owner, Sir John Dalrymple, who had married the Makgill heiress and gained the lands, to designs by Robert Adam, in 1782. It was again given a new aspect in 1842, by his son, created Baron Oxenfoord, who succeeded as eighth Earl of Stair. So little that is ancient is evident about the present large impressive mansion. The interior is very fine, with much Adam decoration.

Near Oxenfoord stands isolated the parish church of Cranstoun, a very sparsely populated parish indeed. The church, set here, would be convenient only for the occupants of Oxenfoord Castle. It is a quite good Gothic edifice of last century. There were originally two baronies of Cranstoun, Upper and Nether. This section was the Nether, and called Cranstoun-Riddell – it still is, although the Riddells left it in the fourteenth century. It came into the hands of King Jamie's Lord Advocate, David Makgill, in 1582; and his grandson became Viscount of Oxfuird and Lord Makgill of Cousland in 1651. That title was dormant for many years but has recently been revived, and accepted by the House of Lords, for the due descendant. Upper Cranstoun belonged to the Cranstouns of that Ilk, who became Lords Cranstoun in 1609. The eleventh lord died in 1869; and though claim to the title has not been established officially, there is still a head of the family, descendant, known as Cranstoun of that Ilk, who lives in Lanarkshire. Here at Cranstoun was a hospice of the Melrose monks, midway between that of Soutra and Edinburgh – of which more under Moorfoot. There is no village nearer than Cousland two miles to the north, a place spoiled by mining – although there *is* one nearer as the crow flies, but much further by road, to the west. This is Edgehead, at the other side of the ridge, on the high side-road between Ford and Dalkeith – it is only three miles to Dalkeith from here. This is a comparatively little known community strung out along this lofty road above the Esk valley, about 400 feet higher than Dalkeith, and not seen from the main highways. A former windmill here – an unusual feature for Scotland – has been imaginatively converted into an interesting dwelling. And in this vicinity another rarity for Midlothian – an oil-well. It has been known for some time that there was oil at D'Arcy, on a ridge to the west of Edgehead, and there have been various attempts at exploiting it. The present-day preoccupation with fuel-extraction has produced further efforts. What the future holds for this area remains to be seen.

And on that question we may leave the Esks and their valleys, within sight of where we started.

V

MIDLOTHIAN - MOORFOOT

First of all the name, which sounds such a nonsense for a double range of hills which rise to over 2,000 feet. As has been indicated under the South Esk, they are called after the former monkish grange and community of that name in the lap of the said hills near the South Esk's source, now at the head of Gladhouse Reservoir. But this is no suitable description even for that place, amongst the surrounding steep hills, all fairly non-moorish. However, a little research reveals that the lands which David I granted to the Abbey of Newbattle in the early twelfth century were called Morthuweit or Morthwait, not Moorfoot, which might be translated from the Norse, a cut-off or remote place. Which sounds more like it.

The Moorfoot Hills, as a range, are a rather vague entity, distinct enough on their northern escarpment but merging with the Lammermuirs on the east and fading into the general Borderland hill-mass on the south. It is almost impossible to say where they end in that direction. Most of their wide and undefined area is probably in Peebles-shire, some small part in Berwickshire, some might even be said to be in Selkirkshire. But for the purposes of this account I am using the name to apply to the entire upland area of Midlothian, so unlike the rest, which projects itself south-eastwards for many miles, like a spearhead into the Borderland, to reach to within four miles of Galashiels and five of Tweed.

Apart from the South Esk and a few minor burns all this large area of perhaps 170 square miles, drains southwards into rivers which run eventually into Tweed, the entire terrain as it were turning its back on Lothian and the coastal plain. So it is very strange that it should be part of that territorial entity. The probable reason for this will appear when we come to its 'capital', Stow. In the entire area, in the main the womb of the Gala Water and its tributaries, there are no towns - although

Stow likes to be thought of as such - only one other real village and a very few hamlets, with some small estate communities. The total population, Stow included, is less than 1,500.

To start where we left off, at Moorfoot itself, we are confronted with a north-facing escarpment about fifteen miles long, rising quite abruptly from around the 1,000 foot level to a series of summits between 1,600 and 1,900 feet, but reaching over 2,000 on occasion, the highest being Blackhope Scar (2,137 feet) out of which rises the South Esk. These heights are less rounded, less green and grassy, than the Lammermuirs, but nevertheless make fair sheep-country. So there are many hill-farms. The collecting of water for Edinburgh is important on the north; there are no reservoirs on the south-draining major part. This main northern ridge is very distinct and quite narrow, with burns running off north and south within distances of a hundred yards or so, mainly southwards to join the Heriot Water.

One road crosses these heights at this north-eastern end, the B7007, from Middleton to the Leithen valley and Innerleithen in Peebles-shire, a lonely, lofty route, over Middleton and Wull Moors, and rising to 1,324 feet near the sort of pass of Windy Slack, 200 feet higher than the better known Soutra summit. Two miles beyond this pass another road, B709, comes in on the east, from the Heriot Water valley, from the main A7 highway down the Gala Water, of which more presently.

East of this the hills sink in height and contour to the extensive Fala area, which forms the uplands behind Borthwick, Crichton and Pathhead. Fala used to be a civil parish on its own, but is now combined with Soutra. It was once more important than it is today, but clearly, on these high levels, it can never have been very populous, most of the area lying above the 1,000 foot level, moorland, moss and heather. There is a small village of Fala, which is also called Blacksheils, sometimes both. This is because the parish church of Fala is here, small and plain on a mound at the east end of the village - really only a hamlet; and the former large inn of Blacksheils stands prominently on the main A68 road at the west end, near the foot of Soutra Hill, eye-catching and dating apparently from the late seventeenth century.

Fala Moor, nearly 400 feet higher, is an extensive tract, now much drained, so that the little loch in the middle, Fala Flow, was once much larger. It used to be a great place for digging peats too. There is the ruin of a peel-tower to the north, which must have been on the verge of the loch once, known as Fala Luggie – luggie means a hut or lodge-house, a horned owl or a crop-eared person, so one takes one's choice. Only a part of one wall remains, but sufficient to see that it had a vaulted basement.

This bleak moorland expanse is bounded on the south by an interesting six-mile-long side-road, B6368, which links the main A68 and A7 highways, through the eastern Moorfoots, rising to 1,212 feet. It is not an important route now but it was once; for this was the line of the old monkish road from Melrose and the other Border abbeys, to Edinburgh and the North – and in those days these were the main creators of wealth in the land, a fact that is often forgotten. They provided hospices on the roads for the shelter of travellers, often in the most inhospitable places and remote spots – and there is a tradition that the staffing of these uncomfortable outposts was frequently a punishment for brothers who had earned the abbot's or prior's disapprobation. Such a place, rather more important than the usual run, was Soutra Aisle, now so-called, formerly the hospice and church of the Holy Trinity, founded before 1164. It was its own parish before the Reformation, and many famous folk have stayed here. United with Fala in 1589, it dwindled away without its monks, its stones carted off to build dykes in the usual fashion, until only that vaulted aisle of the church, which had been appropriated as a burial crypt of the Pringle family, remains today. These names ending with an 'a' – Fala, Gala, Soutra, Caitha, Sherra and so on, in this area, are odd, but probably not significant, save as local pronunciation, for none seem to have similar derivations.

A couple of miles south-west of Soutra Aisle the road begins to drop from the heather ridge down into the attractive quiet valley of the Armet Water, passing the lonely hill-farms of Gilston and Nether Brotherstone – Upper Brotherstone is a couple of miles up the narrow side-glen of the Brothershiels

Burn northwards. Surely there can be few such remote and cut-off establishments as this, and its neighbour, Brothershiels farm, only fifteen miles from a capital city? In winter snows the occupants must seem as though in another land. Prehistoric remains around here show, however, that this area was not always so empty.

This B9368 road eventually joins the A7 in the upper Gala Water valley at the Borthwick estate of Crookston. Before dropping to the main valley-floor it passes the high-set Old Crookston House, a very attractive, modest mansion, mainly of the seventeenth century, but which has grown out of a tower of the late fifteenth or early sixteenth century, this forming the eastern portion of the present T-plan. It is four storeys tall, and whitewashed, with the usual crow-stepped gables and dormer windows, and has been vaulted, with very thick walling and a turnpike stair, the doorway being notably low-browed, as a defensive feature, forcing all visitors to stoop uncomfortably. The original tower is said to have been built in 1446, when John de Borthwick, second son of the first Lord Borthwick, acquired Crookston from Sir Alexander Ramsay of Dalwolsey. The Crookston Borthwicks became the hereditary standard-bearers to the Lords Borthwick and eventually themselves fell heir to the chiefship, their present representative still living in the larger and later mansion-house in the woodlands below. There is a family tradition that it was Young Crookston who aided Mary in her flight from Borthwick Castle to Cakemuir.

Just north of Crookston the Heriot Water joins the Gala from the West Moorfoots in a quite major valley, in the mouth of which lies the scattered village of Heriot itself. It may be that this is where the name of that family originated – but not necessarily so, for the word merely means the payment to a lord of a fee on the death of a vassal, and the name could, and does, apply to a number of places, often corrupted to such as Harrietsfield and so on. Heriot village is not large, but its community extends a long way up its valley, the parish church indeed being two miles up, small and rebuilt in 1835. There is a large fort on the hill above the church, called Corsehope Rings, with four distinct lines of ramparts; and another, smaller nearer the Gala Water, of the early Iron Age. Also two stone-circles high on the hills in the vicinity. So this has been an important area. There is also a stone where witches were burned, of a later but no less superstitious period. The Heriot B709 road proceeds for a further three miles, passing the attractive little side-glen of Carcant, to join the afore-mentioned B7007 from Middleton to Innerleithen, a lonely route. We are nearing the Peebles-shire border again here, deep in the hills. But before reaching it, on the extraordinarily straight road which runs for six miles almost without a bend, something scarcely believable in hill country, in the valley of the Dewar Burn, we pass the notably isolated and large sheep-farm of Dewar. The name is significant, for a dewar was the hereditary custodian of the relics of a Celtic saint, and not many of such are to be found south of the Forth. It would be interesting to know which saint's relics this dewar's croft represented. St Ronan's Well at Innerleithen, in Peebles-shire, immortalized by Scott, is only about eight miles to the south, of course; so that might be the connection. There are two landmarks at Dewar worthy of mention. Some stones called the Piper's Grave, said to mark the spot of a foolhardy and fatal cantrip of a Peebles piper; and a large monolith on top of Dewar Hill known as Lot's Wife.

Back at the Gala Water - the name may be from the Gaelic *geal* meaning white (water) or *guala* meaning a shoulder of hill, or perhaps old Welsh *gwala*, a full stream - two roads run southwards down this fine valley, the A7, busy on the east side of the twisting river, and a lesser and more winding and older road on the west side. Down this latter, four miles from Heriot, is the hamlet of Fountainhall, pleasantly tucked into a re-entrant of the hillside - not to be confused with the Fountainhall House in East Lothian. There are the remains of what is alleged to be a Roman camp at Pirntaton here - although so often these sites prove to have been Pictish.

On the other side of Gala Water there are no communities but some estates and farms. One of the latter, on the high ground unseen from the A7, a mile south of Crookston, is called Hoppringle, and this too is a significant name. For this is how the well-known surname of Pringle used to be spelt, and this was the originating place of that Border clan. There would be a peel-tower here once, no doubt. Actually, the

Probably the most perfect example of Norman church architecture in Scotland. Interior of Dalmeny Kirk.

(*Above*) Hillend artificial ski-slope on the north face of the Pentlands, with Edinburgh, the Forth and Fife behind and (*below*) the new campus of Heriot-Watt University amongst the Midlothian fields at Riccarton, with the Pentland Hills behind.

(*Above*) South Queensferry's High Street, with the Tolbooth on the left and (*below*) the road and rail bridges over the Forth, looking north from Queensferry harbour.

Blackness Castle, West Lothian, an ancient state prison on the shore of the Forth.

Where much Scots history was made. Linlithgow with its palace, St Michael's Kirk and loch-side modern developments.

(*Above*) the bings or slag-heaps of the shale-oil workings which dot the West Lothian plain – this at Winchburgh, and (*below*) red deer being raised in Beecraigs Country Park in the Bathgate Hills.

(*Above*) in Bathgate Hill Country Park and (*below*) hill-top Bronze Age burial cairn, with chambers cut out of the living rock – Cairn-papple.

(*Above*) Torphichen: the preceptory of St John, medieval priory and now the parish church, and (*below*) the new town of Livingston, ambitious newcomer on the West Lothian scene.

family is still represented locally, at Torwoodlee estate further down the Gala Water into Selkirkshire, a property held by the Pringles since 1509.

Five miles on down the Gala's remarkably twisting course – the former railway which shared the valley with road and river had to cross it no fewer than seventeen times – we reach Stow – more properly Stow-in-Wedale – and at last we come to the reason for the inclusion of this lengthy peninsula of Borderland in Midlothian. It was, as might have been guessed by this time, on account of lands held by the Church. It so happened that all the many lands in Midlothian belonging to the archiepiscopal see of St Andrews were erected into the important establishment of a regality, with judicial and fiscal power, as well as ecclesiastical. And the lands of Stow-in-Wedale were actually what was called mensal, that is part of the bishop's own benefice, or 'for his table'. The Bishops of St Andrews, who were, of course, Primates of the Scottish Church, had a private palace here at Stow. So they wanted the place included in their jurisdiction of Midlothian – and it was so. However, Stow claims a much earlier fame than any Bishop of St Andrews could give it. For here, it is claimed, was fought the Battle of Guinnian, one of the twelve battles of King Arthur, when he routed the Saxons. The story is that Arthur himself founded the first church, dedicated to the Virgin Mary, and endowed it with a fragment of the True Cross. It became a place of pilgrimage, naturally, a relic of which was a great boulder allegedly bearing the footprint of the Virgin herself – although this seems to have disappeared. This ancient chapel's remains stand about a mile south of Stow itself, near the inevitable Our Lady's Well, which is still pointed out. Gradually the emphasis seems to have shifted the mile north to where the bishop's palace was established, and here in 1242 another church was consecrated, also to St Mary, in what is now the village itself. This was not only a place of pilgrimage, but actually of sanctuary, shelter for wrong-doers. Indeed, 'the Black priest of Wedale' was one of the three persons in all the land to whom the privileged law of Clan MacDuff applied, for some reason. So this was a very important place. And not only in matters religious and legal, it seems; for we read that the English chronicler, in advising his monarch how to bring Scotland to its knees, wrote:

> To send ane hoste of footmen in,
>   At Lammesse next, through Lauderdale,
> At Lamermore woods and mosses over-rin,
>   And eke therewith the Stow of Wedale.

This name of Wedale is most mysterious, the valley of the Gala Water today. Various suggestions are made as to why it was so called – but none as to why it stopped being so called. One story is that it was the Valley of Woe, referring to the sanguinary defeat of the Saxons by Arthur – but this is patently a nonsense. Another connects it with the Norse *Ve*, meaning a temple or church, to make it the dale of the holy house or sanctuary – which seems slightly more likely. A third suggestion is that it derives from the Vale of the Goidel, one of the Celtic races; but this also seems far-fetched, even though it might be argued that the word Gala could come from the same source. That early peoples were strong hereabouts is evidenced from there being no fewer than seven ancient camps in the parish of Stow. Anyway, it is a long time since the name Wedale dropped out, save perhaps in ecclesiastical records – which is strange since the quite well-known sur-names of Weddell and Waddell derive from it.

Stow itself is a pleasant place which likes to call itself a town, not so very large village as it is, huddling compactly between two burns which join the Gala from the east. To substantiate its municipal pretensions it actually has a town-hall, built in 1854, quite ambitious as to architecture. Even more ambitious is the present parish church which stands on a shelf above road and river, claimed indeed to be one of the finest such buildings in Southern Scotland, built in 1876 in Early Decorated Gothic style with a spire no less than 140 feet high, with seating for 700 – which considering Stow's popula-tion cannot be much more than 500, seems to represent wishful thinking. Near the church, and seen from the A7, is the delightful and graceful pack-horse bridge over the Gala, now disused but kept in repair. The term pack-horse bridge is used for one with especially low or non-existent parapets, so that laden ponies were not impeded from crossing.

South of Stow there is still five miles of Midlothian. On the east side of the river, after Our Lady's Chapel, is the ancient estate of Torsonce, with its old mansion renewed. After this the Gala Water takes a remarkable loop to enclose a half-mile of wide open haughland, highly unusual in that valley, wherein lies the farm of Bowshank, on the west side. On the east is the old estate of Bowland and the tiny hamlet of Bow. Also the hill of Bowcastle. It is tempting to assume that all thus emphasis on the word bow is because of the bow-shaped bend of the river, and therefore of the A7 road likewise. But this may be too simplistic. Bow is a purely English word and unlikely to be used as a place-name before comparatively modern times. Whereas *bo* is the Gaelic word for cattle, and might well apply to this open and level area of pasture in a generally steep sheep country. *Bu* is also the Norse word for a farm; so the two may coincide. Up the side of Bowcastle Hill, at the 1000-foot contour, is the site of a broch, one of those extraordinary Pictish – or even earlier – circular, beehive-shaped towers, which are so rare south of Forth and Clyde. Indeed there are only ten between Tay and Tweed, although there is another at Torwoodlee not far away. This one, perched on the lip of the drop to the valley and surmounted by a tall modern cairn, has walls 15 feet thick enclosing an inner open circular yard 31 feet in diameter. When excavated in 1890 and again in 1922 Roman remains were found, including a bronze brooch representing a cock.

There are other proto-historic relics in this Gala Water neighbourhood, burial-cairns in especial across the river in the Lugate area, revealing that this was once a comparatively populous country. The Lugate is a quite major stream, not so very much less so than the Gala itself, which comes rushing down a five-mile-long glen, passing the scanty remains of two peel-towers, Ewes Castle, nearly two miles up, and Lugate itself a mile nearer the confluence. Although so few folk live on the Lugate Water today, there are no fewer than 30 entries under the name of Leggat, Leggatt or Leggate – which derive therefrom – in the Edinburgh telephone directory alone. The Selkirkshire boundary rims this high valley on the south, so this is the end of Midlothian, at a succession of summits at around 1,600 feet.

From all this, and what has gone before, it will be evident that Moorfoot is something of a world unto itself, out on a limb from the rest of Lothian, included therein only by accident, as it were. But it is an attractive terrain, well worth exploring and knowing.

VI

MIDLOTHIAN – PENTLAND

SUPERFICIALLY this central section of Midlothian might well be thought to be fairly similar to that of Moorfoot, being basically a range of quite lofty hills with their valley systems and foothill communities. But in fact it is very different. The hills themselves are different, much less remote, their skirts more populous, all less hidden and secret. These are R. L. Stevenson's "hills of home"; and though no doubt he was associating them largely with his boyhood's links with Swanston Cottage and village under the north-eastern escarpment, nevertheless he knew and loved them all. The Pentlands are indeed the hills of home for many Edinburgh folk, as well as for Pentland's own population, even though parts of them are as far away from the city as almost anywhere in Moorfoot.

The double range, with its central valley of Glencorse, runs in a slantwise north-east and south-west direction, the northern tip within the Edinburgh city boundaries, the southern twenty-five miles away in the Biggar and Carnwath area of the Upper Ward of Lanarkshire, after having passed through part of Peebles-shire also. With the foothill areas on either side the Pentlands average about five miles in width, at least within Midlothian, broadening towards the south. The individual summits are usually much more shapely and individual than either the Moorfoots or the Lammermuirs, and therefore make the more impressive and challenging skyline. On the whole they are slightly less high than the Moorfoots, none reaching the 2,000-foot mark; but because they tend to rise from a lower base above sea-level, they seem higher. Scald Law, the highest, is only 1,899 feet, yet looks a fine mountain, only three miles from Penicuik as the crow flies. That name itself is interesting, a *skald* being a Norse or Viking storyteller or sagaman. The hill names are indeed a great mixture here. Scald Law's neighbour on the east is Carnethy, a fairly typical

133

Gaelic name meaning the burial-cairn of Ethy or Athyn, possibly Aodh, our modern name Hugh, where the Ay of Mackay comes from. Whereas on the other side are the Kips, from Gaelic *ceapan* a little stump or cap, apt enough. Not far away is Caerketton which could be Welsh or Brythonic-Celtic fort of refuge. And next to it, Allermuir, sheer Lowland Scots for the moor of the alders. The name of Pentland itself is generally accepted to mean Pictland, like the Pentland Firth; but whether this is so is at least doubtful. Why describe any limited area as Pictland when the whole country was inhabited by the Picts? If it is suggested that these heights were where the Picts retired to in face of invaders – that is not the way the Pictish nation came to an end. They were not wiped out after any last-ditch stand; merely gradually taken over and accepting the name of Scots. But having registered my doubts as to Pictland I must confess that I can offer no very valid alternatives save perhaps the pent lands, pent meaning shut in, an Anglo-Saxon word.

These hills, of course, are an enormous asset to Edinburgh and Midlothian, as a scenic background, a 'lung' and recreation area, a salutary halt to urban sprawl, a blessed wilderness, and in more material respects a source of water supply. They are what used to be termed sheep-walks also, although less vitally so than the Lammermuirs or even the Moorfoots. At Hillend, which is sufficiently descriptive, where the steep slopes of Caerketton drop down to the city's outliers, the Edinburgh local authority has established a park area, and here is the popular feature of an artificial ski-slope and Centre, with chair-lift. There is also an old-established golf-course.

This district is within the Edinburgh city boundaries and so outwith the scope of the present survey. Any description of Pentland and its communities has to be in two sections, the north and south flanks, parted by an interior virtually empty. Since we have been dealing with the Esk valleys, we shall deal with that south and east side first.

After Hillend, we come to a lower-lying district on a side-road, which itself is called Pentland, Old and New Pentland, Pentland Mains and Grove. Whether there is a clue here to the origin of the name is not clear. It seems odd if the entire range of hills, some 200 square miles, should have taken its name from this small and unimportant community. Equally strange that this spot, of them all, should have been given the name of the hills. At anyrate, this Pentland could not be called a village or even a hamlet today. It is a scattered community loosely spaced around a crossroads, just managing to keep clear of the mining area of Bilston-Loanhead. It was however a parish before the Reformation, one of the original possessions granted to the new Abbey of Holyrood in 1128 by David I. It became an independent charge the following century, under the patronage of the St Clairs of Roslin and Orkney. We read that its southern section comprised the barony of Falford, now Fulford, two miles away, now a few houses near Woodhouselee, not very baronial-looking.

Nearer than Fulford, and tucked into a sort of corrie of a spur of Castlelaw, one of the Pentland summits, is the sheep-farming experimental station of Boghall, one of the original establishments out of which grew the great complex of the Edinburgh Centre of Rural Economy, generally known as the Bush. The Bush is an estate, a mile to the south, with a pleasing mansion-house which is now the Centre's headquarters. From here is administered an ambitious and valuable project of important agricultural and scientific testing units, on a very large scale, covering no less than 4000 acres, with many bodies co-operating, including Edinburgh University, the Department of Agriculture, the East of Scotland College, the Forestry Commission and sundry others, providing a most notable service for agriculturalists not only in Scotland but throughout the world.

Across the Glencorse Burn here is Glencorse House and estate, and the ruined former parish church of the name. The latter, built in 1665, replaced an earlier building, and was never large. But it has become famous, largely through R. L. Stevenson who used to worship here, and who loved it so much that, far away in the Pacific, he wrote: "Do you know where the road crosses the burn under Glencorse Church? Go there and say a prayer for me . . . see that it is a sunny day; I would like it to be a Sunday . . . shut your eyes, and if I don't appear to you, well it can't be helped!"

Scenes for his *Weir of Hermiston* are set here; also the Resurrectionist dramatics in *The Body-Snatcher*. The parish

was set up, after the Reformation, out of parts of Pentland
and Penicuik. The mansion is not ancient, and belongs to the
Inglis family, one of whom was Lord President of the Court
of Session. The name of Inglis is interesting, and derives from
English – so presumably the founders of the family were
'incomers'. I have heard some of the name hotly deny the
imputation – but the proof is to be found far back, in the
writings of none other than Sir David Lindsay of the Mount,
who was friendly with one of them, a cleric who became
Abbot of Culross, a writer of ballads. He writes in his
Testament of the Papingo:

> Quho can say more than Schir James English says,
>   In ballattis, farcis and in pleasaunt plaies . . .?

Nearer to the hills, on the A702 Hillfoots road, is the
hamlet of Easter Howgate, five miles even as the crow flies
from the better known Howgate on the other side of
Penicuik. Close to it is the estate of Woodhouselee, of some
renown. Here again is a confusing duplication of names,
Midlothian being particularly prone to this. *Old* Woodhouselee Castle perches on the Esk ravine three miles away, near
Auchendinny. It belonged to the wife of the notorious Hamilton of Bothwellhaugh, in the sixteenth century, and is said to
have been forfeited by the Regent Moray, James VI's uncle,
for the benefit of one of his greedy courtiers – who was
responsible for the well-known and terrible murder, by turning the lady out of her house in the depth of winter, in her
husband's absence, to die with her new-born child in the
night's snows. And as a consequence, Hamilton of Bothwellhaugh assassinated Moray at Linlithgow in 1570. Whether the
death of the lady is historical fact is not certain; but the
murder of the Regent certainly is. The transference of the
name to its present site seems to have been occasioned by
the Edinburgh lawyer, William Tytler W. S. who purchased
the old barony of Falford, previously mentioned, in 1748.
What his connection with Old Woodhouselee was is not clear,
but he brought most of the stones of its castle to build up the
ruin of Falford into his new mansion, the vaulted basement of
Falford Castle still being incorporated in the present eighteenth-
century house. His son was Lord Woodhouselee, of Session,

and *his* son, Patrick Fraser-Tytler, was the famous historian.

The hill above Woodhouselee, Castlelaw, rises to 1595 feet, and is notable for the fine fort and souterrain, preserved on its eastern flank by the Department of the Environment. It is an early structure pre-dating the Roman arrival, with multiple ramparts and ditches. The souterrain is somewhat later, probably third century A.D., sited between two of the ramparts of the fort. The stone-lined walls of its corridor and side-chambers are impressive witness of the Pictish ideas. An army firing-range adjoins.

The Glencorse Burn emerges from the main central valley of the Pentland Hills at Flotterstone Bridge, on the A702, where a private road strikes off westwards, the start of many a walk – for cars must be left behind here. This road runs for nearly five miles, with innumerable foot-tracks branching off, for hikers and climbers, offering walks of differing lengths and challenges, all in splendid scenery. A mile up, commences the L-shaped Glencorse Reservoir, a valley flooded in 1828 at the then great cost of £200,000. It has made a delightful loch, with its wooded islet, even though it drowned the historic chapel of St Catherine, claimed to have been founded by the famous Sir William St Clair of Roslin, who fell on the renowned crusade, led by the Good Sir James Douglas, with Bruce's heart, to fight the Infidel, in 1330. The story is that St Clair had earlier wagered his head against his hounds, Help and Hold, with the King, to pull down a noted white stag before it could cross the Glencorse Burn here – the prize being these lands. He won, and built the chapel as thank-offering. And on the won lands he erected Logan Tower, the ruins of which lie beside the small mansion of Logan House, just beyond the head of the reservoir, this tower being added to by a successor, the third Earl of Orkney, in the fifteenth century – he who escorted young James I to the Bass Rock and on to captivity in England.

Almost a mile up the valley is another and smaller reservoir, Loganlea, narrow and only half a mile long, the landscape becoming wilder here, the hills rising more steeply from the water's edge. Halfway up on the north side is the ruin known as the Howlet's Yett or House, howlet being the Scots word for an owl and yett for a gate. Often in such a connection the word has a ghostly reference. Howlet can also be a term of reproach. Despite its name it has probably been another chapel.

Above Loganlea the valley closes in quickly. Here is the farmhouse called the Howe; and some have claimed that this is the true Habbie's Howe, of Allan Ramsay's *Gentle Shepherd*, finding likenesses to the scene he delineates. But almost certainly this is not so, and the real location is southwards across the hills in the Ninemileburn vicinity. After all, Ramsay says:

> Gae faurer doon the burn tae Habbie's Howe,
> Where a' the sweets o' spring an' summer grow,
> An' when ye're tired o' prattling side the rill,
> Return tae Ninemileburn, an' tak a gill.

If one had to return to Ninemileburn from the Howe at Loganlea, over the Kitchen Moss and the Kip Hills, you would certainly need that gill!

At this farm the private road ends and the main footpath bends away northwards for Bavelaw and Balerno, five miles. Due westwards the Logan Burn itself drops from the high tableland of the Kitchen Moss in a series of cascades within a narrow cleft. The Moss is a wild and desolate moorland quite extensive, in the very heart of the Pentlands, empty and lonely, extraordinary to be only a few miles from Edinburgh's suburbs. Only two rough tracks cross it, two miles apart, both in a north-south direction.

The hills flanking this central valley and the Moss behind, are on the north side rounded and not particularly interesting. But those on the south are very different, a range of five fine peaks, with their outliers, which make a magnificent ridge-walk, with much up-and-downing between. Turnhouse Hill, 1,500 feet, directly above Glencorse Reservoir, is the first and lowest, the least dramatic save that it has, in its great east-facing corrie up at the 1,200-foot-contour, the site of the Battle of Rullion Green, in 1666. This was a sorry affair, scarcely to be designated a battle really, in which a retreating and exhausted force of less than 1,000 Covenanters were trapped up here by some 3,000 government troops under the dreaded General Tam Dalyell of the Binns, who had learned his ruthless soldiering in the Russian wars. Defeat was certain; but those who fought to the end and died were probably the best off, in the end. For there was no mercy for the prisoners. Many were hanged, ten on one gallows in Edinburgh, thirty-five before their own doorways, as example, and the remainder shipped as slaves to the sugar plantations of the West Indies. All this in the name of preferred worship and good government.

The next hill is Carnethy, a great and satisfying peak, probably the noblest of all the Pentlands, shapely and rising to a fine summit, at 1,890 feet, topped by an ancient burial-cairn, presumably the grave of Ethy or Athyn or Hugh. It *looks* the highest of the range, although actually it is nine feet lower than its next neighbour, Scald Law, a mile to the west, but with a 500-feet drop between. Scald Law we have already spoken of with South Black Hill a lofty shoulder to the east. Beyond it are the twin peaks of the Kips, East and West, green grassy hills these, where the others are largely heather-covered. West Kip catches the eye from all directions, being an almost perfect cone, steep and graceful, its summit a narrow knife-edge at 1,806 feet. The ridge-walk of these hills, with its steep short climbs and dips, and superb views on every side, is one of the finest challenges to the young-in-heart anywhere near Edinburgh – which is saying quite a lot. Oddly, there are two hill-farms tucked into the corrie quite high on the south slopes of the Kips, called Eastside and Westside, both about the 1,100-foot contour.

The A702 road runs along the foothills of this range at about the 900-foot level mile after mile. After leaving Flotter-stone Bridge, it passes a house with a white cross topping its gable. This used to be the old school-house of Glencorse parish; and the cross was found and put there some time ago, presumably connected with the Rullion Green deaths. A little further is House of Muir farmery, where formerly great sheep-markets were held. And three miles on is the hamlet of Silverburn, reminding us that silver and lead used to be mined in these foothills. Usually it proved more economic to use the product as lead, although with a high silver content. In this connection there is the amusing story of the lead on the roofing of George Heriot's School in Edinburgh, which came from these parts in the seventeenth century. In modern times it was decided to renew the roofing – and hearing of this, a former pupil with a good memory, presumably in the building trade, offered to prove his affection for his *alma mater* by offering to reroof his old school free of charge. Somebody however thought this suspicious, realized that the philanthropist would be keeping the old lead, had a sample analysed, and confirmed that it contained a very high proportion of silver. George Heriot's Trust, needless to say, made other arrangements.

A mile beyond Silverburn is another instance of peculiar nomenclature. Here is Eightmileburn; and a mile and a half to the west is the hamlet of Ninemileburn. This has puzzled some folk. Where are these eight and nine miles from? Edinburgh is nearly twelve miles northwards. Yet, since Eightmileburn is the Edinburgh side of Ninemileburn, the measuring must be from that direction. The answer is, of course, that the Scots mile of old was considerably longer than the mile we now use, 1,976 yards against 1,760. Burns refers to "the lang Scots miles" in his *Tam o'Shanter.* So these were milestones on the old stage-route to Lanarkshire and the south-west.

Ninemileburn was quite a celebrated staging-point, with its inn still extant, probably the first changing-place for horses after Edinburgh. There was also the necessary blacksmith's establishment, Robin Tamson's Smiddy, of Alexander Rodger's song. George Meikle Kemp, aforementioned, was born here in 1794. Determined, after viewing the Prentice Pillar at Roslin, to become an artist in stone, this shepherd lad worked his way across Europe for two years, walking all the way, and working as an ordinary stonemason, whilst studying Gothic architecture. He was a great walker, forty miles a day being quite normal for him. Once, working in England, he decided that he must visit York Minster; so he walked there, fifty miles, and having inspected the place, turned and walked back again. His father shepherded for the laird of Newhall, the estate here. The property has a mansion with an ancient nucleus of vaulted basement, mural chamber and slit-windows, which was rebuilt in 1703 and again in 1785. Its position is strong, on the lip of the North Esk's wooded ravine. At Kemp Senior's time the estate belonged to John Forbes, a cousin of the famous Lord President Forbes of Culloden, and he gathered round him a notable galaxy of the literary and artistic lights of Edinburgh in its Golden Age, Newhall becoming one of their favourite haunts. It is here that the Habbie's Howe of Allan Ramsay is accepted to be sited, a beauty-spot on the sylvan ravine of the stripling Esk.

Two miles on from Ninemileburn is Carlops, where the Esk comes down out of the hills. This is the Peebles-shire border-line, with almost all of Carlops in that county. Some description here, however, is suitable. It is a pleasant smallish village, founded as such only in 1784 as a weaving colony, although lime-burning in kilns had been established as an industry around here long before that. The abandoned kilns still dot the area. There is another well-known inn, the Allan Ramsay Hotel, and a church, a post-office and not much else save for the cottages. The name is a corruption of Carlin-loups, carlin being the Scots for witch, and loups for leaps. An extra-ordinary thrusting and isolated outcrop of rock in the village is pointed out as the place where the carlins used to loup in their high jinks; but this may well be a more comfortable story for children, instead of declaring it the spot where the unfortunates were tossed over to their deaths. Admittedly the normal penalty for witchcraft was 'worrying' - that is half-strangling - then burning. Perhaps their Carlops fate may have been the kinder. Another tradition is that a notorious witch lived in a cottage up the Esk's glen behind the village and used to leap across between two rocks there.

The river rises in the North Esk Reservoir, one and a half miles above the village, not a large sheet of water, embosomed in the hills. Up here a public foot-track, once a drove-road, climbs to the Bore Stane pass at about 1200 feet, and on by Listonshiels across the west end of the Kitchen Moss to the upper Water of Leith west of Balerno, a long, lonely but favoured walk.

Retracing our steps the dozen miles to Hillend, to deal with the other, northern side of the Pentlands, we are faced with the situation that the first five miles thereof are not in Midlothian at all, but within the city boundaries of Edinburgh. Since 1975 and the regional reorganization, even these

have been enormously extended; but for our purposes we shall
ignore this, leaving the Midlothian boundary just west of
Juniper Green. Between Hillend and there, I only mention
Swanston village, where Stevenson grew up, nestling under the
Tee Wood below Caerketton's great screes; the historic inn of
Hunter's Tryst, another haunt of the Edinburgh luminaries of
the past; the great army barracks of Redford and the estate of
Dreghorn Castle nearby, both giving title to one-time Lords
of Session – as do so many properties around Edinburgh; the
former Water of Leith village of Colinton, now a major
suburb of Edinburgh, where is the well-known Merchiston
Castle School; Bonaly Tower, a famous house, largely built by
the celebrated Lord Cockburn, and one more haunt of the
literati; and Juniper Green itself, its village status lost in
spreading suburbia. All these lie along the Pentland foothills,
with the small but picturesque reservoirs of Torduff and
Clubbiedean hidden away in a fold of the hills above them;
and the Water of Leith, in its deep valley, flowing below.

A mile west of Juniper Green, and nowadays scarcely to be
distinguished as a separate entity, is Currie, the Midlothian
boundary between. Currie has, inevitably, grown vastly since
it was a milling village with a fourteenth-century bridge and
two snuff-factories. The name may come from corrie, a
circular deep hollow; although some associate it with *Coria*, a
Roman name for the 'capital' of the Damnonii, one of the
Pictish tribes. It certainly has a long history, both as village
and civil parish – which it still remains. Originally it would all
be contained within the deep wooded valley of the Water of
Leith. On the southern lip of this are still the ruins of Lennox
Tower or Castle, sometimes called Lymphoy, this probably
being the original name, before it came into the hands of the
Stewart Earls of Lennox. Mary Queen of Scots was here
frequently, for of course her second husband, Lord Darnley,
was son of the then Earl of Lennox. James VI used to hunt
from here, into the Pentlands. Later the property passed into
the possession of George Heriot, it is said, no doubt as stake for
one of the King's many loans from his jeweller and banker.
The castle has been of great strength, with thick walling, in a
very defensive position. The accommodation would be much
enhanced by the courtyard buildings to the south, now gone.

Both the basement chambers and the first-floor great hall were vaulted.

The parish church of Currie used to be a subsidiary of the collegiate church of Corstophine; but became independent. A new one was built on the site of the old in 1785, remarkable for having false painted windows. Kinleith Mill, at Currie, formerly a large paper-making establishment, is now converted into a small industrial estate.

All around, the modern housing spreads. But there are still open spaces, both south and north. Baberton golf-course, lying to the north-east, helps to keep the urban sprawl at bay. And the historic mansion of Baberton House was once the residence of Charles X of France. Riccarton estate is still further to the north, and is now taken over by Heriot-Watt University, some of whose endowment comes from the same George Heriot. Great developments are going on there, up-to-date indeed, with the Institute of Offshore Engineering, connected with North Sea oil extraction, one of them. Curriehill House, with the site of a former castle, to the north-west, was a great place for producing legal luminaries. Lord Clerk Register Sir John Skene was laird here until 1612, his son Lord President Sir James Skene until 1633; John Marshall, Lord Curriehill, and his son and namesake, also Lord Curriehill, in the eighteenth century.

On the south side of the Water of Leith the ground rises steadily over a lengthy, wide, open slope whereon are Easter, Middle and Wester Kinleith, odd names in that they certainly do not apply to the head of the Leith Water, which is what the name means. The river's name itself is interesting. Many assume it to be called after the town of Leith at its mouth – but that is not how rivers are named. Anyway, the town used to be called Inverleith, which is more accurate. The river rises in the Pentlands, in headstreams around Harperrig Reservoir, five miles west of Balerno, not far from the already mentioned Bore Stane and Listonshiels. Nearby is Leithhead farm. One suggested derivation of the name is from the Old Welsh *lleithio*, meaning overflowing – and certainly the river is liable to sudden spates. Another could be from the Gaelic *leac* meaning a hill-face.

Only a mile or so on from Currie is Balerno which,

although expanding also, has managed to retain its village atmosphere much better, partly because of its site in a branching hollow away from the main A70 road. The name is straightforward Gaelic *bal-eornach*, meaning the barley-land farm. Paper-making still goes on at Balerno Mills. The village used to be the terminus for a branch railway-line, a great boon for commuters and hill-walkers alike. This has been closed, but a walk-way has been established along its route, through the Water of Leith valley, a pleasing development. Balerno, only nine miles from the city centre, has become a favoured residential area.

There are three fine and ancient mansions in this vicinity. The nearest is Malleny House, to the north-east, a fairly typical, tall, early-seventeenth-century laird's house with additions, in an old-world walled garden. An earlier building is incorporated, but the house as it stands was almost certainly erected about 1634 by Sir James Murray of Kilbaberton, the King's Master of Works. It passed soon however to a branch of the Scott family, one of whom distinguished himself as a hero of the American War, General Thomas Scott. Its estate was large and productive enough to have a rent-roll of £4351 in 1882. There is a good, rectangular gabled doocot containing no fewer than 915 stone nesting-boxes. These pigeon-houses played an important part in providing fresh meat in winter. The mansion and gardens are now in the care of the National Trust for Scotland.

The House of Cockburn, now the seat of Viscount Balerno, lies two miles to the west, a highly attractive and unspoiled old-world building of the later seventeenth century. It is on the usual L-plan, with octagonal stair-tower, crow-stepped gables and dormer-windows, one of which bears the date 1672. The builder, one William Chiesley, seems to have been preoccupied with the passage of time, for he inserted two sundials into the walling, one to north and one to south. Presumably he was connected with the infamous John Chiesley of Dalry, who murdered the Lord President Lockhart in 1689, for having adjudged against him in a court case, Dalry being only a few miles away and the name very uncommon. At any rate, eight years later the property was sold again – so the time element may have been significant indeed.

The third house is Bavelaw Castle, the oldest of the trio, situated on a shelf of the hills three miles south of Balerno, above the large Threipmuir Reservoir. It is a notable fortalice, still occupied and in good repair, which at first sight seems also to belong to the early seventeenth century but on closer examination shows much earlier work, with wide splayed gunloops, thick walling and very small windows, odd floor levels within betraying different periods of construction. There is a small pine-panelled chamber on the first floor known as Queen Mary's Room; Mary, despite the brevity of her reign, seems to have seldom slept at home! Although the property was in the hands of the Braid family as early as 1230, it came to Dundas of that Ilk in the sixteenth century, who presumably built the castle largely as we see it today. There is a tradition that Bavelaw was once a royal hunting-seat; but this does not seem to be borne out. Often, of course, monarchs hunted from such places, but as guests of the lairds.

Threipmuir below is the largest of the North Midlothian reservoirs, three miles long and with an extension to the east called Harlaw, formed by damming the Bavelaw Burn, the greatest of the Water of Leith tributaries. It is a lonely place but quite scenic and a great haunt of wildfowl, narrowing notably near its west end, where a bridge actually crosses it. This carries the road up to the castle, and is also the route of the popular foot-track across the Pentlands, by the Kips, to Eightmileburn and Ninemileburn.

Beyond this area the land changes notably in character, rising into high and fairly bare moorland, with little population other than that of hill-farms, before the borders of West Lothian, Lanarkshire and Peebles-shire are reached. At the headwaters of the Water of Leith, Harperrig Reservoir, almost as large as Threipmuir but not so long, lies in bleak surroundings. Its moors are crossed by the Lang Whang, a descriptively-named stretch of the exposed A70 highway to Carnwath and the Upper Ward of Lanarkshire, which runs almost straight at near the 1,000-foot level for about seventeen miles, without a village, Harperrig not quite halfway. At the west end of this reservoir stands the ruin of Cairns Castle, a lonely hold indeed, which once guarded – or threatened – the outcome of the Cauldstaneslap drove-road from West Linton in Peebles-shire. The castle is said to have been built about 1440 by the notorious Sir William Crichton, Chancellor of Scotland, he who was the death of the young Earl of Douglas and his brother at the Black Dinner in Edinburgh Castle that year. This grim hold looks entirely suitable to its builder's reputation. The drove-road, now a quiet challenging walking-path of ten very rough miles, climbs to a point not far from the summits of the East and West Cairn Hills, both over 1,800 feet, before dropping down by Baddinsgill Reservoir and the infant Lyne Water on its way to Tweed. The Peebles-shire boundary is crossed on the ridge between the Cairns summits.

There are some miles of Midlothian westwards beyond Harperrig, but hardly in Pentland, and dealt with in the next chapter.

VII

MIDLOTHIAN – ALMONDALE

IN CALLING this chapter Almondale, for want of a better description, I am admittedly stretching things, Almondale or Amondell is an old name for the vale of that river, and there is still an estate so called. But it would be extravagant to suggest that the parts of Midlothian which remain to be described, west of Edinburgh but east of the West Lothian boundary and seawards of the Water of Leith valley, could be all included in this vale of Almond. How else conveniently to define the area, however, is not evident. In fact, for much of its course, the River Almond *is* the West Lothian boundary.

For all that, most of the places still to be dealt with under Midlothian are either in the Almond's vicinity or in its drainage area. The river rises in north-east Lanarkshire, near Kirk o' Shotts but flowing north-eastwards soon enters West Lothian in the Whitburn area, and Midlothian just beyond Livingston New Town, thereafter flowing by the Calders, Amondell, Newbridge, Kirkliston and Cramond to the Forth. From Midcalder to the sea its west bank is the West Lothian border. The pre-1975 Edinburgh city boundary extends westwards to Cramond, Turnhouse where is Edinburgh's Airport, Gogar and Long Hermiston, to Juniper Green. So the area under discussion here is a long and narrow triangle with its apex near Cramond and its base back on the high moorlands which we have touched on in the Lang Whang district where the three counties join. If this sounds complicated, I apologize; but it is the geographical situation, and this tract is still to be covered.

Actually it is probably the least attractive part of Midlothian, although it has its redeeming features and even beauty-spots. Topographically it looks as though it should belong to West Lothian, and the outliers and detritus of that county's shale-mining industry spreads over into it. There is much other industry, increasing population and a great amount of main road and motorway development, for this is the beginning of the central industrial belt between Edinburgh and Glasgow. And, of course, the westwards sprawl of the city reaches out its tentacles. Nothing could be more different from rural *East* Lothian. Nevertheless there is much of interest and fascination here, of historical as well as industrial note. West Midlothian is not to be dismissed as dull.

For our purposes it is probably best to commence where we left off under Pentland, up on the south-westerly heights in the Harperrig-Cobbinshaw vicinity, the base of the triangle, amongst the 1000-foot-high moors. Not that there is much to describe here, save vast distances of heather and peat and deer-hair grass, with a few sheep, and traces of abandoned mineral workings. Cobbinshaw Reservoir is large, over a mile and a half long, and was created to supply the old Union Canal. In 1877 it was stocked with 20,000 salmon and sea-trout ova from the Tay, which did well. But it is in very bleak surroundings. Its outflow is called the Bog Burn, which is sufficiently descriptive. The only item of interest hereabouts is the site of a Roman fortlet or camp, on Camilty Hill to the north-east, perhaps one of Agricola's marching camps on his western route from the Clyde valley to Inveresk.

Nearby to the north is Harburnhead. There is a collection of Har names hereabouts flanking the valley of the Harwood Water. No doubt all are a corruption of Hartwood or burn. One estate is spelt that way, whilst another close by misses out the 't'. The ruined castle of Harburn, it is claimed, was fortified by Cromwell to overawe the mosstroopers of these wild moorlands.

The Harwood Burn or Water leads down to West Calder and the beginnings of the shale-mining country – beginnings in more ways than one, for it was here at West Calder in 1865 that Dr James (paraffin) Young first produced oil from shale, and set up at nearby Addiewell the first distillation plant of an industry which was to spread over and alter the face of most of West Lothian and parts of Mid. This Calder area is extensive, East and West Calder being six miles apart, on the A71. West is the largest of the three Calder villages, really a small town, with a population of over 1000. It is situated quite high above the Almond valley, not picturesque and with little that is old. Before 1865 it was a tiny place. Addiewell, nearby to the west, used to be something like Grangemouth is today, a sprawling industrial conglomerate of factories, workshops, retorts, sheds and so on covering over 70 acres, for the production of paraffin-oil and wax, naphtha, candles, and ammonia. The great red shale-bings rise around, ever-present reminders that this is where the great modern oil-industry was born.

The country between West and Midcalder becomes much more attractive, gradually sinking in height and with much more woodland. Here are a number of estates, including Hermand, which gave title to a famous Lord of Session; and Murieston whereon are the ruins of a former castle. There is the small village of Bellsquarry, which name speaks for itself; and a farmplace with the wonderful name of Contentious. And nearer the hills, on the Linhouse Water, is the highly interesting fortalice of Linhouse, still an occupied mansion. It belongs to two periods, the sixteenth and seventeenth centuries, forming three sides of a square. It is unusual in that, though the stair rises within the re-entrant angle, it is not in a stair-tower, but projects within the building; and its head, curiously, is vaulted, to support a parapeted look-out platform at roof-level, this last reached by a tiny stairway in a corbelled-out turret with a conical stone roof. It would be interesting to know what brought about the construction of this almost unique architectural provision. A family called Tennant held the lands of Linhouse from an early period, one of them, Francis, being Provost of Edinburgh in 1571, taken prisoner while fighting for Mary Queen of Scots. His provost-ship probably accounts for the motto of *Nisi Dominus Frustra*, which is that of the city, being carved on a lintel here, with the date 1589. In 1537 there was a trial at Lanark for "the cruel murder of Archibald Tennant of Lennox" – apparently Linhouse was frequently called Lennox. The seventeenth-century part was added by the Muirheads, who then acquired the estate. In the Covenanting wars the laird was a stout royalist, and came into frequent collision with the parish minister, who was of the other persuasion, and who complained about him. In 1646 we read that "James Meik in

Trobainhill deponit that Jone Muirhead of Lynhous, at Torbainhill, came ryding with twa swordis and askit his purse, bot quhidder in joke or earnest he knew not".

Midcalder village, where the Linhouse Water joins the Almond, is a pleasant old-world place of some character, Z-shaped at a complicated road-junction. The old main road from Edinburgh to Glasgow used to pass through, and the inn here was a halt for the stage-coaches. The parish church is ancient, founded by Duncan, Earl of Fife in the thirteenth century and partly re-built in 1541 by the then Sandilands of Calder. There is an apsidal choir and an elaborate sixteenth-century tracery window, and at the east end the burial place of the Sandilands family. The gates to Calder House estate are nearby, where the Sandilands, Lords Torphichen, are still in possession. They have been here for six centuries and their story is an interesting one. James Sandilands of that Ilk (in Douglasdale, Lanarkshire) in 1346 married the sister of the first Earl of Douglas, his chief, and widow of Bruce's nephew, the Earl of Carrick, getting these lands of Calder with her. His son, also James, was a famous character whilst the Stewart line was rising, and married a daughter of Robert II, Bruce's grandson, the first of the Stewart kings. Their fifth descendant was a Reformer and close friend of John Knox, who celebrated his first Communion in the Protestant rite here in Calder House in 1556. *His* son, at this time held the office of Preceptor and Prior of the Knights Hospitaller of St John, at Torphichen, in West Lothian, an extraordinary position and the only one of its kind, which carried with it a lordship of parliament, with the title of Lord St John of Torphichen. At the Reformation, by good management and the payment of 10,000 crowns, he got a grant of all the Order's lands and property for himself and his heirs, with the hereditary title of Lord Torphichen - which continues. Calder House is a tall, old, uncompromising mansion with much very ancient work surviving although giving the general appearance of the seven-teenth century, the walls extremely thick. It has a strange rounded buttress where the ground-level falls away sharply, and in the vaulted basement kitchen is a deep draw-well.

A couple of miles to the north-west, and very near to the West Lothian border, is the smaller estate of Alderston, at one time also in Torphichen hands. The old mansion has developed from a tower-house, of the sixteenth century, built by one Henry Kinloch after 1556. This part of the building still retains its corbelled-out projection at roof-level in the crow-stepped gable, called a machicolation, a device for the dropping of missiles and general unpleasantness upon unwelcome visitors, the original doorway, now a built-up window embrasure, being just below.

The West Lothian boundary here makes an odd oblong diversion northwards, away from the Almond, for some reason no doubt connected with the ownership of lands, enclosing an area of about four square miles, which includes the shale-mining community of Pumpherston. There was once an old castle here also; but the name had dropped out of all gazetteers and reference-works until, in 1884, an oil-refinery was opened by Young's paraffin company, which at its height employed no fewer than 1,750 persons. The usual by-products of shale were developed, and in this case, when the extraction of oil by this process died away with the modern oil-well technique, in the 1960s, two of the subsidiary productions continued to flourish at Pumpherston, brick-making and a large detergent plant. So the shale-bings are not entirely a profitless eyesore.

Near where the county boundary comes back to the Almond is the quite large village of East Calder, not especially attractive. Yet it is a very old place with a quite romantic background. The barony was given by David I's grandson, Malcolm IV (1153-1165), to one of his Norman supporters, Randulph de Clere. From him it took the name Calder-Clere to distinguish it from Calder-Comitis, belonging to the Earl of Fife – now Midcalder. Bruce gave these lands to James Douglas, not the Good Sir James but a kinsman, in 1306. His descendants became Earls of Morton, and still own Dalmahoy locally. There are lands in this area called Mortoun, and some claim that this is where the title arose, not in the parish of Morton in Dumfries-shire, which also belonged to the Douglases, but not so early. East Calder was anciently a parish of its own, and the ruin of its church still stands in its old graveyard.

Two miles east of East Calder on this A71 road is the

hamlet of Wilkieston, notable for being the site of the Scottish National Institution for the War-Blinded training-centre, a splendid and most worthwhile establishment comprising work-shops, hall and housing, in the pleasant grounds of the former small estate of Linburn. This place has done and is still doing noble work. This is in the parish of Kirknewton, the village for which lies some way to the south-west, on much higher ground, somewhat out of the way and reached by side-roads. It is quite a pleasing place and unspoiled. The old parish church is now gone, although its kirkyard remains, with the graves of no fewer than three Lords of Session therein, the present church being removed some way to the west in 1750, enlarged and 'gothicized' in 1872. Southwards about a mile, on still higher ground, is the large Ritchie Camp, where a big American air-force base was established during the Second World War and for years afterwards; now it is a depot of the Queen's Own Highlanders. There is an industrial estate called Raw Camps nearer to East Calder. Oakbank is a former shale-mining village nearby.

Not far east of Kirknewton is the large district of Dalma-hoy, stretching from Dalmahoy Hill and Crags, only two miles west of Balerno, down to Dalmahoy Golf Course, on the A71, and the Episcopal Chapel of St Mary. There were Dalmahoys of that Ilk once, and the surname is still met with occasionally. The first recorded was Sir Alexander, who in 1265 granted permission for the monks of Newbattle to pass through his lands. His son, Sir Henry, signed Edward I's Ragman Roll in 1296; but he must have supported Bruce later, since the Dalmahoys came out of the Wars of Independence intact. They remained here until 1720, when they sold out to the Dalrymples. The present mansion, large, substantial and plain, seems to date from fairly early in the eighteenth century, so presumably it was built by the Dalrymples, possibly to designs by William Adam. The seventeenth Earl of Morton bought Dalmahoy in 1750, so the Dalrymple tenure was brief. The property still belongs to the Douglas Earls of Morton, but the mansion has not been used as a seat for some time, but as a hotel. There are other plans for the estate and golf-course pending, we hear. Dalmahoy Hill (808 feet) is crowned by an Iron Age fort. Oddly there is another, which has been even larger, on the adjoining hill-summit of Kaimes, less than half a mile to the west – although this is being steadily eaten away by quarrying, as at Traprain Law in East Lothian. The two represent different structural periods however before and after the Roman occupation. Dalmahoy Crags present a bold escarpment to the north-west.

The Gogar Burn flows through Dalmahoy estate, and on north-eastwards to cross the Edinburgh city boundary in less than two miles, with its own little scattered community of Gogar pleasantly sequestered in a shallow valley between the busy main roads. Until the Reformation, Gogar was a parish, with its own church, a fragment of which remains. Gogar was the scene of a skirmish between the victorious Cromwell and the defeated Leslie, a week or two after the disaster of Dunbar, when there seems to have been something of an artillery duel – and on this occasion the Lord Protector was less successful. He himself writes of its thus:

> We marched westwards of Edinburgh towards Stirling, which the Enemy perceiving, marched with as great expedition as was possible to prevent us; and the vanguards of both armies came to skirmish upon a place of bogs and passes. ... We being ignorant of the place drew up ... our cannon and did that day discharge two or three hundred great shot upon them; a considerable number they likewise returned to us: and this was all that passed to each other. Wherein we had near Twenty killed and wounded, but not one Commissioned Officer. Seeing they would keep their ground, from which we could not remove them and our bread being spent – we were necessitated to go for a new supply; and so we marched off about ten or eleven o'clock on Wednesday morning.

Actually this marching off was back to Edinburgh and thence to Musselburgh and on.

There are no bogs here now. The Gogar Burn actually flows under the old Union Canal, and after passing through the various Gogar localities suddenly changes its course notably from east to north-west, and flanking Edinburgh Airport, forms the city boundary until it joins the Almond.

There is only a narrow point of Midlothian here, the apex of the triangle. In it, just west of Gogar, is the estate of Ingliston, with its typical early Victorian Scottish baronial mansion of 1846, taken over as the Royal Highland and Agricultural Society's permanent showground in 1960, mecca each year for so many visitors. Agricultural research takes place here. Westwards of it is the village of Newbridge, now swamped in industrial development, and the hub of two motorways, the M8 to Glasgow and the M9 on the way to Perth. The bridge referred to crosses the Almond into West Lothian. Newbridge's sad claim to fame is that its population was all but wiped out by cholera in 1832.

Away from all this concentration of development and modernity, on the higher ground to the south, is the village of Ratho. Quite sizeable, in essence a single long street climbing a slight hill above the Union Canal, it still manages to retain something of its rural atmosphere. Curiously, this retired place, notably off the beaten track, was once a principality with regal jurisdiction. This came about because Robert the Bruce granted it as dowry for his daughter Marjory when she married Walter, the High Steward – presumably prior to that it had belonged to one of the forfeited lords who had supported the English interest in the Wars of Independence. On the accession of this couple's son, Robert II, Ratho became part of the property attached to the King's eldest son as Prince of Scotland, with all sorts of privileges. It suffered a sad declension in the eighteenth century, its poet, Joseph Mitchell in 1724 declaring it to "look like Troy, a field of corn". It has picked up considerably since then. The parish church is part old, a cruciform structure dating from the twelfth century, with a Norman doorway, but much altered in the seventeenth century, the Dalmahoy aisle bearing the date 1683.

South of Ratho just over a mile is another place which has sunk greatly in importance, the estate of Hatton. It is now only a farming property, the former great mansion, built round a major castle, demolished. It was once very prominent on the Scottish scene, for it was the lairdship of the brother of the famous – or notorious – Duke of Lauderdale, who ruled Scotland for Charles II. Since Lauderdale was kept very busy in England, being the member of the infamous Cabal – his name providing the L for that word – although Secretary of State for Scotland, his brother, Lord Hatton, a Senator of the College of Justice, did much of the work for him. And, of course, became a source of patronage. So Hatton saw much coming and going in the later seventeenth century. He built up the old castle, which he had gained by marriage with the heiress of the Lauders, who had owned it since 1377, into a palatial mansion; but all was demolished between the recent wars. The famous Lord Jeffrey occupied Hatton as tenant for some time, when it became another of the haunts of the Edinburgh literati.

At the hamlet of Bonnington, with its old estate, near here, we are back at the Almond, ending this Almondale section of Midlothian – for the actual Amondell estate lies on the other, West Lothian bank of the river.

Before finishing with this county altogether, there is a small area which falls to be mentioned and which has, as it were, slipped between the bars of my dividing-up process. This is the district south-east of the city and north-west of Dalkeith, not large, another triangle with four-mile sides and a three-mile base, its apex on the Forth just west of Fisherrow harbour, Musselburgh. At a stretch it might have been dealt with under the Esk valley. There is not a lot to describe here. Again, it is a thoroughly industrialized area, largely the civil parish of Newton, consisting of the coalfield districts of Monktonhall, Woolmet and Millerhill, with the large industrial estate and housing complex of Danderhall, and an extensive railway marshalling-yard in the centre. Not territory which lends itself to description. But there are pockets of other than industrial interest remaining.

The parish church of Newton itself, for instance, which is in the Danderhall vicinity. This was built in 1742, succeeding an earlier building of which only the tower remains, a mile to the west. It is interesting for its miners' gallery, which was erected by the miners themselves five years after the church was built, on the complaint that they were unable to get in to worship on account of the landowners, their staffs and families. They had to construct an outside stair for this, so that they would not have to rub shoulders with the rest of the congregation – an extraordinary indication of the contempt with which miners were treated as lately as 1747.

At the other, west, side of Danderhall, is the hamlet and

estate of Edmonstone, now largely lost in development, an ancient property which gave name to a family which played quite a prominent part on the Scottish scene. One of its early lairds married, as her second husband, the Princess Isabel, daughter of Robert II and widow of the second Earl of Douglas, who had been murdered at Otterburn by Bickerton of Luffness. Then his successor married that lady's niece, Princess Mary, daughter of Robert III, as her fourth husband. The Stewart ladies were as lively a lot as their menfolk. Their son married the granddaughter of Robert II's brother, the notorious Duke of Albany. And so on. They lost Edmonstone at the beginning of the seventeenth century, however, The Wauchope family held the estate until recent years, one of whom was Lord Edmonstone of Session.

Woolmet, nearby to the east, suffered a worse fate than merely being encroached upon by creeping suburbia. For here the highly interesting and attractive large seventeenth century mansion was first menaced by pit-workings, and then demolished some years ago, a place which certainly ought to have been saved. It was L-planned with two round towers and one square tower with a handsome balustraded parapet reached by a narrow turret-stair. The early owning family was named Biggar of Woolmet, who do not seem to have made any major impact on the national scene.

The village of Millerhill, always a mining community, had a shot-in-the-arm in 1964 when an important new colliery was started here, with very deep shafts and notable production. A mile or so to the east, beyond the vast marshalling-yards, is Monkton House, happily still managing to keep development at bay, near as it encroaches. This is a solid and substantial building of character which has grown, by four stages, from a plain, free-standing tower of the early sixteenth century, or even previous to that. It stands within high old walls, and at one time was in great neglect; but it has been lovingly restored and is again an inhabited home. The main house, which is the tower, with mid-sixteenth and early- and late-seventeenth-century additions, forms an 'L', with a semi-octagonal stair-tower in the angle. And across the courtyard is a detached sixteenth-century building, notable for its excellent mullioned dormer windows, practically unique in Scotland.

The basement of the main block is vaulted, one chamber being the kitchen, with a great arched fireplace provided with stone drain, salt-box in the wall, and oven. Monkton, as its name implies, was another grange of the Abbey of Newbattle; and the mullioned-windowed block to the west is the monks' work. It passed to the Hays of Yester after the Reformation; and then to the Falconer family, who lost it for their share in the Jacobite Rising of 1715, when it was purchased by the Hopes of Pinkie. Monktonhall golf-course is nearby to the east, with the Esk beyond. Midlothian, as will be all too apparent, has been a difficult entity to describe, much cut-up, far-flung and with little coherence in geography or character. That it is full of interest none can deny. This survey, unavoidably, has touched only on a small proportion of it all.

VIII

WEST LOTHIAN – THE COASTAL BELT

WEST LOTHIAN is the smallest in area of the three counties, comprising only 76,000 acres; but it has a quite large population, and growing with the advance of Livingston New Town. Because it has been heavily industrialized it resembles Midlothian more than it does East; but again there are large areas of unspoiled country, much of it very picturesque and less known than it deserves to be, in general. And it has not had the encroaching city to contend with.

It probably best can be described as was East Lothian in three lateral and parallel belts – the Forth coastal stretch, the inland central area and the uplands. This chapter will deal with the shoreline and its immediate hinterland.

Starting from the east and the city boundary across the Almond at Cramond – the name is merely a corruption of Caer-Almond, the fort on that river – West Lothian has a most attractive introduction, with the very large estate of Dalmeny stretching along the coast for five miles, all the way to South Queensferry, still in the hands of the Earls of Rosebery and so far spared any major development save for the offshore one of the oil-terminal at Hound Point – a great blessing for West Lothian and Edinburgh likewise, for the Almond here runs within six miles of the city centre. Indeed West Lothian is fortunate in its coastline altogether, for on the other side of South Queensferry, the Abercorn and Hopetoun Palace and Binns estates save another five miles of it, to a large extent, so that at least ten miles out of a total of about seventeen have, as yet, been saved from spoliation. Some, of course, will resent all this land being in private hands, with consequently few public roads; but there is access for the ordinary walker and the landscape is preserved.

And a fair landscape it is, although very different from the East Lothian shore. Here are no great sandy beaches and cliffs or even major bays, but a fairly quiet and level coast, green with old woodlands coming right down to the water's edge. The Drum Sands admittedly extend far out and for three of the miles, reaching north to Cramond Island a mile from the shore. But these are tidal flats rather than golden beaches, with a certain amount of mud – nevertheless with their own attractions, rather similar to those of Aberlady Bay, and likewise a haunt of wildfowl. The Forth here is altogether more of a wide river's estuary and less of an arm of the sea, narrowing in at Hound Point to only two miles from the Fife shore, this of course affecting not only the character of the coast but the scenic background. Fife's proximity is much more evident. The islands of Inch Mickery and Inchcolm and the skerries of the Cow and Calves, Oxcar and Car Craig, all enhance the prospect. None of these are in West Lothian however, so do not fall to be described here.

The Dalmeny estate is unusual in having two mansions, Dalmeny House itself, a large early-Victorian sham-castellated structure but quite attractive, the Rosebery seat; and the older Barnbougle Castle standing at the shore half-a-mile to the north, its predecessor. The former was visited by Victoria and Prince Albert in 1842, the Queen commenting: " ... beautiful, with trees growing down to the sea ... the grounds are very extensive, being hill and dale and wood. The house is quite modern. Lord Rosebery built it and it is very pretty and comfortable." There have been other royal visits since then. Barnbougle, an odd name which sounds rather as though Sir Walter Scott had invented it, was in a ruinous state when the then Lord Rosebery rebuilt it in the late nineteenth century. Most of the present building is a reconstruction therefore, and it is difficult to say just when the original was built. But Sir Robert Sibbald, writing in the seventeenth century, says: "Barnbougle Castle is also old and is yet inhabitable". It makes a tall and massive pile, and has been used as a private museum. As Queen Victoria said, the estate is a delightful one, of low, undulating wooded hills and open parkland, Mons Hill rising to 387 feet. There are many driveways. Sir Archibald Primrose bought it in 1662 from the Earl of Haddington, and his son was created Lord Primrose and Dalmeny in 1700 and Earl of Rosebery in 1703.

Hound Point, to the west, still within the estate but almost a couple of miles from the mansion, thrusts out not really as a headland but more a major inclination of the coastline north-wards, bringing West Lothian to less than two miles from the Fife shore and reaching out to the edge of the Drum Sands shallows, to deep water. Off-shore here has been established recently a feature which is having a marked effect on not only the estuary scene but on the national economy. This is a sort of artificial island to house the terminal and pumping-gear of the pipeline from the north whereby the flow of oil from the North Sea can be loaded into great sea-going tankers, for export, the deep water allowing these large vessels to moor at the isolated jetty. So now, off this quietly peaceful wooded shore, is a futuristic construction, with its myriad of lights at night looking like a forest of Christmas-trees, and the huge ships queueing up in the Forth awaiting their turn to load. Often three at a time are lying off Aberlady Bay. In one way it is an inspiriting development - no pun intended; but conservationists watch with mixed feelings.

Inland from Dalmeny policies is pleasant rural country, through which the approach-roads to the Forth Road Bridge drive their busy way. The red shale-bings had crept close - but at least some of the material of these has been quarried and taken away to be used as road and motorway bottoming. On the Almond bank itself is the pleasant estate of Craigiehall, its classical mansion now the headquarters of Scottish Command, with various army installations around. The river here is spanned by a rustic bridge over a cascade, this leading to a folly in the shape of a classical temple.

In over three miles from Cramond Bridge westwards there is no community until the village of Dalmeny itself is reached, only green fields and woodlands - rather astonishing so close to a city, a happy alliance between the Rosebery estates and the planning authorities. Dalmeny is a most attractive place, with its cottages grouped around an extensive village-green. Its parish church is deservedly famous, the most perfect example of Norman architecture to be found in Scotland. Dedicated to St Cuthbert, the twelfth-century building consists of chancel and nave, the former with a stone-vaulted ceiling. In 1927-37 a splendid restoration and cleaning-up was carried out, thanks to the enthusiasm of the then minister, the Reverend William Neil Sutherland, and since then much that is fine of modern workmanship has been added to the ancient work. The original entrance, on the south side of the nave, is notable, its triple arches elaborately carved with animals, heads and interlacing in twenty-two designs, a peculiar pillared arcading above. Internally, a progressive narrowing of the high arches eastwards, gives a striking prospect to frame the altar-area. The pulpit is probably unique in Scotland in having a carved misericord. Modern stained-glass windows presented by one of the Polish war-time soldiers who fell in love with this church are very fine. Altogether Dalmeny is a place to visit.

A mile to the north-west, on the much lower ground of the coast, is South Queensferry, a small town and royal burgh – I cannot bring myself to put that in the past-tense merely because of some bureaucratic decision of 1975. It has had a long and chequered history. It was inevitable that here should develop an important place, transport-wise, for this is the narrowest part of the Forth, where a prominent peninsula on the Fife side comes to little more than a mile of the southern shore. If this Fife promontory had been no more than a mile or so to the east, opposite Hound Point, the firth would either have been blocked altogether or constricted into a dramatically narrow channel. It is noteworthy that in the Celtic period this represented the end of the Scottish Sea or Scotwater, the Firth of Forth being only the stretch westwards towards Stirling.

Malcolm Canmore's famous Saxon Queen Margaret the Saint, who had a shrewd eye for more than religion, was the first really to develop this potential – hence the names of Queensferry, North and South. Her husband's palace was at Dunfermline, four miles into Fife, where she initiated her self-appointed task of transforming Scotland religiously by changing the Celtic Church abbey there into the first Roman Catholic church establishment in the country, building a great stone minster to the Holy Trinity – the Celts did not go in for stone churches. Her building is still the nucleus of the present Dunfermline Abbey church. Here Margaret installed her precious fragment of the True Cross of Calvary, inherited from either Edward the Confessor of England, her grand-uncle, or St Stephen of Hungary, her mother's father, and which was known as the Black Rood. Eventually this was moved to her new chapel in Edinburgh Castle – St Margaret's Chapel – and later to the new Holyrood Abbey, hence its name. But while it was at Dunfermline the Queen encouraged people to come and venerate the relic, and a great pilgrimage traffic grew up – all part of her determined and successful efforts to Romanize the Scots ideas of worship. It was to save the pilgrims from the south the long journey round by Stirling, that Margaret personally instituted the ferry across the Forth here, and a free ferry at that, with hospices at either end to cater for the waiting travellers. When the Black Rood was taken to Edinburgh, the pilgrim-traffic was encouraged to continue and go on to St Andrews, which was likewise being built up as a sacred national shrine. So the Queensferries, north and south, grew and prospered, and for long after pilgrim days were over. The ferry-boats continued to ply right up to the building of the Forth Road Bridge, erected after prolonged public agitation in 1964. Although as road-traffic developed the long queues of cars and lorries at both sides constituted a weariness, it was still usually quicker to wait than to make the long detour to the west. The great bridge took six years to build, and longer to fight for, so that the estimated cost had risen from £3,000,000 to £20,000,000 before it was finished. It is one of the longest suspension-bridges in the world and contains 39,000 tons of steel, its total length 2,415 yards, the height of its main towers rising to 512 feet above the waves. There are two carriageways, two cycle-tracks and two foot-paths. Vehicles must pay a toll, by government decision, although this was hotly contested locally, since the bridge is an integral part of the road network.

The huge and renowned railway bridge had been established at almost the same spot in 1890, just a little to the east and using the islet of Inchgarvie as a 'stepping-stone', then one of the world's most advanced feats of engineering, of cantilever construction not suspension. It is actually 51 feet longer than the road bridge, with its approaches, and vastly more massive-seeming. Of the 5000 men employed in building it no fewer than 50 died and 500 were injured. The testing of it must have been a dramatic business especially after the disaster of the collapse of the Tay Bridge eleven years before. When the last rivet (of over 6,000,000) had been driven in, two heavily-loaded trains, each pulled by two engines and pushed by a third, were sent across side-by-side, weighing between them 1800 tons. There must have been a lot of hearts in mouths. But all was well and the 50,000 tons of steel-girders reacted exactly as calculated, and have continued to do so. So side-by-side these tremendous engineering triumphs reach out from the Lothian shore, still calculated to draw gasps of admiration from visitors, so different in aspect.

Huddled beneath and between, so far below, the ancient burgh of South Queensferry is by-passed by both. The town has reverted to a decent quietness after being for so long choked with traffic - although there might be two points-of-view commercially. Nevertheless the Provost of South Queensferry was a stalwart member of the National Forth Road Bridge Committee which spearheaded the fight for the bridge, and the burgh played its part. Although the town has spread, or climbed, or recent years up the steeps to the higher ground where are the bridge-ends, in essence it remains a long main street, narrow between the tide and the hillside, some of the houses on the north side all but projecting above salt-water. There is quite a lot of authentic vernacular architecture remaining, some particularly noteworthy. The Hawes Inn, at the east end, dates from 1683 and features in Scott's *The Antiquary* and in Stevenson's *Kidnapped*, successor to Queen Margaret's hospice. Not far to the west is a tall, crow-stepped, gabled house known as Black Castle, of the seventeenth century, one of its three dormer windows having a pediment inscribed with a heart and a love-knot and the initials 'WL' and 'MS' and the date 1626. It would be the town-lodging of some Lothian laird, but is now divided into flats. A very handsome stone fireplace is in the former hall. The parish church stands on slightly higher ground behind here, a plain building of 1633, with a belfry, its bell inscribed in Latin to inform that it was cast by one Michael Burgherhuys, no doubt a Dutchman as so many bell-makers were, and adding in English: "David Ionking [Jenkin?] maerchant of Edenbvrge giftid this bell to the Kirk of the Qveens Ferrie cvrsed be they that takes it frae the ... anno domino 1635." The Tolbooth, which stands above the main street on the south side, also has two bells, one gifted by the fishermen of the burgh in 1694. The old building was remodelled in 1720, when the tall square tower surmounted by a short steeple and clock, was added. To the west again is Plewlands House, a very large seventeenth century mansion to be found within a burgh. It does not seem to have been built as a town lodging but as the seat of the laird of Plewlands, a property which lies to the west and is now incorporated in the Hopetoun estate. It is typical L-plan, harled, with a semi-octagonal stair-tower in the angle, and was built by Patrick Ellis of Plewlands between 1641 and 1644. He was also of Elliston in this county, of which more later. The house is now taken over by the National Trust for Scotland and divided into flats. There is yet another building worth mentioning in this old town, still further west, the truncated remains of the Carmelite priory of St Mary of Mount Carmel, dating from as early as 1332, founded by George Dundas of Dundas. This fell on evil days, part being reserved as the burial-place of the Dundas family, the nave ruinous and the tower let as a shop and stable. But in 1890, happily, the place was restored as the local Episcopal church. It has a fine vaulted ceiling.

Queensferry has by no means had an easy passage down the centuries. Even when, before 1640, it was made a royal burgh, the county town of Linlithgow seems to have resented this increase in its status – and rival privileges – and objected to the Scots parliament, declaring that its representative has "neither riddin, sittin nor voyced in parliament for the Queensferry". There were other insults hurled, and the burgh reacted strongly. In 1641 parliament put Linlithgow in its place, and the new royal burgh was allowed its due representative in parliament, until sixty-six years later the auld sang ended and there was no parliament at all. But that was not the end of the burgh's troubles, for it actually went bankrupt in 1881 – obtaining a discharge on payment of 12s. 6d. in the pound next year. When we learn that it had a corporation revenue of precisely £120, we can perceive the size of its problems. Once twenty vessels, most of them 'large brigs', were based here; and shipbuilding was an industry. Nowadays Sandersons, the VAT 69 distillers, have a large establishment, built fairly high up the slope, a blocklike place which tends to dominate the prospect from the north.

There is a smaller harbour at Queensferry itself, west of the former ferry quay. But west of the town further, is the much larger former Royal Navy station of Port Edgar, which was known as H.M.S. *Lochinvar,* an offshoot of the great naval base of Rosyth across on the Fife side. It was named after Queen Margaret's fourth son, the first of the three Margaretsons, as they were called, to succeed to their father's throne – an unfortunate young man. Port Edgar was not particularly modern, even if it appeared so latterly, for here in 1822, George IV embarked for his return to London, after the first and famous visit of a reigning monarch of the Hanoverian line since the Jacobite times. The harbour has recently been taken over by the local authority, and there are ambitious designs to convert it into a yachting marina and sports centre.

Inland from Queensferry is the large and fine estate of Dundas Castle, whence originated the family of the name. Although themselves never ennobled, the heads of this house have a most illustrious ancestry, being descended from the old Cospatrick Earls of Dunbar and March, the first of the line to take the name of Dundas, early in 1100, being Helias, who was probably a son of the second Cospatrick. They are thus direct descendants of the old Celtic royal house of Scotland, like the Dunbars themselves and the Homes. Twenty-six generations of them remained at Dundas until, in 1875, James Dundas of that Ilk, who had presumably over-stretched himself in building his great new mansion to replace the old castle, had to sell to the up-and-coming Stewart-Clark family. Subsidiary branches of the house climbed the hill to being Marquises of Zetland, Viscounts Melville and baronets of Arniston and Beechwood; but the chiefs remain Dundas of that Ilk and of Inchgarvie. The massive keep of the name stands in a strong position, and is still in repair although greatly altered internally – astonishingly so, for of all things, it was at one time converted into a distillery. We know exactly when it was built, for in 1416 Dundas of that Ilk received a warrant from the Duke of Albany, Regent, to erect this fortalice; and in 1424 a second warrant was issued by James the First to add to it. John, thirteenth of Dundas, was to have

been created Earl of Forth by James III, but the monarch's
death at Sauchieburn prevented that. The castle is a tall
L-shaped parapeted tower within a courtyard, with much
vaulting on various floors and mural chambers contrived in
the thick walling. It was strong enough to sustain a siege in
1449, soon after it was built. It received a visit from Cromwell
in 1651. Charles II had already been there the same year,
inspecting the fortifications of the island of Inchgarvie in the
Forth, of which Dundas was owner and keeper, so presumably
Cromwell was on the same errand. But its stark strength was
not comfortable enough for the twenty-sixth laird, James,
who commissioned the later famous William Burn to build
him the large Gothic residence nearby, in 1818, the architect's
first major work, a typical sham castle of the period, all
pointless towers and useless crenellations, but commodious as
well as splendid within. There is a very handsome fountain
and sundial combined here, which used to be in the courtyard
of the old castle but was moved to front the later mansion. It
has a Latin inscription, which informs those able to read it
that it is under the protection not only of the castle but of
guardian spirits to frighten evil-doers; that it was built by Sir
Walter Dundas in 1623; and that friends and strangers are
invited to use the gardens, the sundials, the fountain and the
cushions available on the seats. All rather pleasingly odd. Odd
too how it came to be erected. The story is that Sir Walter
saved up enough money to buy nearby Barnbougle Castle, but
was much disappointed to discover that the new Earl of
Haddington, Tam o' the Coogate, had beaten him to it; so he
used his hoard to build this splendid garden-ornament instead.
Which of his successors was responsible for turning the old
castle - which, after all, adjoins the new mansion - into a
distillery is not recorded. The estate is a very scenic one,
extending most of the way to Kirkliston, in wood and
parkland, and enclosing a half-mile-long loch.

West of Port Edgar the coast is fairly featureless, but quite
pleasantly so, for a couple of miles, until the oddly named and
rather decayed hamlet of Society is reached, in the great
Hopetoun estate. This huge property, like its mansion, is one
of the most impressive in southern Scotland, and represents the
swallowing up of a whole cluster of lesser and older lairdships

- Abercorn, Philipstoun, Stonehill, Midhope, Duntarvie, Craigton, Duddingston, Plewlands and others, witness to the enormous power and riches of the early Hopes who garnered all this, and erected one of the greatest houses in all Scotland, at the end of the seventeenth and beginning of the eighteenth centuries. It still belongs to their descendants and is, of course, one of the show-places of the land. To do any sort of justice to Hopetoun would demand a book in itself, for superlatives apply. The Palace, palatial indeed, was built between 1696 and 1752, replacing the modest but attractive fortalice of Midhope nearby - the name is a coincidence, Midhope Castle's story having nothing to do with the Hopes. Sir James Hope, Lord Hopetoun of Session, purchased Midhope and other land around in 1678, his grandson being created first Earl of Hopetoun in 1703. He employed the famous Sir William Bruce to design the ambitious mansion, which many have called that architect's masterpiece. Later extensions were added by both William Adam and Robert his son, to complete a magnificent structure of a great four-storeyed central block, with curved arcaded wings and two-storeyed end pavilions, surmounted by cupolas, the whole front measuring no less than 520 feet. The grounds are landscaped to obtain fine prospects in all directions, from this terrace-site above the Forth, the gardens alone covering 12 acres and planned in the style of those at Versailles. Internally the palace is a treasure-house of decorative work, panelling, fine furniture and notable pictures. It is open to the public, and a most popular venue. Sir James Hope, Lord Hopetoun, was the sixth son of Sir Thomas Hope of Craighall, the founder of the family fortunes, mentioned under Luffness, and two of his brothers were likewise Lords of Session, as Lords Craighall and Kerse. Sir James did not make all his great fortune out of the law, however; but marrying a Lanarkshire heiress he acquired valuable mineral properties there, including the silver and lead mines of Lead-hills. It seems suitable that he should have become Master of the Mint in 1641. The seventh Earl of Hopetoun was, amongst many other offices, the first Governor-General of Australia, and was created first Marquis of Linlithgow in 1902. The present Marquis is the third. Midhope Castle, within the same deer-park and policies, but so very different a place, was built in 1582 by a member of the Drummond family but passed to the Livingstones, Earls of Linlithgow, before the acquisitive Hopes took over. Unfortunately it is now ruinous, but could still be saved, a splendid example of its kind. Philipston House, further to the west; now let, is another most attractive E-planned house of the late seventeenth century, and was long the residence of the Hopetoun factor. There is a hamlet of Philipstoun further inland, with a shale-oil background.

Seaward of Midhope is another portion of the vast estate, Abercorn. This is, historically, the most important of all, a very resounding name in the nation's story. Today it is a quite sizeable hamlet and a civil parish, also giving title to a dukedom – although the said dukes now live in Ireland. Abercorn was most famous as the Lothian seat of the old Earls of Douglas, the senior or Black Douglases – as was Tantallon of the Red Douglases, Earls of Angus. But long before the Douglases got it, Abercorn, or Abercurnig as it was then, was a noted monastery, founded about 675 under St Wilfred for the administration of his northern territories. Just why David I, that great benefactor of the Church (the *Romish* Church, of course) handed over these Church lands to Sir William de Graham, one of his close Norman friends, is not clear; but it may have been part of the campaign to pull down the Celtic Church, which still persisted in surviving. In due course the Douglases got them, as they got so much else – probably by marriage. In the fourteenth and fifteenth centuries they were the greatest and most powerful family in the land, notably richer and more influential than the royal house of Stewart – which naturally led to all sorts of problems. It is strange that they never seem actually to have aspired to the throne, however much they dominated it and made a point of marrying their sons and daughters into the royal family, generation after generation. Time and again they could have taken over the crown, and probably have been accepted, for the early Stewarts were frequently neither effective nor popular. They all used Abercorn as a base more convenient for national affairs than their home territories of Douglasdale in Lanarkshire and Threave in Galloway. Particularly associated with the place was James the Gross, who before he succeeded as seventh Earl of Douglas in the 1440s was best known as

Lord of Abercorn, an unsavoury character of whom, probably, the less said the better, but father of the eighth Earl, who was the most illustrious since Bruce's companion-in-arms, the Good Sir James, and who had the distinction of being stabbed to death by none other than his own monarch, James II; the only known case, surely, of a king personally murdering one of his great nobles, however many may have been disposed of by proxy. Under all these, Abercorn was near the centre of national activities. In 1662 Sir Walter Seton obtained the property; and there is still a baronetcy of Seton of Abercorn, although the family have not lived here since, a few years after gaining estate and baronetcy, they sold the former to Sir James Hope.

The ancient church of Abercorn is most interesting and picturesque, still the place-of-worship for the civil parish. The building was old when it was refitted in 1579, after the Reformation, and renewed again in 1838, its Norman doorway, with typical zigzag carving, turned into a window, and now built-up. It is remotely situated within the Hopetoun estate, with only the hamlet near. On a grassy mound nearby is the site of the old Castle of Abercorn. Most notable in the church is the highly elaborate and decorative laird's-loft, or gallery-pew, with sky-blue coved ceiling and innumerable coronets, designed by the aforementioned Sir William Bruce for the new earls - it rather gives the impression, however fine, that the party to be worshipped herein was the Earl of Hopetoun rather than his Maker. There is also the Binns Aisle, much more discreet, for the Dalyell family to the west, still under its stone-slabbed roof. Beneath the Hopetoun loft is a sort of cellar, reached from outside, and here have been deposited a number of highly interesting stones and relics which ought to be made much more of. There are two Celtic cross-shafts, one tall and unfortunately broken in two, with most handsome interlacing and animal carving; and another still upright but less tall - these no doubt from the original Celtic cashel of Abercurnig. Also there are two of the rare hog-backed tombstones commemorating Danes who fell in some Viking invasion here. There is a sad stone within the church on the chancel floor. It bears a shield with only the initials I.M. on the sinister side, representing a wife. The sorrowing husband left room for himself and his initials – but by the time he died, the new Reformed Kirk had disallowed burial within the church and he was interred outside. One would have thought that an exception might have been made. The graveyard, manse and its garden are attractive. Newton of Abercorn, the village over a mile away to the south-east, on the A904, is quite pleasant but lacks particular character.

Still moving westwards beyond all this spread of the Hopetoun estate, is more lairdly property, the lands of Binns and Mannerston. The former is, of course, the home of the famous Dalyell family – pronounced Deeyell. Dalziel, the commoner way of spelling the name, is in North Lanarkshire, where the family originated however they spell the name. A grandson of a sixteenth-century Dalziel of that Ilk bought this estate of Binns, mentioned as early as 1335, from one of the Livingstones. This was in 1612, and his son was the renowned or notorious General Tam, born in 1599. A prominent Cavalier officer, General Tam – he seems always to have been called that, although his father was Thomas – fought throughout the Civil War, and at Charles I's death vowed never to shave until the Stewarts were restored to the throne. He was expressly excluded from the Act of Grace by Cromwell, and went into exile, to sell his sword to the Czar. He grew famous in Muscovy and brought a dire reputation home with him when he came back, at the Restoration. To escape forfeiture, the Binns estate had been handed over to his brother-in-law, William Drummond of Riccarton, who duly handed it back in 1667. Whether the Muscovy general was as black as he was painted is doubtful, but he certainly became one of the most execrated names in Scottish history, mainly for his savage dealings with the Covenanters, not only at Rullion Green battle. Allegedly when annoyed, he used to chew up wineglasses. Possibly that is as true as the story that the Devil himself spirited away his corpse from the Binns Aisle burial-place in Abercorn church. It was said that he learned to roast his prisoners in the Russian wars – and certainly these were a tough training-ground for any soldier. Bishop Burnet records that he did threaten to spit and roast prisoners here in Scotland. Be all that as it may, he it was who first embodied the Scots Greys Regiment, here at the Binns in 1681. And here, in 1971, that celebrated regiment made its last parade before being amalgamated with others to form the Royal Scots Dragoon Guards. General Tam's son was created a baronet in 1685, the same year in which his father died – and it seems that the old warrior arranged both the entail of the estate and the descent of the baronetcy carefully, to avoid the issue of his other children, that all should stay with this eldest son's line, male or female. So both have passed three times through the female line since then. Sir John Graham Dalyell, sixth baronet, was in his own way as extraordinary a character, as author and antiquary and scholar. An indication of his versatility may be gauged from the fact that he published books on such diverse subjects as monastic antiquities, the chronicles of Pitscottie, Martial's Epigrams, the darker superstitions of Scotland, animal physiology, music, nature study and poetry. What either of these predecessors would have thought of their present-day descendant, Tam Dalyell of the Binns, Eton-educated Labour M.P. for West Lothian, himself a former trooper in the Royal Scots Greys and determined fighter against devolution for Scotland, there is no knowing. The name of Binns itself is odd and less than dignified-sounding perhaps. The usual suggestion is that it is no more than a corruption of bens, the Gaelic *beinn* meaning mountain. If so, it represents very modest mountains indeed, for the ridge on which the place is situated is only 200 feet above sea-level. On the other hand, across the Forth at Burntisland, there are two low hills known as the Binns, East and West; and another not much larger at Kinfauns in Perthshire. The house of Binns is mainly old, although it does not look it. It was built by the General's father between 1621 and 1630, but was unfortunately subjected to a severe Gothic rebuilding about 1820, that alleged Golden Age of enlightenment when the architectural taste of the *cognoscenti* was largely sham, pretentious and anti-Scottish. So today the Binns looks all ornamental towers, crenellations and Gothic ornament, externally. But internally it remains very fine. It has some excellent plaster ceilings, that of the drawing-room particularly, dated 1630 with the initials of Thomas Dalyell and his wife. Another is slightly curved up into the roofing, with elaborate pendants. The Binns was the first historic house in Scotland to be brought into an arrangement with the National Trust for Scotland. So although the Dalyells remain in possession, the Trust takes responsibility for much of the maintenance, and the public is welcomed.

The lesser but still ancient property of Mannerstoun lies on the lower ground nearer the Forth. It may indeed be more ancient than the Binns, for we read that a relative of the General Tam's father, the Bishop of Dunkeld, had to intervene in 1616 with the Presbytery to win for Dalyell the right to re-edify the Mannerstoun Aisle and turn it into the Binns Aisle, in Abercorn church. It probably takes its name from the Norman de Mesnieres family, another of David Margaretson's importations, a line which in England anglicized their name to Manners, but in Scotland first to Meyners then to Menzies, whence the Highland clan of that name. The mansion of Mannerstoun has late seventeenth century work in it.

At the coast below Binns and Mannerstoun is the rather special castle of Blackness, still in good order and in the care of the Department of the Environment. It stands on a rocky promontory, and it is perhaps suitable that it should be in government hands, for it appears to have been so for most if not all of its story. Most of the present double building appears to date from the fifteenth century, and stands within strong later curtain-walls gapped for artillery. It is, in fact, a fortress rather than a true castle, which has been much altered during its various phases of governmental occupation. Whether it was ever a house, either private or royal, is uncertain. But from an early period it was in fact a state prison, for noble and prominent transgressors or inconveniences, rather than common malefactors. Many an illustrious captive has been immured here, including distinguished Covenanters – who must have been the more uncomfortable to have General Tam so close. Not that all the prisoners had to be uncomfortable; many of them were installed here merely to keep them from activities awkward for the powers-that-then-were; and so long as they paid for it they could have all home comforts. The castle was burned in 1443 in the conflicts of James II's reign; again by an English fleet in 1481. James III and his rebellious nobles met here in 1488 to try to bring about a reconciliation. Ten vessels which had taken refuge in its haven were burned by an

English fleet in 1548. And so on. It was one of the chief
fortresses of Scotland guaranteed by the Treaty of Union of
1707 to be maintained as a national strength - yet at one time
was held as fort only by a single man. By the 1870s it has sunk
to be the central magazine or ammunition depot of the
country. At this stage further buildings were added as barracks
and stores. But it still looks impressive, oddly shaped like a
ship. Its harbour was anciently the port of Linlithgow before
this was removed to Bo'ness. Some say that here was the
original eastern extremity of the Roman Antonine Wall,
usually placed at Carriden two miles to the west. There is
quite an attractive village here, with church and hotel.

We are now nearing the western end of the county, and
still this seaboard is protected by this prolonged line of estates.
There is one more before Bridgeness commences the Bo'ness
industrialized area - Carriden House. Here is another early
seventeenth-century mansion, considerably altered but still
showing its original face, the old portion, dated 1602 over one
of the windows, being a tall L-planned structure of five
storeys, with angle-turrets and many gunloops, the ground
floor vaulted. The roof unfortunately has been lowered in
pitch, detracting from the appearance. Although the lands had
long belonged to a Cockburn family, the builder of the present
house was Sir John Hamilton who became first Lord Bargany.
It eventually passed to the Hopes, like so many another. There
is a parish of Carriden, the church, near Bridgeness at the
shore, dating from 1766, the village now more or less a suburb
of Bo'ness, but quite pleasing. The name was Caer Eden or
Eddyn, the fort on the front. Gildas, writing about 560,
describes it as a most ancient city, the terminus of the
Antonine Wall. Here at Bridgeness, during excavations for an
iron-works in 1868, a notable Roman carved distance-slab was
unearthed. The coast hereafter, westwards over the Bo'ness
area, has been much reclaimed from the sea, a process started
by using the slag from the iron smelters.

After all the rural and picturesque country and coast, with
no community larger than Newton of Abercorn's hundred or
two, it is with something of a jolt that we come suddenly
upon Bo'ness and its unlovely environs, at the extreme western
limits of West Lothian, more akin to the Grangemouth-

Falkirk area of Stirlingshire, apt to be heralded ahead by a pall of smoke. The name Bo'ness is usually accepted to be a contraction of Borrowstoun-ness, 'burrostoun' being a quite common Scots form of burgh. There is still a suburb of the town called Burrowstoun. Nevertheless some authorities have derived its name otherwise. Apart from the New Town of Livingston it is the second-largest community in the county, with a population of just over 10,000, and a not very long but chequered history. The parish used to be called Kinneil, and that was an ancient entity; but Bo'ness only became a burgh of barony in 1748 and a police burgh in 1880. The Industrial Revolution caused it to rise fast, so that although the population in 1800 was 2,768, by 1880 it was 6,000 and still growing. Nevertheless, Bo'ness had claims to be the third seaport of East Scotland at one time, although this seems scarcely believable. But there is no question but that it became a major port, towards the end of last century, largely through the export of coal and the import of timber – indeed until not very many years ago it was the principal timber-importing centre for Scotland, convenient for trade with Scandinavia, and there are still great timber-yards. Then, with the opening of the Forth and Clyde Canal, Grangemouth grew up, a few miles to the west, and quite outstripped Bo'ness; and the great woodyards, sawmills and seasoning-stacks, which stretched along this level coast, began to wilt. As well as these, collieries also thrust out towards the firth; and there were shipbuilding-yards, four iron-foundries, two engineering works, two chemical factories, two brick-yards, a pottery a distillery and other ventures. Some of all this still remains, of course, but there has been decline for long now, and the town centre has become distinctly dejected. This, like South Queensferry, stretched along the level and narrow coastal shelf – narrow before the reclamations seaward – with steep braes climbing the hillside southwards to the later and residential areas. These upper environs show no signs of decay. And happily there are efforts, and quite ambitious plans, to reinvigorate the lower town, to give it a face-lift and encourage industrial revival. Also there is an imaginative project for about 100 acres of reclaimed foreshore, which could greatly improve the appearance here, with the Scottish Development Agency taking a hand to the extent of £500,000. It is hoped to set up an open-air industrial and maritime museum; to use the closed dock-area as a 'home' for old ships; and to have a mile-long railway for steam-trains, with the Scottish Railway Preservation Society interested. So perhaps Bo'ness's day is by no means done. Grangepans, the eastern suburb of the town, was once an independent community, where salt was produced. James Watt's first steam-engine was put into use at the former Burn Pit colliery, in 1765. One final word on Bo'ness. Here, in 1679, five witches and wizard were tried and burned; and two years later a peculiar group of twenty-six, known as the Sweet Singers of Borrowstounness, marched off to the Pentland Hills behind their leader, Muckle John Gibb - who called himself King Solomon - there to look down, hopefully, on the smoke and utter ruin of that sinful and bloody city, Edinburgh.

West of Bo'ness is the formerly great estate of Kinneil, the rump of which is now a public park. Industrial development overtook Kinneil - Kinneil Collery still functioning - thereby no doubt producing much revenue for the ducal house of Hamilton. Of the former Kinneil Palace only part remains, not exactly as a ruin but as a reduced establishment. The original mid-sixteenth-century keep was partly demolished as early as 1570 by the Regent Morton, who hated the Hamiltons, but the western walling remains, overhanging the steep ravine of the Gil Burn and forming part of the now roofless great central block. An L-shaped seventeenth-century addition was erected to the north, and this remains more or less intact, in the care of the Department of the Environment. It is fairly typical, commodious but plain externally. But within are some fine rooms with handsome mural tempera paintings. In what is called the Parable Room are six magnificent episodes from the parable of the Good Samaritan, life-size figures against a background of rocks, trees and walled-cities. The Arbour Room has further Bibilical scenes below a frieze of animals and birds. These murals are probably amongst the finest in Scotland. Bruce gave the barony of Kinneil to Sir Walter Hamilton. When the Hamilton Earl of Arran was acting Regent for the infant James V, the country was largely ruled from here. Its last tenant, with the Hamiltons still owning but departed, was the famous metaphysician, Dr Dugald Stewart, one of the Edinburgh luminaries of the Golden Age. Before that it was occupied by Dr Roebuck, the co-founder, with Cadell, of the Carron Ironworks, near Falkirk. He was James Watt's patron, and the young engineer laboured on the invention of his steam-engine in an outhouse here, still preserved.

Kinneil Kerse – the same word really as carse, a low-lying flood-plain – stretches for over a mile westwards to the mouth of the River Avon at Inveravon, enclosed by the rampart of the Antonine Wall and the rising ground. The Avon is the Stirlingshire boundary. Beyond lies the vast, spreading, futuristic landscape of Grangemouth's oil-refineries, cracking-plants, flare-chimneys and storage-tanks, a success-story of a sort. But not for this survey. Here ends Lothian.

IX

WEST LOTHIAN - THE CENTRAL AREA

UNLIKE East and Midlothian, the central part of this county cannot be divided up conveniently into river valleys. The two real rivers of West Lothian, the Almond and the Avon, form the boundaries east and west, both running slantwise north-east and south-west. So this chapter makes no attempt to follow any river-line but deals arbitrarily with a stretch of country reaching from one river to the other, about ten miles in length from east to west and varying in width from five to eight miles, a heavily industrialized area in the main, but not without its pleasant and unspoiled portions, some indeed remarkably sequestered. There is some hilly terrain to the west, reaching to over the 1000-foot contour, in what are generally known as the Bathgate Hills; but there are no major heights.

Starting at the Almond again and dealing with the more northerly section first, we follow the A9 highway, not the new M9 motorway, and in a mile come to Kirkliston, a quite large village, with some industry, notably an old-established distillery, most of it well south of the main road and hidden therefrom. It is an old place but not especially attractive, although its situation is good, just above the Almond. It is a parish as well as a village, and an oddly scattered parish at that, part of it in Midlothian, and a small section detached and far away on the Pentland Hills, called Listonshiels – which was mentioned under Pentland, set in the middle of the plateau of the Kitchen Moss, and now merely a farm. This peculiar arrangement was because all the Listons were originally Knights Templar lands, and the Order was powerful enough to have them all united in the one local jurisdiction. The church which gives its name to village and parish, is sufficiently ancient, dating from the twelfth century probably, and retaining a fine Norman doorway. The tower is of the unusual saddleback-roof variety. The attractive bell-cote on the east gable is of seventeenth-century construction. Alterations and additions were made in 1822. The Newliston aisle here is the burial-vault of a number of early members of the Dalrymple of Stair family who owned Newliston estate nearby until 1753. Interred here is Margaret Ross, Viscountess Stair, who was the prototype of Lady Ashton in Scott's *Bride of Lammermuir*, and the famous second Earl of Stair, her grandson, one of Marlborough's field marshals.

Newliston House stands to the south over a mile, its woodlands said to have been planted by the said second Earl to represent the lay-out of the various formations at the Battle of Dettingen, where he played a prominent part. The present mansion was not his, but was built in 1789 by Robert Adam after the lands had been bought by Roger Hog. It was near here that King Edward of England camped his army in 1298, on his way to the Battle of Falkirk, and had to put down a mutiny by his Welsh troops, who put to death no fewer than eighteen English ecclesiastics who were sent in to act as peacemakers. The reason was that the English army was very hungry, with Wallace's scorched-earth tactics, and the English spearmen were doing better than the Welsh archers. Eighty Welshmen were dispatched.

Two miles on from Kirkliston and still in its civil parish is the even larger village of Winchburgh, dominated by its great shale-bings. By its looks and name this would seem to be only a typical modern industrial community. But not so. It was so called in Wallace's time. The name has nothing to do with winching machinery, but represents the borg or burgh of one Winca, possibly a Viking. But only the name is old, the relics of the oil industry being less than scenic. However, to north and south there are points of interest. A mile southwards, behind a shale-bing, is the ruinous castle of Niddrie, most of it still surviving, and well-known by travellers on the railway between Edinburgh and Glasgow, the line passing close by. This is a notably historic fortalice, and should be better cherished and made a place to visit. Tourists would love it, if it was tidied up and made weather-tight. For here it was that Mary Queen of Scots was brought, to spend the first night after her romantic escape from Lochleven Castle in 1568, by its owner Lord Seton. It was from here that the unfortunate queen sent a letter to her cousin, Elizabeth of England – with ultimate results we all know, the Battle of Langside and an English prison for the rest of her sad life. The original keep was built in the late-fifteenth-century by George, fourth Lord Seton, who fell at Flodden. In the seventeenth century, to give added accommodation, it was built upwards above the parapet and garret storey, as at Preston Tower in East Lothian, the only two such I know of. L-planned and massive, with nine-foot-thick walling, it was known as Niddrie-Seton, to distinguish it from Niddrie-Marischal near Edinburgh and Longniddry in East Lothian. It has a most unpleasant pit or prison in the vaulted basement of the wing, small and dark, lit only by a narrow slit and gunloop. Niddrie was one more estate bought by the Hopes to extend their great demesne.

North of Winchburgh an equal distance is another castle which might yet be saved and restored, also part of the vast Hopetoun property, Duntarvie. It is, or was, quite an ambitious building, although now roofless but complete to the wallhead, a long main block of three storeys with tall square towers at each end, their upper floors reached by tall stair-turrets. Once this fine-sixteenth-century house was surrounded by elaborately planned gardens and walks, now rough pasture. Few people even used to see it, for Duntarvie is remote on side-roads, but the new M9 motorway passes near enough to afford a good view. The Durhams of Duntarvie were the lairds here, presumably the builders; but by 1628 it was in the hands of the Hamiltons, Earls of Abercorn. We read that the Countess wife of the second, for nonconformity (religious presumably) was confined in the Tolbooth of Edinburgh along with the common malefactors. "This loathsome prison procured her many heavy diseases", and she was given licence to visit the Baths at Bristol. Cured, she was brought back for another six months in the Canongate jail, but subsequently permitted to reside at Duntarvie, on condition that "she sall contein hereself therein so warily and respectively as she sall not fall under the break of any of his Majesty's laws".

The countryside is pleasant around Duntarvie and remains so westwards of Winchburgh for some distance. In this area is the farm of Aldcathie, once a parish on its own and a district of some importance, a detached portion of Dalmeny parish now, for obscure reasons. There would be a pre-Reformation church here somewhere. The name Aldcathie is frequently to be met with in old documents. Now not one in ten thousand would know that it ever existed. The name is Gaelic *allt cach*, the burn of the battle, the battle as unknown as the parish.

A couple of miles along the A9 westwards is the hamlet of Threemiletown, amongst woodland, another example of long Scots miles, four present-day miles from the county town of Linlithgow. The ground is beginning to rise, now, the skyline southwards becoming hilly in a modest way. Up there above the mining village of Bridgend, enlarged by a housing scheme of this century, is the old barony of Ochiltree, still with its inhabited castle although this is now a farmhouse. Sometimes called Ochiltree Place, an old Scots word which has the same derivation as palace, this is an excellent and attractive example of a late-sixteenth-century fortalice, added to in the seventeenth, typical with angle-turrets and steep roofing and dormer windows. There is a remarkable doorway-porch, a 1610 addition, bearing the arms and initials of Sir Alexander Stirling of Keir and his wife Dame Grizell Ross. The angle-turrets contain tiny chambers, one being entered from the second floor, the other from the third, an unusual arrangement. The name Ochiltree is strange and has nothing to do with either the Ochil Hills or trees. Ochiltree is a parish in Ayrshire, but there seems to be no connection. However, the suggestion is that the name is corruption of *uchel tre* Old Welsh for a high house. I am not convinced. But there is another of the name in Galloway, so there must be a general application.

South of Ochiltree, on the side of Binny Craig, is the farm of Oatridge now an agricultural college, with the neighbouring farm of East Broadlaw included. This was set up by local authority initiative in 1967, and has dairy and beef cattle units as well as going in for pig-husbandry, sheep and hill-farming and arable research and education, for day-release classes and full-time courses.

West of this is the Riccarton area, not to be confused with the estate of the same name in Midlothian where the Heriot-

Watt University has established itself. The word, of course, merely means Richard's Town, and there are at least four others in Scotland including a large parish in Ayrshire. The Riccarton Hills here rise to 833 feet. This property was held by a family of Drummonds, descended from the Innerpeffery branch of that great Perthshire clan. Henry Drummond who died in 1561 no doubt got the place when he married Janet Crichton, of a Lothian family. Their descendant it was who held the Binns estate for General Tam Dalyell whilst he was a forfeited exile, a century later. A mill is recorded here in 1282, so the original Richard must have been a Norman incomer, for it is not a Celtic name. All this is in the great West Lothian Bathgate Hills Country Park – of which more here-after.

Back on the A9 is the old hamlet of Kingscavil, once expanded by shale-mining but now reduced again, the mining-rows demolished in 1938. The name has nothing to do with kings cavilling, although as usual elaborate tales have been concocted. In the fifteenth century it was Kincavil, which might be derived from *ceann caibeal*, Gaelic for head chapel. It was a Hamilton place, and in 1501 Sir Patrick Hamilton, illegitimate son of the first Lord Hamilton, was the hero of a jousting tournament held before James IV. His son, also Patrick Hamilton of Kincavil, has the distinction of being the first Protestant martyr of the Reformation in 1528. He was Abbot of Ferne, in Easter Ross and his mother was a daughter of the Duke of Albany, but he was burned at St Andrews, aged only twenty-eight years, refusing to retract his Lutheran sentiments. Two centuries later Prince Charles Edward slept at the old mansion, now gone, on his way to Edinburgh and the Battle of Prestonpans, in September 1745, whilst his army of Highlanders lay at Threemiletown. The shale-mining developments here were really on the nearby estate of Champfleurie, but failed despite the romantic name. There is still a mansion of that name across the road at Kingscavil, comparatively modern. There are suggestions that this place was given its name by Queen Mary of Guise, admiring the flowers – but this sounds too facile and it is probably a corruption of something Celtic.

We are now approaching the county town of Linlithgow, a

place of renown of which much ought to be written. It is attractively situated in a hollow on the shores of its own quite large loch, its narrow streets now happily relieved from the thundering traffic of the A9, with most of this being carried on the new motorway across the loch to the north. The town itself is long and narrow, strung-out on account of its site, and contains much of interest and importance - although some very modern architecture right in the centre, close to the loch-shore and the most historic features, is scarcely an enhancement. Also the main Edinburgh-Glasgow railway-line drives right through the town.

It is a royal burgh, being promoted to be one of the famous Four Burghs of Scotland in 1368, to replace Berwick-on-Tweed which had fallen into English hands. After all this time, it seems fatuous that under the new local government arrangements control of the West Lothian District has been removed to Bathgate. The population is about 4,500. Its history is very much the history of Scotland, so little can be related here. The name is Brythonic, *llyn lled cu,* the dear broad loch; and there seems to have been a Pictish settlement here in Roman times - although the semi-mythical King Cay's Stone, supposedly named after the Achaius we spoke of connected with the famous battle at Athelstaneford, is doubtful history. But we do know that it was important place enough to have a royal residence in the twelfth century, for David I granted to St Andrew's Priory the chapel and lands at Linlithgow "as well within the burgh as without"; and at the same time, to the Abbot of Holyrood the skins of all the sheep or cattle used at the castle on his demesne here. In the Wars of Independence Linlithgow played a prominent part, and here Edward I lay before the Battle of Falkirk, and took up his quarters for the winter three years later, in 1301, erecting a new castle "mekill and stark". Part of this is incorporated in the present palace. But it was the Stewarts who gave Linlithgow its great importance, for one after another they added to and improved their residence here, until it became the finest palace in the land, and the favourite seat of some of them. David II, Bruce's son, rebuilt Edward's stark castle, and James I began the palace we now see. James IV added splendidly to it - and his account-books tell us the names of the masons engaged in his "paliswerk". James V was born here, as was his daughter Mary Queen of Scots. And so it went on. Charles I spent the night in the palace, in July 1633, the last monarch to do so – though Cromwell was here in 1650, and Charles Edward visited it in 1745. It was, suitably enough, left to the Hanoverian troops to sound its knell when, in 1746, they set it on fire, accidentally or otherwise. Yet though that was the end of the Stewart cause, it was not quite the end of the palace, for in 1914 George V actually held a Court in the Great Hall; and the present Queen has also held a reception there. The building, on a green knoll above the loch, is as romantic-looking as its story sounds, a great quadrangular structure of warm brown stone, surrounding a courtyard, with square towers at the angles and parapeted wall-walks above all faces. Most of the basement is vaulted, some of it groined, and above that, on the first floor, are some of the finest apartments in Scotland. The Great Hall, on the east side, also called the Parliament Hall, so many Scots parliaments having been held in it, is 100 feet long by 30 wide, with a most magnificent triple fireplace, near where would be the royal dais. On this floor was also the banqueting hall, a lesser dining-hall and a withdrawing-room, a large chapel and one bedroom of great size, presumably the King's. There are six stairways, and may have been more. Some of the doorways, both outside and within the courtyard, are magnificent; and the elaborate fountain in the yard, built by James V, is notable – that at Holyrood in Edinburgh is a copy. The palace is now kept in excellent repair and is a show-place indeed, its grounds an attractive park leading down to the loch – which James II stocked with perch and eels for his table.

Sharing the mound with the place in pleasing harmony is the church of St Michael, declared to be one of the most handsome parish churches in all Britain. Which was there first, church or castle, has been argued about; but almost certainly the church must win; for a chapel was on the site before David I's accession in 1124, and so far as we know, he was the first to have a residence here. No doubt there was a Celtic Church establishment at Linlithgow, which David would convert to the Romish order. In 1242, Bishop de Bernham, a tremendous dedicator of new churches, opened a new one here, probably incorporating something of the old But most of the present building dates from James III's reign, for church and town both had been all but destroyed by fire in 1424. The tower was then finished off with an open stone crown, similar to that of St Giles in Edinburgh. This was enhanced with a vane decorated with a hen and chickens, a favourite theme of James's, representing his care for his realm. But a new roof put on in 1812 seems to have been thought insufficient to support the weight, and in 1821 the fine crown was taken down. As late as 1964 the space was filled by a somewhat spiky wood-and-aluminium spire which at least is eye-catching. The building is very fine within, almost of the aspect of a cathedral. It has seen some stirring and unusual scenes. In 1559, the Lords of the Congregation (Protestant nobles) marching from Perth to Edinburgh, destroyed all the altars and images in the building – with the exception of St Michael himself, who happily still remains, winged and armoured. In 1646, when plague was raging in Edinburgh, the University classes were removed here, and the interior was partitioned to form classrooms. The shoemakers' craft in Linlithgow had the privilege of holding their annual meeting in the south transept. And, of course, Cromwell stabled his horses herein. Oddly, one of the three church-bells bears the name of Meg Duncan. Some of the windows are suitably fine.

There are many other notable features in Linlithgow, of which only two or three can be mentioned. On the south side of the High Street is the Friars' Brae and the Friars' Well, relics of a Carmelite Priory instituted here in 1290. There was a Dominican Priory also, further to the east. Also a leper-hospice dedicated to St Magdalene, believed to be an establishment of the Military and Hospitaller Order of St Lazarus of Jerusalem, which still takes an especial interest in the alleviation of that disease. This would be outside the town-gates, of course, lepers always being excluded; and the St Magdalene Distillery now stands some little way to the east of the town, probably on the site. The other chivalric Order, of St John, had a large establishment here also, unfortunately pulled down last century. Apart from the Friars' Well there were many others, such as the Lion Well, the Dog Well, St Michael's Well, and more than one Cross Well. Why this plethora of wells, when the loch was so close, is not clear; but an old rhyme says:

> Glasgow for Bells,
> Lithgow for Wells.

The Scots Mint used to be housed here, for a time, in the St John's building, James I striking a coin which actually bore the legend *"Villa de Linlithe"* inscribed. At the west end of the town still stands the venerable and handsome West Port House, like Plewlands at Queensferry a country laird's mansion set just within a town. It was built in 1600, but incorporates earlier work, a Hamilton place, from which line, in course of time, came that famous figure of the First World War, General Sir Ian Hamilton. The house is tall and plain, with a curious rectangular stair projection in the L's angle; and there is a circular shot-hole still apparent. It remains a private house.

Today there is considerable industrial development and a small industrial estate, engineering, paper-making, distilling and road-services. The loch is a bird sanctuary and used for yachting and fishing. And the disused Union Canal, which passes by, is given over to recreational purposes.

Linlithgow and West Lothian both finish at Linlithgow Bridge, the paper-making suburb where the A9 crosses the Avon. North of this area, between the town and Bo'ness, the land rises to 559 feet at a ridge of hill variously called Irongath, Bonnytoun, or, splendidly, Glourorem, or Glower-o'er-em. Outstanding on the south face of this, seen from far and wide is the large modern mansion of Grange, belonging to the family of Cadell, of Cockenzie and Carron fame. They brought the name with them from an earlier late-sixteenth-century mansion of Grange, between Bo'ness and Carriden and behind Grangepans, a most attractive house unhappily demolished thereafter. And sadly, too, on the other, north side of this ridge of Glower-o'er-em, was until fairly recently another delightful fortalice, of 1591, named Bonhard, likewise demolished. On a gabled doocot nearby were the arms of Cornwall of Bonhard and Seton of Abercorn, with the motto: "WE BEIG ZE SE VARLE" (we build, you see, warily). The estate is now partly a golf-course.

Returning to the eastern end of the central belt, to deal with its southern half, now on the axis of the old A8 road, two miles along this from the Almond at Newbridge is Broxburn, a small town that was never a burgh, one more which grew from hamlet dimensions with the rise of the shale-mining industry. There used to be a colliery here also. These have gone, but other lighter industries have come in their place and there is an industrial estate. At 7,500 the population is larger than that of Linlithgow. Yet in 1880 it was only 660. Like most communities which grow too fast, and unplanned, it is not a place of beauty. It consists mainly of a very long and fairly wide street, this reaching almost to Uphall, so that the two places all but run together. Halfway between, on the north side, is the former estate of Kirkhill, which became a farm, with a much-altered old house of various dates, much of it late seventeenth century. The eleventh Earl of Buchan, a well-known character who founded the Society of Antiquaries of Scotland, lived here. As well as antiquities, he was a patron of the arts and of literary men – his brother was the still more famous Henry Erskine, of the Golden Age – and also of astronomy. It is this last which interests here, for the Earl established an astonishing outdoor replica of the solar system on his estate of Kirkhill. In his garden he erected a great square pillar, intricately carved, topped by a round ball for the sun. And all around, in every direction, at precisely calculated distances to the scale of 12,283 miles to the inch, he raised other stones, with balls, to represent the other planets, one as far as one-and-a-quarter miles away. This nobleman died in 1829.

Uphall is much more ancient than Broxburn but until the Reformation was known as Strathbrock, not only the village but the parish, a better name, for the Brocks Burn (meaning badgers) runs eastwards through the area, forming a shallow vale, much more meaningful than Uphall, which was probably only one small property in the parish. Strathbrock was a Douglas patrimony, and in the early fifteenth century these Douglases held the office of Keeper of Linlithgow Palace, a position of some influence. Their castle is long gone. The parish church stands high, almost a mile to the north of the A8 road, and contains a twelfth-century nucleus although much is mid-seventeenth-century work, with a Romanesque doorway to the south. An outside stone stair, dated 1644, gave access to the laird's loft. The bell is the oldest in West Lothian, inscribed *"In onore Sancte Nicholae Campana Ecclesia de Strabrok Anno Dni 1441"*.

On the south side of the main road, west of the village, is Houston House, a splendid example of a tall old fortified mansion of 1600, still in good repair. We know the exact date, for Sir John Shairp, Queen's Advocate wrote in that year: ". . . the mansion house, biggings, tower and fortalice begun to be built, and, God willing, to be finished as soon as possible". He had obtained Houston in 1569, so this may well have been Church lands previously, parcelled out at the Reformation. He received from Mary Queen of Scots a pair of hawking gauntlets and a glass cabinet, long preserved here. Nevertheless there had been Houstons of that Ilk before that, one of whom gave a charter of Alderston in 1556, Houston is now a hotel.

South of the Broxburn-Uphall area is a corner of land enclosed by a major bend of the Almond and the Midlothian border again, in which are the two interesting entities of Illieston and Amondell. Illieston, more properly Elliston, remotely situated, is now a farm, but retains its old mansion, another fortalice of the late sixteenth century, T-planned with tall stair-tower and angle-turret. Internally the house has been much altered. A scullery addition covers an old draw-well 18 feet deep. The Ellis family seem to have been quite important in Lothian in the sixteenth-seventeenth centuries, lairds of Plewlands, Stenhouse near Edinburgh and Southsyde near Dalkeith. Amondell or Almondale, until fairly recently the seat of the Earls of Buchan, is now a Country Park under West Lothian District Council, with riverside walks. There is a nature-trail created by the Scottish Wildlife Trust. The mansion, built by Henry Erskine, is demolished.

On the other, northern side of Uphall-Broxburn is a still more picturesque area, largely unspoiled scenically by industry and still very sparsely populated compared with the rest of the county. Another part of the large Bathgate Hills Country Park, this is essentially the upper valley of the Niddrie Burn, with the surrounding low hills, at its centre the sequestered village of Ecclesmachan. We come near to this from the other

side, at Oatridge and Ochiltree. Ecclesmachan, a civil parish as
well as a village, goes back a long way historically, as its name
reveals – *Eaglais Machan,* the church of the Celtic St Machan.
In its wooded vale, the village is less known than it deserves to
be. The new Country Park connection may help to change
that. The original church was old, no doubt a typical small
Celtic timber-and-turf sanctuary, when the present building
was erected in 1244. It was renewed in 1710, and is very small,
but interesting in having stained-glass windows commemorating another Celtic saint, Madoc, as well as Machan.

The area to the west, still higher ground, is now called
Binny – Binny Craig (710 feet), Binny House, and so on. It
was formerly Binning and earlier still Benyon, no doubt
having the same derivation as Binns, merely meaning hilly.
The district has its interest. Oddly enough this is where the
great Binning Woods of *East* Lothian got their name. The
famous Tam o' the Coogate, who became first Earl of
Haddington, prior to that owned this property as Sir Thomas
Hamilton of Binning. His first lordly title was indeed Lord
Binning and Byres; and the heir to the earldom is still called
Lord Binning. So, when one of his improving successors
planted the great beechwoods near Tyninghame, they gave
them this name. Silver-mining took place here, of which more
later. Binny quarries used to yield a notably high-quality
yellowish sandstone, from which much of Edinburgh's New
Town was built, including the Register House, the National
Galleries and the Scott Monument. The present Binny House
is an early-nineteenth-century mansion with an eighteenth-
century doocot.

On along the A8 two miles from Uphall is the large
Bangour Hospital, two hospitals, general and village. The
Bangour estate was another Hamilton property, its eighteenth-
century laird being the Jacobite poet William Hamilton,
whose best-known work was *The Braes of Yarrow.* There is an
ancient bridge here, which formerly carried the Edinburgh-
Glasgow road. The district is rather bare, the A8 reaching
550 feet. The area to the south is now part of the great spread
of Livingston New Town – but that will be dealt with in the
next chapter, for we are reaching the upland south tract of
West Lothian. On the main A8 road, we now enter Bathgate

parish and more major industrialization.

Bathgate itself is the largest town of the county – again excluding Livingston New Town – with a population of over 12,000. It is scarcely a handsome place but it is pleasantly sited on the south-facing skirts of its own hills, and makes a busy, bustling community, since 1975 the headquarters of the West Lothian District. Here are most of the attributes of a major centre – good shops. offices and multiple stores; social and working men's clubs; industrial estates; a local newspaper; an abbatoir; a library, a golf-course, parks and so on. And, to be sure, a large and well-known Academy, founded by a former native, who made his fortune in Jamaica. This establishment now actually boasts an artificial ski-slope. Bathgate is an old place, a burgh since 1663, with quite a stirring history. Indeed it was once a sheriffdom on its own, its hereditary sheriff, the then Earl of Hopetoun, getting £2000 for the privilege of withdrawing, at the abolition of such jurisdictions in 1747. But the town was quite small, for all that, until the mid-nineteenth century, with a population of only 2500 in 1800. Then shale-oil came along, and coal-mining and brick-making also. Some of this has gone, leaving the inevitable detritus. But fortunately other industries have taken its place, including the great British Leyland Truck and Bus Division works, employing 5000 men. And there are two iron-foundries.

.There was a large medieval castle here in the fourteenth century, royal property, which Bruce gave to his son-in-law Walter the High Steward as part of his daughter Marjory's dowry. Indeed Walter died at Bathgate in 1328, a year before his master. In due course, the Steward's own son became King. It is apt that the site of this castle, with other land around, should have been presented to the town by the Royal Stewart Society, 18 acres in extent, as Kirkton Public Park. The Covenanting army passed a night here in 1666, prior to its disastrous defeat at Rullion Green. Amongst distinguished natives was Sir James Young Simpson, pioneer of chloroform. Much land-improvement now goes on here.

The interesting Bathgate Hills area lies to the north, between the town and Linlithgow, rising to 1017 feet at the Knock, in a couple of miles. This is the territory, covering 24 square miles, which has imaginatively been turned into the extensive country park of that name, also Beecraig Country Park, an excellent development, most if it still private property, estates and farmland, but with access developed, and nature-trails, picnic-areas, ancient monuments and places of interest made evident. There is considerable forestry.

Three miles north, passing the ruined Hamilton castle of Ballencrieff, is the pleasant village of Torphichen, with its renowned Priory church, one of the most interesting places in all Lothian. Part of the original building still stands in its kirkyard, and is now the parish church, a highly unusual edifice, as much fortified strength as a place of worship, its keep-like tower soaring to parapet and wall-walk. The chancel and nave of the Preceptory of St John are gone, replaced by a plain post-Reformation kirk, but this tower remained, rising above the crossing and transepts. This was, of course, the headquarters of the Order of St John of Jerusalem, in Scotland, until 1560. The building is most characterful, with traceried windows, turnpike stair, effigies and memorials. David I introduced these Knights into Scotland, as he did the Templars; and after the suppression of the latter, in 1312, this Order inherited their rivals' vast properties and became exceedingly powerful. Their Preceptors made good use of their mandatory seat in parliament; and almost all took a major part in the affairs of the realm, filling important offices such as Treasurer, Justiciar and Justice-General. The last Preceptor, Sir James Sandilands of Calder, achieved a bargain on joining the Reformers.

As well as having many other privileges, the Order had the especial one of sanctuary - that is, in an area all around of a mile's radius, fugitives from justice who could reach here were free from arrest by other authorities, royal, baronial or religious. Whether the knights took it upon themselves to dispense their own justice is not clear; but these sanctuaries were greatly prized by their 'owners' as well as the refugees, and must have carried substantial advantages other than mere escape from the consequences of wrong-doing and blood-feud. They were probably a relic of the Celtic dispensation; the Clan Macduff one has been mentioned, and there was another at Dull, the Celtic Church college in Strathtay. A squat stone pillar in the kirkyard at Torphichen marks the centre of this one, and other stones at various points Scots miles around have been discovered as marking the perimeter, that at Craigmailing, for instance, inscribed with a double cross.

The village, with its steep main street, is pretty to be so close to such industrialized territory. The name Torphichen means the Hill of the Raven. Here the only extant charter issued by William Wallace, as Guardian of Scotland, was signed. Wallace's Cave is pointed out near the Avon to the west, but this would be his refuge on another occasion, if at all. The tradition was that he hid here after the disaster of the Battle of Falkirk in 1298. It is generally held that, after that battle, the hero, wounded and distressed, hid in the great Forest of Torwood, on the other side of Falkirk altogether. But practically every locality in Southern Scotland seeks to show some link with the great patriot, and Wallace's Caves are legion. At Torphichen Mill, at a bend of the Avon, was born in 1767 Henry Bell, first man successful in applying steam to navigation. His famous *Comet* was laid down in 1811.

East of Torphichen rises the hill of Cairnpapple, another fascinating place. For on the summit of this, at 1000 feet, is one of the most remarkable prehistoric sites in the land, and one covering a lengthy period of use and occupation. Excavations in 1947 revealed that from 2500 B.C. down to the Roman period and possibly later, here was a henge-monument or sun-worship temple, on the stone-circle principle, with astrological conceptions. The upright monoliths of this were later used as kerb-stones for a huge Bronze Age burial-cairn with stone-lined chambers, and later still Iron Age tombs cut out of the living rock. The cairn is now preserved by the Department of the Environment and open to the public, a most valuable exhibition of our remote ancestors' culture and ideas. The view from up here is superb.

Craigmailing Hill lies just to the north, less high. On the east side of this is a large, natural boulder inscribed to the effect that here was preached a sermon, by the Reverend Mr Hunter in 1738, on a text from the third chapter of Ezekiel. Craigmailing was a noted place for conventicles – but 1738 seems late in the day for that. This stone is thought to be one more of the Torphichen sanctuary marks.

East of Cairnpapple and south of Craigmailing is the site of a silvermine with an amusing story. A collier named Alexander Maund, in 1607 discovered stone here containing silver. Quickly this got to the ears of that shrewd operator Sir Thomas Hamilton of nearby Binning, Lord Advocate, who managed to procure a charter from his absent monarch in London of the entire mineral rights of the area of Bathgate, Torphichen and so on. We do not hear what the miner Maund got out of it, but Tam o' the Coogate did very nicely – until James in London began to hear stories, even there, and promptly cancelled his charter, ordering his Lord Advocate and others to continue silver-mining but only on his royal behalf and as managers. Soon thereafter the venture failed, or appeared to, and King Jamie quickly withdrew. One wonders, London being a long way from the scene of operations? Actually one of the mines, at Hilderston to the west, was reopened in 1873 for the extraction of nickel, but the seam ran out. Sir Tam did not have things all his own way, however, even as King's manager. For one Ross of Tartraven, who seems to have felt deeply about his amenities – or perhaps merely loathed Hamilton – became so incensed at the invasion of the area by miners and mineral works that he gathered together his neighbours and descended in force on the mines, drove away the workers and filled in the shafts with earth and ruble. Scotland's silver-mining always seems to have been beset with troubles.

North of Torphichen a mile is the reservoir of Lochcote, the name indicating that it is only an extension of a natural loch. It is attractively placed in a hollow of green hills, and boasts a crannog or small artificial island, once a defensive dwelling. A later defensive fortalice, Lochcote Castle, is represented now only by a vaulted cellar. And not far to the east is another, Kipps Castle, now wholly ruinous but occupied until comparatively recently. It dates from 1625 and was the home of the historian Sir Robert Sibbald, who was physician to Charles II. He also was a naturalist, antiquary and geographer – indeed he was Geographer Royal for Scotland, and started to write, at the King's command, a general description of the entire kingdom, including particular histories of the different counties of Scotland. However he did not get this enormous task finished. At Kipps he cultivated rare and exotic plants. He had heired this small castle from his mother, of the Boyds of Kipps. Nearby is a cromlech, where three boulders have supported a fourth, now fallen. Courting couples used to plight their troth by clasping hands through the gap.

On the Avon, to the west is another place of interest, Carribber and its glen, with a smaller reservoir. Carribber Castle's scant ruins are often called Rob Gibb's Castle – and thereby hangs a tale. Rob Gibb was court-jester to James V, allegedly – but no sort of a fool. He improved his position under the young King so as to become, first, Stirrup-Holder, then Master of the Stables, and a man of consequence. He further enhanced his position by marrying one of the King's mistresses, Margaret Shaw. So he rose in the world and was granted the barony of Ogilface, in 1538, building thereon Carribber Castle, and proving that there are more ways to eminence than one.

Carribber is close both to the Avon and Linlithgow, which was James V's favourite palace. Towering above the town is the hill of Cockleroy or Cocklerue, 912 feet. Many have been the attempts to invent anglicized reasons for such a name – the favourite, that it refers to cuckold-le-roi, allegedly commemorating some occasion when that amorous monarch had the tables turned on him and his queen yielded her virtue to some enterprising courtier up on this hill – even Rob Gibb, it has been suggested. This is rather hard on Mary of Guise. There is no reason to believe that she was not a faithful wife, despite her husband's notorious activities as the Gudeman of Ballengeich. A slander on Rob Gibb too. The name is almost certainly derived from the Gaelic *cochull ruadh* meaning the red-capped hill. There is another Pictish fort on Cockleroy, large, with ramparts measuring 410 feet by 200.

Back at Bathgate, in contrast to this interesting area to the north, that to the south is rather dull and flat scenically, heavily industrialized with the aforementioned collieries and foundries – producing of course infinitely more wealth and employment. These level lands, once marshy flats as indicated by the names Boghead, Mosside and West Inch, are now drained, and criss-crossed by the A8, the M8 and their feeder roads. Beyond flows the Almond and the area to be dealt with in the final chapter.

There remains to be described in this central belt only the corner of land west of Bathgate to the county boundary, which here takes a major loop westwards and contains the highly industrial district of Armadale. Most of this is the large civil parish of Torphichen, stretching far from that village itself, and the basin of the quite sizeable Barbauchlaw Burn, an important feeder of the Avon, which has given its name to a productive coalfield.

Armadale seems a strange name to find here. There are three or four other Armadales or Ormidales in Scotland, the name seeming to come from *Eorm*, Norse for a great worm or dragon – but all the others are in very lovely country, in the Highlands and Islands. It is to be feared that there is nothing very lovely to be seen hereabouts, and probably never was, even before the nineteenth-century environmental defacement and utilitarian spread of coal and shale extraction, iron-foundries and brickworks. And yet it may have had its fairness too, once, as names around indicate – Birkenshaw, the Glade of Birches; Harthill, the Hill of Stags; Torbane, the Fair Hill; and so on. Armadale was a mere hamlet until 1851, but proved to be sited amidst rich fields of coal, limestone, ironstone and brick-clay. It quickly grew to become a police burgh, and now has a population of over 6000, even with its Academy School.

The West Lothian boundary is only a mile to the south of the town, yet because of the great westwards bend made by the Avon and another of its main tributaries, the Drumtassie Burn, which the boundary follows, there is still five miles more of the county due westwards, rising, bare land, largely consisting of pasture and the moorland-type country of the Blawhorn Moss, around the 700-foot-contour. In the midst is another colliery village, Blackridge, almost on the border, with much modern housing, not formerly provided with a church but only with a preaching-station, which has a somewhat pioneering and missionary ring about it. Bedlormie Castle, nearby, now only a ruin, must have been an unfriendly hold indeed, an outpost of the Livingstone family, Earls of Linlithgow, lording it over these remote uplands.

But north of Armadale the valley of the Barbauchlaw Burn is more attractive and rural country, although not without its scars. Here was the ancient barony of Ogilface, a name which has faded right out of use, although it was important once and quite large. It will be recollected that this barony, or part of it, was given by James V to his ex-fool, Rob Gibb, who built his castle at Carribber – which lies over five miles to the north of Armadale. Ogilface Castle itself lay in this Barbauchlaw valley. It is gone; but about a mile to the north stands its successor, Bridge Castle, still intact and now a hotel – although a century ago it too was said to be a roofless ruin. It is handsome building on a rocky eminence overlooking the burn, and dates from three periods. The north-east portion is a massively constructed early-sixteenth-century L-shaped keep with parapet and wall-walk; and to this has been added a lofty seventeenth-century wing, and later, more modern work. There has been much internal alteration but the feeling of antiquity remains. It formerly was called Little Brighouse, and the fortalice thereof, in the barony of Ogilface, was sold to William, Lord Livingstone in 1578. Like the other Livingstone lands, this was forfeited for the Earl of Linlithgow's share in the Jacobite rising of 1715.

And so we come back to the Avon again, at Westfield with its paper-mill, Stirlingshire across the river.

X

WEST LOTHIAN - THE SOUTH-WESTERN CORNER

THE LAST section of West Lothian left to survey, until a few years ago could have been described perhaps as the least interesting of all. But that was before the advent of Livingston New Town. Now, in one respect it is quite the most dramatic.

The area concerned is comparatively small, thanks to the odd shape of the county and the pronounced bend of the Almond which largely forms the Midlothian boundary. It consists of territory west of Midcalder and south of West Calder parishes and contains as well as Livingston the villages of Blackburn, Whitburn and Longridge. Much of it is fairly high and bare pasture and moorland, again pitted with industrialization, with the lower and more attractive parts to the east, now largely covered by the spread of Livingston.

Despite all the modernity and development, Livingstone was an old and renowned name long before the famous explorer and missionary made it a household word. The surname is usually spelt with an e, the place-name without. The village here, on the bank of the Almond, was an ancient place, not large and latterly somewhat decayed. It was, and still is, also a civil parish. The name is thought to come from one Leving, one of the Flemings imported by Alexander I. The Peel of Livingston, an important stronghold, vital enough to be garrisoned by the invading Edward I in 1302, stood until the mid-eighteenth century, east of the village, surrounded by a wide moat. It was, of course, the original seat of the Livingstones, Earls of Linlithgow, who probably were the descendants of Leving. The mansion which succeeded the Peel was demolished in 1812. It had a very notable botanic garden, founded by Sir Patrick Murray, in the later seventeenth century, who appears to have obtained the estate. On his early death most of the plants were taken to found the old Physic garden in Edinburgh, out of which grew the present and famed Botanic Garden there. Sir Patrick also gifted the silver communion cups to the parish church, dated 1696. The Livingstones themselves had moved their headquarters westwards some ten miles to Haining or Almond Castle first, just into Stirlingshire, then to Callander Park near Falkirk, further west still, once the Celtic thanedom of Calatria. There the Earls flourished and took their part in the uneasy rule of the land, until they were forfeited for their share in the Jacobite Rising of 1715. So Livingston district itself sank into rural peace, no doubt thankfully, its inn on the highway to Glasgow its principal source of excitement. A song, "The Bonnie Lass o' Livingston" refers to the lady of this inn.

In due course shale-oil and coal extraction hit West Lothian and this area did not escape. But the major developments were not at Livingstone itself but a mile or so to the north on somewhat higher ground, where a new community called Livingston Station grew rapidly, near the railway-line, amenity scarcely the major factor. Then again decay and dereliction until 1962. Nearby is the Dechmont area, with its abrupt, volcanic hill rising to 686 feet, and its former hamlet and mansion.

In 1962, then, all this Livingston area, of 6692 acres around, was designated a New Town project and, for better or worse, the great transformation began to turn this rather sad district into the largest community, outside the city of Edinburgh, in all Lothian, with a population target of 100,000.

It is not for this survey to enter into the arguments as to the merits or demerits of such planners' dreams or nightmares. Some see them as an inspiring answer to many social and industrial problems, others as an artificial growth draining the life's-blood away from all the neighbouring and old-established communities and creating vast urban spreads which deface the countryside, neither true town nor true country for the folk who live there. However that may be, Livingston New Town is a great effort, an exciting and ambitious conception, a major experiment in very traditional Lothian. The old village with its kirk, manse, inn and school, is preserved as an attractive centre. Here are the Development Corporation offices.

Statistics can be a great weariness. But some are probably

helpful to define the fuller picture. For instance, the estimated total capital expenditure between 1962 and 1987 is £180 million, £50 million having already been spent, by government, local authority and private sources. The population is already over 30,000, some eighty-five firms and businesses have so far taken up premises, seventy new factories, large and small, have been erected in four main industrial estates, the New Town being a Special Development Area, with the financial advantages that implies. Some 8,000 jobs have been provided, over sixty new retail shops opened and forty more are planned. The district had two small primary schools formerly; now there are ten, with another four under construction or planned, and one secondary opened with 1300 pupils, plus three more to be. There are nearly 9000 houses constructed and almost 30,000 envisaged. And there are eight churches, eleven community halls, two health centres, thirty parks and play areas, a championship-standard golf-course, a library and over 250 clubs and social organizations of one sort or another.

All this, of course, is scarcely to be taken in without a determined exercise of the imagination. Mere numbers can convey little but bewilderment. But something of the size and complexity of the conception may be gathered – and something of the change that has already come over the land and landscape in this vast and ever-growing, if disciplined project – which, it should be emphasized, is not by any means a flat monotony of streets and lamp-posts, harled brickwork, chromium and glass, for the terrain is a rolling one of gentle ridges and valleys, with some woodland preserved and some new trees planted. Some individual touches will perhaps serve to highlight the overall picture. Almondvale, the New Town Centre has already a major department store, as well as the sixty other shops, and an office campus extending to over fifty acres. The Lanthorn project, possibly the most imaginative, is a practical exercise in ecumenical religious activity where the various Church bodies have combined in heartening fashion to create a Christian centre, a light in the community as the name suggests, distinct from the ordinary and separate church programmes, Protestant and Roman Catholic both. The Development Corporation itself has made a contribution of no less than £85,000 towards this scheme. Another excellent conception is the Howden Park Centre. This is an eighteenth-century mansion-house, 30 acres of its wooded policies and its former domestic offices and stableyard turned into a community-centre with a difference, providing a theatre, a conference hall, an art studio and gallery, dining-hall, reception and committee rooms and studies and club premises. This mansion belonged to the family of the famous Scots portrait-painter, Sir Henry Raeburn, and a handsome yet simple vernacular building it is, amidst its lawns and fine old trees. Conferences for as many as 300 at a time are held here. Then there is the Petroleum Industry Training School, with all the most modern technological equipment, ensuring that West Lothian, which pioneered the oil industry, is well to the forefront in the present-day offshore and other developments. Other items well worth mentioning are Techincal College; the special Kirkton Campus; a fifth industrial estate which provides fully serviced sites for factories with a high research and development potential, for close liaison with the research departments of universities; the Craigshill Farm project; and so on. All stimulating – but difficult to create any real sense of an integrated community out of it.

The impact of all this on the fairly limited West Lothian scene is, of course, very great. For instance, the Corporation's own figures show that, at the end of 1975, of the 10,000 workforce, more than half commuted into Livingston from elsewhere. And being a Special Development Area, financial inducements are available for firms to establish themselves there rather than in older communities. So, while providing employment, there is also talk of sucking the neighbouring places dry. Only time will tell. I have heard the New Town described both as a shot-in-the-arm and sock-on-the-jaw!

Of the immediate communities, Blackburn, four miles along the old A705 westwards, is the closest, a cross-roads village which grew up only in the industrial age, but which shows no signs of decay, seemingly expanding, and with a modern St Kentigern's Academy. The Almond runs through it, here at a height of over 500 feet above sea-level. As well as coal found in the vicinity, there were discovered rich beds of ovenstone or picrite, ideal for making ovens. So various workings started up here, including quite a large cotton-mill. But those days have gone. Further on, two to three miles, where the White Burn joins the Almond, is Whitburn, a sort of twin community, which has outgrown its neighbour to become quite a town, a burgh indeed, with a population of some 6000. Yet it was only a village with a population of 700 in the middle of last century. It is not a beautiful place and curiously has been notable mainly for its particularly vigorous church-history, a seed-bed of the Secession movement, its worshippers dividing into determined Burghers and Anti-Burghers, with much controversy. This dichotomy seems to have produced a succession of very prominent ministers, who made their impact far outside Whitburn. One of these produced a book entitled *Free Thoughts on the Toleration of Popery*, which the ecumenists of present-day Livingston might have some views upon. The parish church dates from 1713, but there must have been a church before that; for the famous Donald Cargill, author of *The Queensferry Covenant*, and a real thorn-in-the-flesh of Charles II's episcopal government, preached at Whitburn the Sunday before he made his renowned excommunication of the King, the Duke of York, the Dukes of Monmouth, Lauderdale and Rothes, Sir George Mackenzie of Rosehall and Sir Tam Dalyell of the Binns, at the Tor Wood near Falkirk in 1680. He was hanged for high treason the next year, and beheaded thereafter. After all this religious fervour, it seems very humdrum to refer to Whitburn's mere mineral wealth; but its noted black-band ironstone produced a more than normal percentage of pig-iron, and its coal seams have remained rich, so that the Polkemmet pit was renewed and revitalized in late years when others were being closed, and still employs about 1500 men.

Polkemmet, at the very boundary of West Lothian, is celebrated for more than coal. The large wooded estate here is now being developed as another Country Park by the District Council. It used to be the seat of a baronet family of Baillies, who bought the property from Shaw lairds in 1620. The first of the line fell at the Battle of Kilsyth, fighting for Montrose in 1645. Another was Lord Polkemmet of Session, whose son became the first baronet in 1823. But though the discovery of minerals on the estate brought riches, in time it made the property less than attractive to live on, and the Baillies moved on. Now, there is a new beginning. Polkemmet Moor adjoins.

The mining villages of Longridge and Fauldhouse lie near together on Fauldhouse Moor, at over 750 feet, just where the counties of Mid and West Lothian and Lanarkshire join, so that we have now reached the very end of our survey. Looking back over the entire long story, we can see it, except for that coastal belt, as mainly a record of man's exploitation of the land and its various riches, with greed and haste a deal more common than care and foresight or any concern for beauty and the quality of life for future generations. It should be a thought-provoking exercise. What man has done to the land is highlighted most eloquently in the two Lothians, East and West, by the improvers and the exploiters. Yet who will aver, if coal and oil and ironstone had been found in workably quantities all over East Lothian, that the results would have been so very different from what happened in the west; and that the magnificent agricultural potential of that county would have triumphed over the get-rich-quick fervour? Would the improvers have won their battle? Or even fought it? We have seen what happened at Tranent and Prestonpans.

A new and more caring attitude undoubtedly manifests itself today, with conservation and reclamation schemes, planning, country parks, historical monument appreciation and so on. Even at the dreich wastes of Fauldhouse Moor and its vicinity a major plan is being debated and worked out by the local authority and national bodies, to rehabilitate by widespread tree-planting and landscaping – which is excellent. But if rich oil deposits were suddenly discovered under the most cherished conservation area, would it be safe? If open-cast coal can be cheaply exploited, is the scenery important? Again consider Tranent and Gladsmuir. If anti-pollution measures prove costly, are they always enforced, planners or none? Dunbar, with its cement-factory and Torness nuclear power-station sited on a lovely coast, may provide the answers to these questions. So before we cheer for today and condemn yesterday, let us look around us with a seeing eye.

POSTSCRIPT

So there are the three Lothians, each so very different from the others, yet combining to form a unique entity. This survey, whilst seeming to be in depth and detail, is in fact highly superficial, selective, biased, admittedly. It is one man's portrait of a fascinating area, with an attempt at looking below the surface and showing why as well as what. Forgive the seeming preoccupation with the past. Any country's present is conditioned by its past – and Lothian has had a lot of past! Surely its future will be worthy of this pleasant, lovely, storied land – but only adequately so if the lessons of yesterday are learned and acted upon.

Aberlady,
East Lothian
March 1978

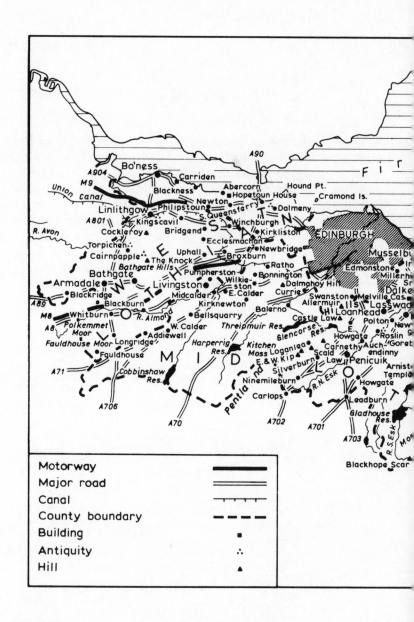

Motorway	
Major road	
Canal	
County boundary	
Building	■
Antiquity	∴
Hill	▲

Based with permission on the Ordnance Survey. Crown Copyright Reserved.

INDEX